BASEBALL TIDBITS

VICTOR DEBS, JR.

MASTERS PRESS

A Division of Howard W. Sams

Published by Masters Press
A Division of Howard W. Sams & Company
2647 Waterfront Pkwy E. Dr, Suite 100
Indianapolis, IN 46214

Printed in the United States of America.

96 97 98 99 00 01   10 9 8 7 6 5 4 3 2 1

Library of Congress Cataloging-in-Publication Data

Debs, Vic, 1949-
      Baseball tidbits / Victor Debs, Jr.
         p.   cm.
      ISBN 1-57028-115-7 (trade paper)
      1. Baseball--United States--History. 2. Baseball--United
States--Miscellanea. I. Title.
GV863.A1D43 1997   96-53576
796.357'64'0973--dc21   CIP

ACKNOWLEDGEMENTS

My thanks to the following people and organizations for making this book possible:

My father, Victor, for providing the line drawings of the players.

Bill Burdick, senior photo associate, for the National Baseball Library; Marcia Lein, AP/Wide World Photos; and Jocelyn Clapp and Sharon Philip of UPI for their help in obtaining photos.

George Kell and Karl "Tuffy" Rhodes for generously giving their time in providing interviews.

Researcher Walt Wilson for supplying the September stats and highlights of Reggie Jackson's career.

The staff at the microfilm department of the New York Public Library and the staff at the main branch and reference section of the St. George Library, Staten Island for their patience and diligence.

Members of the Society for American Baseball Research for their responses to the "Baseball Then and Now" questionnaire.

Finally, thanks to my wife Lola and daughter Jackie, whose love and support inspire all that I do.

Credits:
Cover design by Christy Pierce
Illustrations by Victor Debs
Edited by Kathleen Prata
Cover photos provided by the National Baseball Library, Cooperstown, N.Y.

To the Memory of The Mick

TABLE OF CONTENTS

INTRODUCTION

There are many facets of baseball which make it appealing. The limited success in consistently hitting a round ball with a round bat squarely is known well enough by most who've tried to accept batting expert Ted Williams' theory that it's "the single-most difficult thing to do in sports." Yet, some Sunday participants have found other aspects of the game such as pitching, fielding grounders, judging fly balls, throwing accurately and running the bases nearly as challenging. Our failures on the field, occurring during adolescence or adulthood, help us appreciate the play of professionals.

The attraction of the national pastime lies in more than the skills required of its players. Devoid of records and statistics, the game wouldn't be nearly as interesting to spectators. Should Ken Griffey, Jr. or Frank Thomas belt 62 homers in some future season, would it be as significant an achievement not knowing that Roger Maris once hit 60?

How important would Randy Johnson's 21-strikeout performance seem in the year 2000 if fans were unaware of Roger Clemen's 20-K mark in a 1986 game? Records offer a basis for comparison, and in no other sport are they as meticulously itemized and carefully scrutinized as in baseball.

But America's game is much more than numbers. Its long tradition has spawned countless tales involving player personalities, pennant races and controversies. In some cases, fiction has evolved to legend, adding to rather than tarnishing the game's luster. Fans aid in dissemination of baseball history with delightful descriptions of ballpark memories to children and grandchildren, and it's unfortunate that authors haven't sought out fans often enough in putting together oral histories of the game. The image of Bobby Murcer raising his cap to some 20,000 delirious spectators after socking his fourth consecutive homer in a Yankee Stadium doubleheader in 1970 and his return to the Bronx as part-time player nine years later to win one in the ninth on the day following teammate Thurmon Munson's funeral are two unforgettably dramatic moments, especially for a guy who at one time claimed Murcer was his idol.

Baseball Tidbits contains a smorgasbord of stories regarding our nation's greatest game. That the book at times includes opinions, the author willingly concedes. After all, that is the nature of the baseball fan. At least no pretense is made of offering only the facts.

The reader may also detect in *Baseball Tidbits* a tendency to focus on the winningest team in history and its players more than others. Being a Yankee fan, the author can merely offer his apology and hope the bias wasn't carried too far.

See you at the ballpark.

WILL THE REAL FATHER PLEASE STAND UP?

G iven the spaciousness and grandeur of America, it's not surprising that heroes have emerged throughout its history, their glorious achievements often obscuring their shortcomings. Davy Crockett was killed at the Alamo after surrendering, not while clubbing Mexican soldiers with "Old Betsy." Abe Lincoln was the Great Emancipator, but freed the slaves only after the Confederacy shattered his dream of peacefully preserving the Union. George Custer died a hero, despite the Last Stand massacre being a result of the general's military blunder. At times, our quest for heroes creates outrageous untruths, best exemplified by Abner Doubleday's title Father of Baseball. In all likelihood, he never heard of the game.

Doubleday attended West Point. He became a Union general, described by one historian as a "reliable but not outstanding officer." He was nearly killed by an exploding shell at Gettysburg, then witnessed the inspiring sight of thousands of retreating Rebs the next day. By the turn of the century, Doubleday was considered a hero by most Americans who knew of him.

When baseball authorities initiated a study to determine the game's origins in 1909, it wasn't difficult for them to accept heresay evidence crediting the esteemed Doubleday with its invention. According to an alleged eyewitness, Abner was in Cooperstown

1

in 1839 laying out the game's first baseball diamond. Too bad the general wasn't around to dispute the claim, having died in 1893.

Actually, there were those more accurately being called "Father of Baseball" even before the Doubleday myth took root. Henry Chadwick, baseball's first sportswriter, did more to popularize the sport than anyone else. He covered games for newspapers, published the first rule book, and printed an annual guide which included seasonal statistics of batters and pitchers. Followers of box scores today have their designer, Chadwick, to thank. Henry was baseball's great spokesman and innovator, but not its inventor.

Harry Wright was a former cricket star who was called the "Father of Professional Baseball" after his Cincinnati Red Stockings became the first club to pay its players in 1869. They showed their income was deserved by winning their first 91 games. Wright required his players to wear uniforms, which became the standard still used today. He also held regular workouts, drilling players in how to react to game situations. For managers, Wright was the game's pioneer.

Harry's brother, George, gave up cricket to become baseball's best player. His 1869 stats of 339 runs and a .669 batting average testify to his batting and baserunning skills, but don't explain his defensive ability. Wright's throwing arm was such that it allowed him to play behind the baseline in the infield, a technique used by others much later. George Wright was the game's first superstar.

In 1871, the National Association was formed which was essentially controlled by professional players. By 1876, William Hulbert decided baseball needed a change. He organized the National League, composed of eight clubs whose collective authority was in the hands of the owners, with Hulbert as president (though some would argue dictator). In four years, the new league was the only league. Hulbert was soon labeled the "Father of the National League."

Alexander Cartwright deserves the "father" title more than anyone. Cartwright created the diamond-shaped infield with bases spread 90 feet apart. He established a uniform distance from the pitcher's mound to home plate, though it measured 45 feet, not the 60 of today. Cartwright made three strikes an out and developed rules for catching fly balls and throwing out baserunners which are still used today. When he quit playing, he traveled across the country teaching others the game before settling in Hawaii, where Cartwright made a bonanza as a merchant. He didn't invent baseball, however, but amended an already popular game.

Members of the New York Knickerbocker Ball Club join their captain, Alexander Cartwright (top row, middle) in a mid-19th century pose. (National Baseball Library, Cooperstown, NY)

The truth is, baseball has no founder. Harder to accept is America's pastime having its roots in England, where citizens played "rounders" and "town ball" before their descendants did the same in the States. Modifications were made and aspects of cricket were also incorporated. Voila. . . baseball, after decades of evolution of course.

George Washington should suffice as our father figure. We don't need one for baseball. Anyway, its players have always been the real heroes.

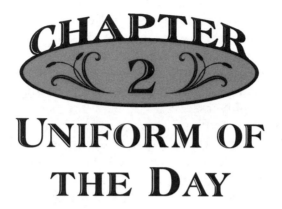

UNIFORM OF
THE DAY

I f baseball evolved from other games, it has never ceased
changing. Since the turn of the century, the height of the
pitcher's mound has been altered a few times. The composi-
tion of baseballs has varied, so that calling one a "horsehide" today
is a misnomer (a "cowhide" is more appropriate). The rules speci-
fying doubles and homers have been modified, as have those for
sacrifice bunts and sacrifice flies. Balk rules have fluctuated,
making it alternately easier or more difficult for anxious base
stealers to "get the jump" on vigilant hurlers anxious to "pick
them off." Managers, allowed limitless trips to the mound in the
past, must be content today with no more than two an inning, a
1967 ruling which no doubt rankles such loquacious leaders and
stubborn strategists as Sparky Anderson and Tony La Russa.
(Imagine the game devoid of that decree, as if three-hour-plus
ball games aren't long enough already!)

Nor have baseball uniforms remained the same. At the beginning of the century, they were made of either 100% wool flannel
or a combination of wool and cotton. Loose-fitting and extremely
heavy, the uniforms were torturous during hot summer months,
one reason perhaps that perspiring players wasted little time on
the field, with games often finishing in less than two hours. Relief came gradually when the weight of uniforms was reduced in

half by the 1940s, but problems with shrinkage continued. After World War II, newly developed synthetic fibers such as nylon and Orlon were incorporated, and in the '60s, a blend of wool and Orlon further improved the comfort, durability and look of uniforms. Flannel gave way to double-knit fabrics in the '70s, resulting in the much lighter, tighter, cooler and durable uniforms worn by today's players.

Caps were of the "pillbox" variety at the beginning of the century, having a flat top with stripes running across the crown and a short sun visor slanted downward. The "Brooklyn" and "Boston" styles had vertical stripes on a round crown, with buttons imperfectly centered on top. Today's cap has a generally larger crown and sun visor than preceding ones.

Spike shoes have always been in use, and until the '60s were predominantly black. A's Owner Charlie Finley revolutionized footwear fashion by introducing chalk-white spikes in the '60s. Since then, black spikes have been replaced by those which match the color of the uniform.

During the late 1890s, several teams were adorned with colored stockings which identified them, namely the Red Stockings, White Stockings and Browns. In 1905, the stirrup stocking was first seen, though the height to which they've stretched to the pants legs has varied over the years.

Washington was the first club to have its nickname, rather than the name of the city, spelled on the uniform when they wore their "Nationals" jerseys in 1905. The Cubs, White Sox and Reds soon copied the idea, and by 1954 each franchise had displayed either its full nickname or initial during at least one season. It remains the preference of most modern ballclubs.

It's commonly believed that the Yankees were the first to experiment with numbers on uniforms when owner Jacob Ruppert identified Ruth's (number three), Gehrig's (number four), and other pinstripers' position in the batting order in 1929. The Cleveland Indians had actually tried it first in 1916, with numbers attached to uniform sleeves rather than the backs. The Tribe abandoned the idea after one season. Though they no longer necessarily revealed batting spots, numbered uniforms not only continued to be worn by New Yorkers after '29, but by all players by 1932.

Baseball fans have witnessed many bizarre uniforms since 1900.

John McGraw was a highly successful manager, but hardly the Pierre Cardin of his profession. In 1901, his Orioles were the subject of much ridicule after a season attired in solid black caps, shirts and trousers, with yellow-orange trim and striped socks, and matching, oversized "O"s on the jersey. The serious-minded skipper again revealed morbid taste when his Giants were made to wear black uniforms with a large white "NY" on the chest during the 1905 World Series. If the odd outerwear incited hilarity, big Mac had the last laugh when New York defeated the Athletics in five games, though similar outfits didn't help the Giants six years later while losing to those same A's in the Fall Classic.

In 1916, McGraw's predilection for outrageous fashion reached its peak when the Giants wore "perhaps the most unusual fabric of any major-league team uniform," to quote Marc Okkonen, author of *Baseball Uniforms of the 20th Century*. As they took the field in the season opener at Baker Bowl, fans were aghast upon seeing the pillbox cap resurrected after nearly 15 years of extinction, and uniforms having a gray shade with black lines which formed two-inch squares, giving a plaid appearance. Socks were red and black. Wrote a *Philadelphia Inquirer* eyewitness, "Mr. McGraw refused to make known the reason for the new style, but fans figured the astute manager believed the lines would confuse opposing ballplayers." The Giants lost 5-4.

Conservative colors haven't been the exclusive choice of ballclubs. Cincinnati's 1936 uniform featured a trimless white top with bright red pants. The Dodgers were probably successful in their attempt to upstage the Reds the following season with green-trimmed uniforms. The rarely-seen grass color wasn't re-used until rebel owner Finley went against tradition with white, gold and green uniforms in 1963. The Seattle Pilots wore an aqua outfit with yellow trim and lettering on the road in 1969. Two years later, the Orioles drew attention with their difficult moundsmen and dark-orange uniforms, which were difficult on the eyes.

Few innovators could top White Sox owner Bill Veeck, as he helped to prove in the mid-70s. He forced his players to wear outlandish, straight-bottomed shirts with open, flapped collars — outside the trousers! Lettering spelled "Chicago" rather than the team nickname, going against most other clubs by then. In

1976, Veeck made disgruntled Sox players wear shorts, a fashion which ended quickly after continuous complaints from the embarrassed employees.

It's anyone's guess as to how much baseball will change during the 21st century. Judging from the past, no team uniform will remain uniform.

IT'S A WHOLE NEW BALLGAME

Baseball has changed to a far greater degree than merely the look of its uniforms.

During the early part of the 20th century, minor-league ballclubs were independently operated franchises which would either retain players on their rosters indefinitely or sell them to major-league clubs, whose owners often dug deep into their pockets. After pitcher Jesse Haines was obtained for the exorbitant price of $10,000 in 1919, St. Louis executive Branch Rickey devised a plan to eliminate the high cost of player purchases. In 1921, he convinced Cardinal owner Sam Breadon to buy controlling interest of several minor-league teams, which would then be used to develop young players with inexpensive contracts. A prospect would be placed on a lower-echelon club, with the opportunity to work his way up the ladder of increasingly better ballclubs. Once reaching the top team, the prospect would be in a position to be placed on the Cardinal roster.

By the late 1920s, clubs in Syracuse, Houston, Sioux City, Fort Smith, Danville, Rochester and Columbus had become part of Breadon's breeding organization, or "farm system." The idea attracted other owners and by the early 1930s, most were using it, leading to a decade in which, as observed by historian Charles Alexander, "farm systems became the dominant element in minor-league operations." Attendance at minor-league parks dropped, sagging still further during the '50s and '60s when television and the introduction of additional clubs made big-league baseball more accessible. Today, interest in minor-league ball appears on the rise, possibly a result of fan disgust with televised major-league games filled with countless instant replays and commercials, as well as the greed and lack of respect for the game shown by major-league players and owners.

Dismayed by less-active turnstiles, minor-league operators thought of ways to innovate. By May of 1930, Des Moines Demons owner Lee Keyser had installed six towers with lights at his ballpark. The Demons's clash with Wichita on May 2 drew national attention, and although the dimly lit field caused difficulty with fly balls, Keyser's innovation was sufficiently successful to cause the installation of lights at most other minor-league parks by season's end.

Larry MacPhail had been a minor-league executive prior to his retention by the Reds in 1935. MacPhail liked the idea of night ball and persuaded club president Powel Crosley to install lights at Crosley Field. With Franklin Roosevelt throwing the switch at the White House on May 24, the first major-league night game became a reality, the Reds defeating the Phils 2-1. Fired for swinging at Crosley during an argument, MacPhail went to Brooklyn in 1938, where lights were first used on June 15. Nor was it a coincidence that MacPhail was a Yankee executive on May 28, 1946, when night ball at Yankee Stadium was inaugurated.

By 1948, all major-league teams were offering lit fields, with the exception of the Chicago Cubs, who finally joined the fold 40 years later. Listed chronologically in the following table are the dates of the first night games played at home by the original 16 major-league teams of 1903.

In 1947, baseball moved out of the Dark Ages when Jackie Robinson became the first black to play in the majors. Robinson had been signed the year before by Rickey, now in the Dodger organization, and played in Montreal that year in preparation for his move to Brooklyn. Rickey's motive for breaking the color barrier is debatable; it being either purely ethical, believing that blacks had long been unjustly denied their right to play big-league ball, or opportunistic, with the issue of integrating the game al-

FIRST NIGHT GAMES PLAYED BY ORIGINAL MAJOR-LEAGUE TEAMS

Team	Ballpark	Date
Reds (N)	Crosley Field	May 24, 1935
Dodgers (N)	Ebbetts Field	June 15, 1938
A's (A)	Shibe Park	May 16, 1939
Phils (N)	Shibe Park	June 1, 1939
Indians (A)	League Park	June 27, 1939
White Sox (A)	Comiskey Park	August 14, 1939
Giants (N)	Polo Grounds	May 24, 1940
Browns (A)	Sportsman's Park	May 24, 1940
Cards (N)	Sportsman's Park	June 4, 1940
Pirates (N)	Forbes Field	June 4, 1940
Senators (A)	Griffith Stadium	May 28, 1941
Braves (N)	Braves Field	May 11, 1946
Yankees (A)	Yankee Stadium	May 28, 1946
Red Sox (A)	Fenway Park	June 13, 1947
Tigers (A)	Tiger Stadium	June 15, 1948
Cubs (N)	Wrigley Field	August 9, 1988

ready being discussed by the baseball hierarchy and his wanting to get the jump on other organizations. Most likely, a combination of both.

Roy Campanella joined the Dodgers in 1948, Don Newcombe in 1949 and Monte Irvin became the Giants' first black ballplayer that same season, ushering in the decade of the integration of baseball, if not yet all of American society. The more conservative American League owners were slow in accepting players from this new talent pool, resulting in comparatively weaker ballclubs during the '60s and '70s, as is indicated by their losing 21 of the 23 All-Star Games from 1960-1979.

In 1959, Rickey helped create another major change in the sport with his plans to start a third league. Feeling baseball was losing popularity, that new ballclubs would be welcomed in cities including New York which had recently lost two National League teams, and that "there is no chance of expanding the existing leagues to 10 clubs due to opposition to such expansion," Rickey announced his plan for the Continental League, which would begin its schedule in 1961. Rickey said, "I am alarmed at the subtle invasion of professional football, which is gaining pre-eminence over baseball." The Mahatma's assessment of owner antagonism towards expansion had been accurate, yet, ironically, by threatening the status quo Rickey inadvertently softened their position. Plans were announced for American League franchises in Los Angeles and Washington to begin play in 1961 (Senators owner Calvin Griffith had already announced his decision to move the old Washington team to Minnesota), and National League clubs in Houston and New York were to begin in '62. The new teams were intentionally placed in cities Rickey had intended as part of his Continental League. Thus his dream for a third major-league vanished, as baseball reluctantly broke a 60-year-old tradition of allowing only 16 competing major-league franchises.

The Pandora's Box having been opened, the gift or evil of expansion (depending on one's point of view) was reused by baseball officials. The number of teams was increased from 20 in 1962 to 24 in 1969, then to 26 in 1977, and to 28 in 1993, with an additional two clubs planned for 1998. The inevitable dilution of the player pool has supplied critics of modern baseball with further ammunition.

For 10 teams in each league to be competing for one post-season spot did little to enhance baseball's image from 1962-1968. Expansion to a dozen per league in 1969 therefore necessitated another change — divisional play. The leagues were divided into an East and West division, the winners of each to compete in a post-season, best-of-five championship series (changed to best-of-seven in 1985) for the right to play in the World Series. Expansion to 28 teams in 1993 prompted a three-division format in 1995, with each league comprised of an East and Central division of five clubs apiece, and a West division consisting of four teams.

Besides being a wonderfully entertaining game, baseball's uniqueness lies in its tradition, yet owners continue to react to pressure from other sports by trying to imitate rather than waiting for the public's inevitable return. In January of 1996, a delighted Bud Selig spoke for owners when he announced that a proposal for interleague play, whereby American and National League clubs would compete with each other in regular-season games, had been unanimously approved and would be put into effect in 1997. In defending the concept, Selig declared, "You're creating excitement, you're creating new opportunities, you're creating new potential." The owners were also creating a World Series that would be even less significant than it had already become after divisional play ensured its participants no longer necessarily reflected the best teams from each league. With interleague play, baseball's hallowed and unbroken custom of "never the twain shall meet, until the Series" will become passé.

As football edged closer to displacing baseball as the most popular American spectator sport, owners looked for other ways to innovate. The Houston Astros, formerly the Colt .45s, built the Astrodome, the first major-league covered stadium, with a dome which reached over 200 feet high. It opened in 1965, not without some problems. The roof consisted of clear glass panels which allowed sunlight to bathe the natural grass below, but whose glare also interfered with outfielders's views of fly balls. The dome was painted, but blocked the sun's rays and destroyed the grass, leading to another innovation — the artificial surface, or Astroturf.

Other owners found the new toy appealing, leading to the constructing of additional roofed stadiums. The Seattle Kingdome, whose roof "looks like its made of thousands of bricks," as noted by ballpark expert Philip Lowry, and whose 42 air-conditioning units "blow air in toward the field which means fewer home runs," (except for Ken Griffey, Jr.), offered indoor baseball in 1977. Minnesota's Metrodome opened in 1982, and Montreal's Olympic Stadium and Toronto's Skydome became the first to use retractable domes in 1989. Owners have only recently changed their thinking, wanting to build more traditional and cozier ballparks, such as those put up in Baltimore in 1992 and Cleveland in 1994.

If roofed stadiums necessitated artificial surfaces, what excuse did owners have for its use at uncovered ballparks, unless they had a preference for high-bouncers that turned routine outs into infield singles or baseballs that skidded through the infield like a cue ball on a pool table? For whatever reasons, artificial surfaces made their debut in Cincinnati's Riverfront Stadium, Pittsburgh's Three Rivers Stadium and St. Louis' Busch Stadium in 1970. Then this man-made surface appeared in Philadelphia's Veterans Stadium in 1971, and Kansas City's Royals Stadium in 1973. Again, mercifully, some organizations are reconsidering; the Cardinals and Royals recently decided to replace the carpet with the real thing.

Baseball purists and reformers still argue over the American League's use of the designated hitter, whereby a batter is allowed to hit in place of the pitcher in the batting order, first used by the Yankees when Ron Blomberg was inserted as the "DH" in the season opener at Fenway Park in 1973. Unquestionably, it has eliminated a certain amount of strategy from the game, such as managers having to decide whether to pinch-hit for starters who are trailing late in the game or requiring their pitchers to attempt sacrifice bunts, but it has also significantly increased run-production. The National League has rejected the designated hitter, and baseball has solved the problem of its use in the World Series by permitting it in games played at the American League park and prohibiting it in the National League parks. The same will hold true when interleague play takes effect, assuming neither league alters its attitude toward the DH by then.

There are those who, perhaps yearning for an innocent period which will never return, can find no fault with America's past. Others are under the illusion that change has always meant progress. In regards to America's game, the same holds true.

CHAPTER 4

KING OF THE DIAMOND

One of the most famous and accomplished ballplayers of the 19th century was Mike Kelly. Born in upstate New York on New Year's Eve of 1857, Kelly began playing professionally at the age of 13, was 21 when he joined the National League's Cincinnati Red Stockings and switched colors in 1878 when White Stockings's player-manager Cap Anson signed him.

Soon, Kelly became, as Ken Burns, creator of the PBS series *Baseball*, acknowledges, "the most popular player of his era." Historian Charles Alexander notes in *Our Game* that Kelly was the "first great player of Irish-Catholic ancestry." So extraordinary were his skills that he gradually became identified as "King of the Diamond."

Even by today's standards of excellence, King Kelly's stats are impressive. He finished with a career average of .308 in 16 seasons. His 1357 runs scored in 1455 games averages to nearly a run a game, and he accumulated over 1,800 hits. King led the league in runs-scored for three consecutive seasons, in doubles twice consecutively and won the batting title twice.

As splendid are his stats, they don't explain his popularity. The tall, well-built Irishman with dark hair and thick mustache looked every bit the dapper, dashing gentleman off the field, complementing a flamboyant style of play on. Stealing bases would be turned into a science by Maury Wills nearly a century later, but King Kelly was the first to become famous for it. His 10-foot leaps into second base culminated in a hook slide that became known as the Kelly Spread which was mimicked by other less successful basestealers. For five consecutive years, Kelly swiped more than 50 bases, reaching a career high 84 in 1887, and once stole six in a game. He became so famed for his foot feats that a song "Slide, Kelly, Slide," written by a namesake, became as popular in the late 19th century as the poem "Casey at the Bat."

Some of Kelly's single-game achievements were astounding, if not unprecedented. In 1884, he became only the ninth player in history to sock a grand slam. The next year, he became the fifth player to bang three triples in a game. In 1887, he was the 10th player to have as many as six hits in a contest, which included a double and homer. That same year, he scored six runs in a game, a still-standing major-league record matched by 11 others.

Kelly was inventive. One source credits him with being the first to use the hit-and-run. As a backstop, he thought of the idea of signaling pitches, and was the first to back up first base on infield grounders. Even when he retired Kelly was an innovator, writing America's first sports autobiography.

Matching Kelly's fame was his notoriety for breaking rules. He suffered no qualms about taking shortcuts from first to third, as long as the umpire (they used only one in those days) didn't catch him missing the second-base bag. As a catcher, Kelly would often throw his mask toward the first-base line, hoping to trip the baserunner, or would place it on home plate as a runner attempted to score. He was even more obstructive as an infielder, often shoving baserunners or grabbing their shirts.

Kelly's clever chicanery matched his versatility. The Hall-of-Famer, who played every position at least once during his career, including pitching, once faked catching a ball hit over the center-field fence in the twilight. Instead of being the game-winning hit, the blow was called the final out by the confused arbiter. Legend has it that in another instance, Kelly was on the bench when a foul pop-up approached him. Seeing it was out of reach of teammates, he promptly proclaimed himself a substitute and corralled the ball for the final out. Though the ploy was legal then, Kelly is appropriately called by one historian "the most notorious rules violator of his time."

Kelly behaved just as badly off the field, his gambling on horses, heavy drinking and late-night activities causing a frustrated Anson to say about the popular athlete, "He has only one enemy — himself." Curfews meant little to the King. He once admonished detectives for reporting to their employer, White Stockings owner Al Spalding, that he had stayed out until 3 a.m.drinking lemonade. Kelly insisted that it was whiskey instead. Once, he told his skipper he'd be at a Turkish bath sweating out excess fat, but detoured to the track where he sweated out races. It wasn't unusual for an intoxicated Kelly to take the field, at times causing teammates to resent his flaunting the rules.

Kelly was in awe of no one but himself. Invited by Grover Cleveland to a luncheon at the White House, the king took the president's gesture of friendship as a challenge. As he recalled the handshake years later, "I squeezed so hard that he winced."

Like some superstars that followed, Kelly was treated with tolerance by owners and managers, realizing his worth to the club and to the gate outweighed his personal excesses and excess salary. Even when Spalding became so disgusted that he sold his star to Boston in 1887, it must have been with some reluctance, considering Kelly's abilities and the storm of protest it precipitated in the Windy City (Clarence Darrow was one of several notable Chicago citizens to become outraged). This was a controversy paralleling Ruth's sale to the Yankees three decades later. The $10,000 Spalding received (who made appreciably more money selling baseballs to ballclubs than selling tickets to see his ballclub) helped assuage any regrets, the figure easily the most paid for a player at that time. So jubilant were the fans in Beantown, that they welcomed their "$10,000 Beauty" with a horse and carriage and new house. (When John McGraw purchased pitcher Rube Marquard in 1908, he paid Indianapolis an extra $1,000, hoping the new record price would gain publicity. It did, but not the way McGraw had hoped, with Rube labeled by newspapers the "$11,000 Lemon" after a 5-13 rookie season.)

Kelly was a charmer, but Boston's benevolence toward their newest star was based more on his reputation as a gifted ballplayer. He had been the key to Chicago's winning five pennants in seven seasons. His aggressive play and underhand tactics

17

King Kelly was known as much for his swagger as for his sliding.
(National Baseball Library, Cooperstown, NY)

so unnerved opponents that they "were whipped before a ball was thrown. They were scared to death," to use Kelly's words.

The King was only slightly less dominant with the Beaneaters, averaging .311, 108 runs scored and 69 thefts in three seasons before joining the rebel Players' League, headed by the talented and cerebral John Montgomery Ward. The mutineers survived one year. Kelly returned to the National League, first with Boston, then with the New York Giants, but was a shadow of his former self. He finished his final two seasons averaging .204 as a part-timer.

Kelly made more than most during his career, and earned additional income during off-seasons working at race tracks and as a vaudevillian. Nonetheless, his extravagant spending on clothes, booze and gambling left him nearly penniless when he died of pneumonia in November of 1894, just a month shy of his 37th birthday.

Can the story of King Kelly end so dismally? As he was being carried on the stretcher to the hospital the dying Kelly fell off, prompting his last words, "I think, me lads, this is me last slide."

CHAPTER 5

LEAGUE OF
THEIR OWN

I n 1885, major-league ballplayers, annoyed with owner policies, organized the Brotherhood of Professional Base Ball
Players. Its goals included promoting high standards of conduct among players and fostering interest in the National League,
but its main purpose was to collectively bargain with owners.
The chief source of their disenchantment wasn't dissimilar to that
which would frustrate players throughout the prefree-agent era
— low salaries and the reserve clause. Wisely, this first players
union chose the qualified John Montgomery Ward as president.

Ward was a sports star and scholar, a rarity even among today's
more sophisticated athletes, but almost nonexistent in pre-20th
century America. The dashing right-hander played college ball
at Penn State, then pitched in the National League while earning a law degree at Columbia University. Ward won 47 games for
the pennant-winning Providence Grays in 1879, leading the
league in wins and strikeouts, and threw the second perfect game
in history in 1880. After developing a sore arm, Ward converted
to shortstop and became one of the best at the position. Intelligent and articulate, Ward published *Baseball — How to Become
a Player* in 1888, rated a century later by one journalist "one of
the best books about baseball ever written by a player." Yet
"Johnny" could be rowdy and violent on the field, often scrapping

with players, even umpires.

Ward and his followers yearned for better pay, but their main concern was the reserve rule adopted earlier in the decade by the two major leagues — the National League and American Association, in a "National Agreement." It prevented any organization from obtaining players already signed with other teams, even at the termination of their contracts. In effect, the rule tied a ballplayer to a club until he was either traded or given a 10-day notice of release. Players felt like serfs on a manor, unable to decide where and for how much they could work, cognizant that salaries would be far more lucrative if permitted to negotiate with any club. They felt cheated when sold "like chattel," to use Ward's label, while receiving nothing in return. The owners' argument was simple — the players' freedom hadn't been denied. They were at liberty to sign their contracts or not sign them.

Chicago's sale of superstar King Kelly to Boston in 1887 "dramatized to players their powerlessness in obtaining compensation for themselves," in the words of historian Benjamin Rader. Ward requested and was granted permission to discuss a new form of contract with the owners committee, called the League Alliance, headed by the comparably competent negotiator, Chicago White Stockings mogul Al Spalding. (The team was renamed "Cubs" by the turn of the century.)

Even for the normally undaunted Ward, it must have been a bit intimidating dealing with the highly accomplished Spalding, who by then was arguably the most recognized name in baseball. The game's best pitcher during the 1870s, Spalding led the National Association in victories from 1871-1875, and his 47 wins with pennant-winning Chicago in the newly-formed National League of 1876 also was a league high. He quit the following season, finishing with a 253-65 mark, probably realizing more money was to be made from owning a ballclub than playing for one (during that era, at least). Necessary funds to purchase the White Stockings were derived from ownership of a sporting goods company which would eventually become a baseball manufacturing monopoly.

If Ward came with the intention to fight, Spalding cleverly outmaneuvered his adversary and by meeting's end, though apparently satisfied that owners had at least been willing to talk, the Brotherhood had gained little. Even the dreaded reserve rule remained unaltered, but seemed less distasteful after Spalding's persuasion, with Ward writing a few months later in his book, "The reserve rule is a usurpation of the player's right, but it is, perhaps, made necessary by the peculiar nature of the base-ball business, and the player is indirectly compensated by the improved standing of the game." The players had been appeased, but conditions would soon cause them to revolt.

As Harold Seymour writes in *Baseball — The Early Years*, "Had the owners been more willing to conciliate, or at least to let matters continue in the same manner, the eruption of 1890 would have been avoided." That eruption took the form of a new league created by the players in which clubs were intentionally placed in cities where National League teams were already located. The Players League was the brainstorm of Ward, who argued it would be more effective and less distasteful to the public than the planned strike by his peers. By drawing all the best players, the new league would force National League owners either out of business or to consent to more favorable contracts in exchange for its liquidation.

What had sparked the rebellion was the Brush Classification Plan, a brazenly autocratic move pushed through by misguided owners while their able arbiter Spalding was overseas on a famed world baseball tour, hoping America's new pastime would appeal to foreigners (it didn't). The classification of ballplayers, which allowed owners to rate them as "A," "B" or "C" players, assign salaries appropriate to player levels with a ceiling of $2,500, and force some lower-echelon players to do non-baseball chores such as collecting tickets at turnstiles, didn't appeal to those players who heard about it at home and who now felt more like cattle than chattel. Ward was met upon his return from Europe by an irate Brotherhood anxious to strike, but the attorney successfully made his case for the Players League. In an effort to avoid conflict, Ward sought out Spalding, but when the Sox owner balked at the players' demand for annulling classification, Ward announced the formation of the third league, which would offer ballgames in eight cities beginning in 1890. Now unable to compromise, Spalding prepared for all-out war.

The 1890 season was characterized more by activities off the field than on. Players and owners waged battles of propaganda, with each side blaming the other in newspaper manifestos. Ward denounced the changed attitude of the baseball establishment, claiming, "There was a time when the National League stood for integrity; today it stands for dollars and cents." Spalding condemned "ungrateful" players, likening them to anarchists and revolutionaries, unpopular labels in late-19th century America, and warning the working public not to show sympathy for those who "engage in light exercise for a few hours" as their means of livelihood and spend the remainder of the day at leisure. As would be expected, both sides exaggerated attendance figures, but Spalding later took advantage by implanting spies near the turnstiles of Player League ballparks who would count the actual number of paid customers, report to Spalding, who in turn made public the actual figures through friendly newspapers, thus making liars of the players.

If the Brotherhood's intention was to ensure the National League would be in the red at season's end, it succeeded. National League losses may have been as high as half a million dollars, and many clubs would have gone bankrupt without support from others. But the Brotherhood's bargaining position remained weak when the Players League lost money as well. Notwithstanding its offering the best ballplayers, the rebel league dropped a quarter of a million dollars, losses too heavy for its financial backers, which included streetcar owners and small businessmen, to dare risk another season of warfare.

The fact that the financial backbone of the league was a group of outside businessmen, not the players, sealed its doom. When Spalding approached the nervous rookie owners at year's end, purposely snubbing the Brotherhood, with an offer to buy them out and permit their investment in National League clubs, all that remained for Ward and his followers was an invitation by Spalding to play under previous contractual conditions without fear of disciplinary action, and a New York barroom toast to a good try.

As Seymour points out, the 1890 season saw "interest in the game decline as the public became more and more disgusted with the chaotic state of baseball." Fans at first chose sides, but later perceived both as being greedy and self-serving, and capable of destroying what had already become America's favorite sport. Fortunately, modern owners and players are more sensitive to the concerns of fans. Financial matters would never compel them to take action which would jeopardize baseball's popularity and future.

Not much.

CHAPTER 6

IT'S MY TEAM AND I'LL DO WHAT I WANT WITH IT!

Among the recalcitrants to have participated in the Players League of 1890 was a righty-swinging, first baseman named Charles Comiskey. In the decades to come, Comiskey either forgot or ignored from whence he came, transforming into a club owner more miserly than any he may have condemned while wearing the spikes.

Comiskey was player-manager for St. Louis throughout the 1880s, then for Cincinnati for three years following the rebel league's downfall. Nicknamed "Commy" (a misnomer considering Comiskey's entrepreneurial ambition), he became owner of the Chicago White Sox in Ban Johnson's newly formed American League of 1901 and saw his Sox take the first junior-circuit pennant that year. Despite his club finishing in the top four in 13 of 18 seasons thereafter, including three first-place finishes and two World Series flags, Comiskey's players were relatively underpaid. With the exception of Ty Cobb and possibly Honus Wagner, Sox outfielder Joe Jackson was the best hitter in the game in the first two decades of the century, yet his salary was nearly half that of other professional ballplayers. Comiskey disdained his employees to the point where their meager meal allowances and soiled, ragged uniforms became the joke of the league. He prevented players from achieving batting or pitching goals by purposely

27

benching them late in the season, and he reneged on promised bonuses by paying off with champagne instead.

By 1919, Chicago players were ripe for mutiny, but with the reserve clause still in place, they had nowhere to turn. Some today blame Comiskey for the desperate conditions which led eight of the Chicago players, including Jackson, to accept bribes from gamblers to purposely throw the World Series of 1919, still the most notorious scandal in sports history. It should be remembered, however, that Comiskey, though possibly the worst of the cheapskate owners, wasn't the only one.

Take, for example, Brooklyn's Charlie Ebbetts, whose first act as majority owner in 1902 was to double his own salary. When the Dodgers won their first pennant in 1916, Ebbetts rewarded his players with pay cuts in 1917. His penny-pinching became renowned in New York, if sometimes exaggerated as was the case when a newspaper reporter claimed the owner interrupted participation in a parade by stooping to search for a dropped dime as waves of marchers avoided him.

Ebbetts's concern for the dollar helped lead to a positive baseball innovation in the Big Apple. Sunday pro ball was banned in most major-league cities at the turn of the century, including New York, a condition which aggravated Ebbetts to the extent that he once thought of a way to get around the "blue law." Offering spectators "free" admission in April of 1904, Charlie's only requirement was that fans pay for diversely priced scorecards, the colors of which indicated the location of seats. Unable to get away with it on a consistent basis, Ebbetts continued his fight to repeal the prohibition until Sunday ball became a reality in 1919.

To various extents throughout baseball history, owners have exhibited decision-making policies reflecting self-interest over concern for fans. Boston's Harry Frazee was never as fond of his Red Sox as he was of his Broadway productions in New York. He sold several key players following the club's World Series victory in 1918 in order to repay show costs. That trend continued the next year when Harry sent Boston's latest slugging sensation, Babe Ruth, to the Yankees for $100,000 in cash and a $300,000 loan. Frazee claimed Ruth's being "selfish and inconsiderate" as his reason for dumping him, but Beantowners were outraged nonetheless. Today, Sox fans still point to the aftermath of that ill-fated sale — the "Curse of the Bambino," as the chief cause of the team's failure to take another Series since.

Cardinal Owner Sam Breadon's trade of Player-Manager Rogers Hornsby to New York following the club's victory in the 1926 Series was no less controversial. By then, Hornsby was a six-time batting champ for St. Louis, having attained .424 in 1924, a record which still stands today. Called the "foremost figure in St. Louis history" by one biographer, Hornsby nevertheless was sent packing by Breadon, who shortly afterward admitted to expecting to "catch hell for the next few months."

Catch hell he did. Newspapers blasted him in editorials. A Cardinal board member resigned on the spot. The St. Louis Chamber of Commerce sought out baseball commissioner Kenesaw Mountain Landis, demanding the trade be rescinded, to no avail. Breadon received hate mail and telephone threats at his home. One resentful fan, spotting the owner in his luxury auto, jumped on the running board and shouted insults through the window.

Conversely, some owners have genuinely sought to please fans. Bill Veeck, Jr. did so to the point of irritating other owners at times with outrageous promotions and gimmicks, like the time he used the diminutive Eddie Gaedel as a pinch hitter in a twin-bill at Sportsman's Park on August 19, 1951. The Browns owner got the idea of using a midget by recalling a conversation between John McGraw and his father decades earlier, when the Giant manager mentioned he was thinking of using a batboy as a hitter to draw walks. Concerned more about publicity than strategy, Veeck hired the 3-foot, 7-inch Gaedel, who was the highlight of festivities at the park which included free beer, ice cream and cake. Gaedel made his surprise appearance by popping out of a giant cake wearing a Browns uniform with the number 1/8, and further delighted fans by stepping up to the plate to open the nightcap. After St. Louis manager Zack Taylor confirmed for the home plate umpire Gaedel's presence on the team roster, Eddie was allowed to bat, which for him meant crouching motionless during each delivery, as ordered by Veeck. Gaedel walked on four pitches. Those pondering the legality of the midget's sole career at bat might check the record books, which indicate his having no official plate appearances, but one base-on-balls.

Veeck was full of surprises. On "Grandstand Managers Day,"

Browns fans held aloft large "Yes" or "No" signs indicating preferences for such managerial decisions as whether or not to steal, pinch hit or change pitchers. As an executive with the Cubs in the '30s, he thought of adorning the Wrigley outfield walls with ivy, making it still the most esthetically appealing of all ballparks. Indian owner Veeck was the Branch Rickey of the American League, with Cleveland's Larry Doby becoming the first black to play in the junior-circuit in 1947. As White Sox owner in the '70s, Veeck had veteran broadcaster Harry Caray sing "Take Me Out to the Ballgame," with crowd accompaniment, during the 7th-inning stretch of ballgames, a tradition Caray carried over to the Cubs when he switched from the South Side to the North in the '80s.

Not all of Veeck's brainstorms were praiseworthy. White Sox fans were treated to "Disco Demolition Night" in 1979. The explosion of records between games of the doubleheader started a fire, and caused such chaos that attempts to play the nightcap were abandoned, with the game forfeited to the Tigers. As a minor-league club-owner, Veeck once erected adjustable fences in the outfield, raising them during the visitors' at bats, lowering them during the home half of innings.

No owner has been as vexing to the baseball establishment, players, and hometown fans as was two-decade Athletic owner Charlie Finley. Acquiring the club in 1961 for $2 million, he began an anti-Yankee campaign by criticizing its past raids on A's talent and bemoaning Yankee Stadium's reachable right-field fence, which he claimed was an unfair advantage for such southpaw sluggers as Roger Maris, Mickey Mantle, Yogi Berra and Johnny Blanchard. Finding Commissioner Ford Frick unsympathetic, Finley fought back in 1964 by announcing plans for a V-shaped plywood fence to be installed in right field at Municipal Stadium which would considerably shorten the distance from home plate. Chortled Charlie, "Now since we can't get the Yankees to conform to honest distances, I'll conform to Yankee distances." When his "Pennant Porch" was declared illegal by Frick, the defiant owner declared he'd build it anyway, but backed off when threatened with forfeited games, announcing plans for a "One-Half Pennant Porch" instead.

A love-hate relationship existed between Finley and fans. Like

Veeck, Finley attracted spectators with unorthodox player uniforms, promotions, and innovative ideas. Players were required to autograph baseballs to be used in games, making more-cherished souvenirs out of foul flies or homeruns caught in the stands. Umpires were provided with baseballs by a mechanical rabbit which arose from the ground. Sheep grazed on sod behind the outfield fence, and livestock shows and milking contests often entertained the crowd.

But Finley loved money more than the fans. As attendance decreased in Kansas City during the '60s, Finley's whining increased, and in 1969 he successfully coerced American League President Joe Cronin into granting his request to move the franchise to Oakland. Following five division championships, and three pennants and World Series flags from 1971-1975, the profit-minded Finley began selling his players, a strategy which outraged Commissioner Bowie Kuhn to the point of declaring Finley's dumping of several stars in 1976 illegal. This prompted Finley to label Kuhn the "village idiot." As the sales continued, team performance declined, with Oakland finishing last or next to last in each of the subsequent three seasons, until the one-time insurance executive finally sold the ballclub in 1980.

Playing for Finley wasn't fun. The annoyance of wearing white shoes and green and gold uniforms was nothing compared with Finley's frequent fines and duels over contract negotiations. Mounting frustration caused Catfish Hunter to become the first free agent in 1974 when, using a late-payment of his salary as a legal excuse to escape from Finley, he signed a $3 million deal with the Yankees, one year before the courts voided the reserve clause and paved the way for free agency for all ballplayers.

"Most owners are in the sport for the money." For Yankee boss George Steinbrenner, it's been one big ego trip since acquiring the most-recognized sports team in the world in 1973. What else would explain a shipbuilding magnate with no prior professional baseball experience to interfere in team affairs to the point of banishing players to the minors as punishment for poor performances, making insulting public remarks about his regulars, and hiring and firing field managers with such rapidity that by 1996, the number of Yankee helm changes under Steinbrenner's 23-year-reign reached 21 — an average of nearly one change per season!

Steinbrenner hasn't always lacked patience. Wasn't he remarkably constrained when Billy Martin managed for three consecutive seasons from 1976-1978? Well, not quite three seasons. Billy was fired in the middle of '78 when hopes for the pennant appeared doomed, but George's benevolence led to Martin's rehiring in 1979. Sure, Billy was history after one season, but sentimental Steinbrenner rehired him in '83, and again in '85, and once more in '88, easily making Martin the most often hired-and-fired manager by one owner in the history of baseball, or perhaps of any business.

While reverently conveying his deep respect for the tradition of the game, Steinbrenner's contradictory actions have spoken considerably louder than his words. One year after becoming owner, George renovated (and desecrated) Yankee Stadium by shortening distances to the spacious power alleys, fencing off the famed monuments to Lou Gehrig, Miller Huggins and Babe Ruth in center which were previously in play and visible to spectators, and eliminating the beautiful facade on the Stadium roof. Despite owning one of the most financially successful franchises in sports, Steinbrenner has often threatened to move the Bombers out of the Bronx, perhaps irritated with a park nicknamed "The House That Ruth Built." As of the Spring of '96, he was still lobbying for a new stadium, a distasteful possibility that seems alarmingly likely in the near future.

Americans are fortunate being able to pursue any profession or business venture with little government interference. It's unfortunate that some baseball owners choose to exercise their freedom at the expense of those who are most meaningful to the business — its fans.

CELEBRITIES AND BASEBALL

C onsidering baseball's long-held status as the "national pastime," its attracting celebrities throughout the century,
either as spectators or participants, has been no surprise.
Billy Sunday was the first great American evangelist, known
for his zealous campaign against alcohol prior to the Prohibition
amendment of 1919, and reputedly converted a quarter of a million people to Christianity. Before gaining fame at the pulpit,
Sunday earned a reputation on the diamond.

Sunday was born in an Iowa log cabin to a Union soldier five
months before the Battle of Gettysburg sealed the Confederacy's
fate. Twenty years later, Cap Anson spotted Billy playing in a
semipro game in the Hawkeye State and was impressed with his
speed. Sunday signed with the Cubs in 1883 and despite an unfortunate beginning to his career, fanning in his first 13 at bats,
played ball for another seven seasons. He became renowned for
swiping bases, if not with the same flair as teammate King Kelly,
with comparable success. Sunday, who once stole second, third
and home on consecutive pitches, amassed 71 thefts in 1888, and
in his final season in 1890, he stole 84.

Legend has it that Sunday was bar-hopping with Kelly one night
when they passed a Gospel wagon from which a speech on the
evils of alcohol emanated. Moved by the message, Sunday turned

to the unaffected Kelly and vowed to avoid the wild life and henceforth live in the service of God. After leaving baseball, Sunday entered a seminary and became ordained as a Presbyterian minister in 1896.

Except for Sunday, Chuck Connors was the most notable celebrity to have once played major-league ball. Born Kevin Connors in Brooklyn in 1921, Chuck was a minor-league first baseman from 1940 to 1943, served three years in the military during World War II, and returned to play both professional basketball and baseball from 1945-1947. He continued his hardball career in Montreal in 1948, where teammate Don Newcombe was still a year away from his big league debut in Brooklyn, and once rushed to the defense of the black moundsman when an opposing batter, resenting a brushpack pitch, charged the mound.

Like Newcombe, Connors's major-league career also began in Brooklyn in 1949. He was brought up late in the season and made one unsuccessful appearance at the plate as a pinch hitter. He returned to play another season at Montreal in 1950, but made the most of his chance at the Cubs spring training tryouts in 1951.

Platooning at first base that year with veteran National Leaguer and former batting champ Phil Cavarretta, Connors accumulated 201 at bats in 66 games with Chicago, hitting an unimpressive .239 while showing little power with two homers and 18 RBIs. He was remembered by teammates mostly for being friendly and funny, and for a propensity to recite Shakespeare and "Casey at the Bat."

Connors was shipped to the Pacific Coast League late in the season, where the new environment worked to his advantage. Hollywood scouts, attracted by his height, recitations, or the way he wielded the bat, envisioned him as a rifle-toting 19th century western farmer (or "sodbuster" as he was often referred in the television show). Cast with teen heartthrob Johnny Crawford, Connors made more money from whirling a Winchester than would have been procured from a career of ballplaying during the pre-free-agent era. (Fans of *The Rifleman* will recall the show's opening tune, "Da-Da, Da, Da-Da-Da," while Chuck fired and twirled.)

Comedians have often used baseball themes in their act, the

most famous being the "Who's on First" routine of Bud Abbott and Lou Costello. Costello's attempt to understand such player names offered by Abbott as "Who," "What," "I Don't Know," and "Why," in the 1945 flick *The Naughty Nineties* was so hilarious that the comedy pair would often repeat the act at personal appearances. They performed it again during one of their television spots during the '50s.

Costello's popularity helped gain off-screen privileges, but he wasn't always successful, especially when dealing with tight-fisted baseball owners. In 1948, Lou traveled from Hollywood to Boston, hoping to catch one of the World Series games between the Braves and Indians. Offering to give a live pregame performance of "Who's on First" for free, Costello was nevertheless spurned a ticket to the sold-out game by Brave owner Lou Perini. Perhaps Perini preferred Laurel and Hardy.

America's foremost humorist, Will Rogers, loved baseball and in 1917 performed his cowboy roping act prior to a game. He became an admirer of Walter Johnson, respecting the humility shown by the successful strikeout artist. Once spotting Johnson at a Ziegfield Follies, Rogers roped the right-hander, pulled him from the back-row seat, and guided him to a more enviable one.

Actor-comedian Joe E. Brown played for a semipro ballclub, owned a minor league team, and was a friend of fireballer Dizzy Dean. When Dean's Cards faced the Tigers in the '34 Series, Detroit hurler Schoolboy Rowe blamed Brown for his losing game six. Rowe had a slightly swollen right hand which was further aggravated after receiving an energetic pregame handshake from Brown. The wide-mouthed celebrity loudly declared his innocence of foul play after the St. Louis victory.

Bob Hope often joked about his part-ownership of the Cleveland Indians, once appearing on an *I Love Lucy* episode with such a theme. Vainly trying to watch an Indian-Yankee game at Yankee Stadium, Hope is continuously distracted by hot-dog vendor Lucille Ball, who is finagling for a spot in his act. At one point, Hope misses seeing an Al Rosen home run, then later is plunked on the head with a foul pop-up while speaking with Lucy. The episode ends happily with Ball, husband Desi Arnaz, and Hope performing as a trio, Lucy apologizing for the bump on Hope's noggin, and Hope shrugging off the injury, declaring in song, "I don't care. It may grow hair."

Owning the Anaheim Angels has been no joke to former singing cowboy Gene Autrey. Since purchasing the franchise in 1960, Autrey has spent more money than any other owner (with the possible exception of Steinbrenner) in trying to bring a World Series to Anaheim. His win-at-any-cost philosophy, which was aptly expressed in his once responding to sportswriter Grantland Rice's two-line motto, "It's not whether you win or lose. It's how you play the game" by snapping, "Grantland Rice can go to hell," resulted in only three division titles during the likable owner's 35-year spending-spree. By January of 1996, Autrey's days as Angel owner appeared numbered, as rumors spread of an attempted buyout by the Disney Group.

Tom Selleck played ball in college long before playing sleuth Thomas Magnum. In preparation for a part in a baseball flick, Selleck once worked out with the Boston Red Sox in 1990. The southpaw batter impressed many with a smooth swing and numerous line drives during batting practice.

Songwriter-singer Paul Simon never played ball professionally but was an avid Yankee fan. As a toddler, he often sat on his father's knee and listened to Mel Allen's broadcasts, and once missed seeing a DiMaggio homer at Yankee Stadium when the adult spectators in front of him stood to watch the flight of the ball. In spite of the famous line from his song "Mrs. Robinson," asking the whereabouts of Joltin' Joe, Simon's childhood hero was Mickey Mantle, who when finding out, asked Simon why he hadn't used his name in the song instead.

Baseball has attracted the notorious as well. Al Capone hobnobbed with actors and actresses, opera singers, and powerful politicians, but liked speaking with ballplayers as well. Invited to Scarface's suite in 1931, Charlie Gehringer, Jumpin' Joe Dugan and two other Tigers were searched by henchmen four times before meeting Capone.

On September 9 of that same season, Capone took his imaginatively nicknamed son, Sonny, to Wrigley Field. Prior to the game, he requested an autographed baseball from the Cubs' Gabby Hartnett. A photographer took advantage, and the photo of America's foremost gangster chatting with a participant of the nation's grandest sport appeared in newspapers throughout the country,

a sight which would have disturbed any of baseball's commis-
sioners, but none as much as the righteous Judge Kenesaw
Mountain Landis. Capone was then in the midst of a tax evasion
trial for which he was convicted and sentenced to 10 years in
federal prison one month after the photo was taken. Hartnett
was admonished by the Mountain, who also sent word to the two
league presidents that conversing between ballplayers and fans
during games was no longer permissible.

*Cub's Gabby Hartnett autographs a baseball for Al Capone and his son, Sonny,
seated to Scarface's right. Behind Capone is his vigilant bodyguard who appears
to be reaching for something inside his jacket. (AP/Wide World Photos)*

Another hoodlum who'd often frequent Wrigley Field was
America's first "Public Enemy Number One," John Dillinger.
Dillinger played second base and pitched in amateur ball during
his teen years before choosing robbing banks as his
profession. While incarcerated in the '20s, Dillinger played on the

prison team and organized baseball pools.

Attending Cub games was different for Dillinger than for "businessman" Capone, who received ovations at Wrigley from crowds appreciative of his frequent Depression handouts and illegal liquor provided at speakeasies. Though Dillinger captured public attention, the wanted murderer could hardly take bows at ballparks. On one occasion in 1931, the normally careful criminal was nearly spotted by a Chicago police captain before sneaking out of the ballpark.

Arnold Rothstein was one of New York's most notorious criminals, though he'd have argued he was never convicted of a felony. The Broadway gambler, who at one time or another had such infamous thugs on his payroll as Legs Diamond, Lucky Luciano and Bugsy Siegel, and who was nicknamed "Mr. Big" for the quarter of a million in thousand dollar bills always present in his pocket, liked baseball and any other sport only as a means to make money. The ignominious figure was almost certainly the brains and money behind the bribing of the eight Chicago White Sox (turned Black Sox) players who intentionally lost the Series of 1919. Ironically, the man who earned a reputation as the consummate gambler was "done in" by fellow gamester Hump McManus for welshing on a bet. Bleeding profusely from a gunshot wound in the stomach, Rothstein was rushed to the hospital, where he responded to deathbed inquiries from police by smiling and placing his forefinger on his lips.

Not all celebrities have found baseball appealing, the wide-eyed, early-century comic Eddie Cantor once pointing out that a ballplayer is considered by many to be "king of the loafers." Nevertheless, when General Douglas MacArthur returned from Europe in 1946 to take in a game at the Polo Grounds and remarked, "It's great to be here, to be able to hear the baseball against the bat, ball against the glove, the call of the vendor, and be able to boo the umpire," the old soldier's sentiment echoed that felt by most Americans, famous and unknown.

PRESIDENTS AND BASEBALL

S howing a considerable amount of patience and diplomacy, President William Howard Taft appeased a group of rebellious women suffragists gathered at a White House luncheon on April 14, 1910, then scurried to Washington's American League Park to attend the first game of the baseball season. The heavyset chief executive, encouraged by the equally rotund Ban Johnson to throw the game ball from his front row seat to the Senator's Opening Day pitcher, Walter Johnson, removed his gloves, took the ball from his wife, and fired a low throw to Johnson, who fielded it cleanly. As observed in *Baseball — The President's Game*, the effect of the toss was to "once and forever wrap the flag and the president around the game."

Since Taft, nearly every chief executive has observed the first-throw tradition at least once, with Jimmy Carter's brief tenure and preference for softball helping to make him the sole exception. Not surprisingly, four-term president Franklin Roosevelt holds the record with 11 opening tosses, while George Bush is a close runner-up with 10.

Taft wasn't the first president to attend a ballgame. On June 6, 1892, Benjamin Harrison watched the then-National League Senators lose to Cincinnati and saw the home team fall to the Phillies later that month. His successor, William McKinley, also attended games and had a chance to set the first-throw precedent in the opener of the 1897 season in Washington, but declined the offer.

Despite its long-held status as the national pastime, baseball hasn't been embellished by all American leaders. Teddy Roosevelt proclaimed it a sport for sissies (he must never have witnessed an old Oriole game), preferred the more manly exercise of boxing, and never attended a ballgame despite receiving season passes. Calvin Coolidge carried on the first-ball tradition during the 20s but, being a lukewarm fan of baseball, did so reluctantly. Ironically, Washington's winning the World Series in October of 1924, with Coolidge gaining publicity by giving verbal support and attending the Series opener (setting a precedent for presidents), helped him to a convincing election victory one month later over Democrat John Dawes. Harry Truman was an avid spectator, but his wearing glasses prevented ball-playing as a youth. Carter didn't enjoy baseball, attending only one game as president, but was a fierce competitor and particularly competent slow-pitch hurler in its close cousin, softball. Bill Clinton preferred playing the saxophone to ballplaying as a youth, but liked following the Cardinals, though he switched allegiance to Chicago after marrying Cub fanatic Hillary Rodham.

Presidents have at times reluctantly refused first-throws. Taft declined on April 19, 1912, a few days after a speeding Titanic rammed into an iceberg in the North Atlantic and sank, killing two-thirds of its passengers and crew. Woodrow Wilson enjoyed the ritual, but appropriately passed during the World War I years of 1917 and 1918. FDR would have added to his record 11 tosses had World War II not interfered from 1942-1944. Lyndon Johnson asked Vice President Hubert Humphrey to pinch-throw for him in 1968, one month after his decision to abstain from a second-term run due to the unpopular conflict in Vietnam.

Most presidents have been kids at heart in terms of their enthusiasm for the game, often a result of past participation. Herbert Hoover played baseball in his youth, and attended nine ballgames, including three Series games, in his single term of office. Dwight Eisenhower was a high school center fielder in Abilene and continued wearing the spikes at West Point while secretly breaking amateur rules by playing pro ball to help pay tuition costs. Texan

Lyndon Johnson played sandlot baseball as a teenager. Bush was a good-field, no-hit first baseman and captain of his Yale team in the late '40s, playing against such future big leaguers as Jackie Jensen and Walt Dropo and skilled enough with the leather to have once been approached by a professional scout.

Boston's John Kennedy was a huge Red Sox fan as a senator, but diplomatically switched allegiance to the Senators as president. Unlike other chief executives, Kennedy always remained until the game's completion, despite lacking a hat or topcoat in the normally chilly openers. JFK's political rival and future president Richard Nixon was probably the most knowledgeable leader in terms of baseball history and loved the game to the point of once wishing he could have been a sportswriter instead. Nixon was so respected by the baseball community that in 1965 he was first offered the position of Player Association president, then baseball commissioner, politely declining both times. In 1995, at a scholarly conference at Hofstra University honoring the 100th anniversary of Babe Ruth's birth, historian David Eisenhower, grandson of Ike, recalled how father-in-law Nixon compiled a list of "Dream Teams" from various periods in baseball history. Surprisingly, Willie Mays was excluded from the 1960-1991 era, with Aaron, Roberto Clemente and Lou Brock chosen for the outfield positions.

Ronald Reagan's connection with America's game is more well-known than that of any other president. Before turning to acting, Dutch delighted radio listeners of the '30s with imaginative recreations of ballgames. Broadcasting from Des Moines, Reagan would receive reports via telegraph from Wrigley Field, then, with a flair indicative of a future Hollywood career, dramatically describe the "play-by-play." In 1952, actor Reagan starred in "The Winning Team," a fairly accurate biography of Grover Cleveland Alexander, and was coached by former big-league hurler Bob Lemon, who later described his protégé as "graceful and easy to teach."

Presidents have begun games with different styles and sometimes with different results. Hoover should have been an accurate tosser, having played shortstop as a youth, but the beginnings of the Depression may have distracted him in 1930 when his throw went sailing over a photographer's head. Roosevelt had a smooth overhand toss and was usually accurate, though he did once break a camera lens. His successor, Truman, made the first lefty toss on September 2, 1945, and again made history five years later by first throwing right-handed, then left-handed in the season opener. Kennedy delighted fans with energetic flings, heaving the ball well beyond front-row players in his premiere toss of 1961.

Some presidents have been eyewitnesses to historical baseball events. Bush met Babe Ruth in 1948, when the Bambino presented the Yale University library with the original manuscript of his autobiography, *The Babe Ruth Story*. President Johnson attended the first game ever played in the Astrodome, a 1965 preseason exhibition between the Yankees and Astros, and watched as Mantle blasted the first-ever indoor home run. Gerald Ford saw Hank Aaron match Babe Ruth's 714 homers with a belt off Cincinnati's Jack Billingham in the season opener of 1974, though he was vice president at the time.

Not all first-throws have been pleasant presidential experiences. Spectators booed Hoover's presence at Shibe Park in game three of the '31 Series, their angry reaction to the Depression and Prohibition. Truman heard it from the crowd at the 1951 opener, a week after relieving General Douglas MacArthur of all commands. Bush's being booed at the All-Star Game in San Diego in 1992, a foreboding of the November election results, was probably a reaction to continuously depressing reports on the economy by all three major television networks.

Though interrupted by Carter, the custom of first-ball tossing by presidents has become another delightful American tradition, one not likely to be supplanted by presidential participation at other, increasingly popular professional sporting events. Imagine the fun Don Imus and Howard Stern would have with a chief executive's throwing out the first football, or shooting the first slap shot, or jump shot. Dare Clinton or any future president take that risk?

CHAPTER 9

LAST INNINGS

J onathan Swift wrote, "Life is a tragedy, wherein we sit as spectators for a while, and then act our part in it." Some play their parts sooner than others.

On April 11, 1909, a record crowd of over 31,000 gathered to celebrate the opening of the season in Philadelphia and the opening of the A's new, half-million dollar Shibe Park. Pregame ceremonies included a parade across the field led by American League President Ban Johnson and A's Owner Benjamin Shibe, and a speech by the Philly mayor, who at 3 p.m. tossed out the first ball to begin play. Two hours later, fans celebrated the A's battering of Boston hurlers for 13 hits in breezing to an 8-1 laugher. However, Connie Mack's crew wasn't celebrating.

One Philly who hadn't contributed with the bat was Mike "Doc" Powers, though his defense and handling of pitcher Eddie Plank that day was "perfect, grand, superb," as one eyewitness wrote. The last of the original A's, having joined the junior-circuit club in its inaugural season of 1901, Powers began experiencing stomach pains during the seventh inning. Though shrugging it off as gas, Powers collapsed by game's end, making it apparent to teammates that Doc, a nickname derived from his studying medicine at Notre Dame, was in need of one. An ambulance rushed him to the hospital, where physicians diagnosed the condition as merely "acute gastritis," assuring Mack that Powers' powers would fully return in a couple of days. Instead, Doc deteriorated to the point where three unsuccessful stomach operations were performed. After hearing his last rites, Doc died on April 26 from strangulation of the intestines at the age of 38.

Memorial Day of 1928 was memorable for fans of Urban Shocker, for it was on that holiday that the four-time 20-game winner made his first appearance of the year, and last of his life. By then, the 38-year-old Shocker was a 13-year veteran with nary a losing season and had been one of the top pitchers on the famed 1927 Yankee club with an 18-6 mark. That outstanding season prompted Urban to shock Yank owner Jacob Ruppert by refusing to sign the following spring. Like most other players who had attempted coerced pay hikes, Shocker's holdout was futile and he relented by mid-May. He was used as a batting practice pitcher for a couple of weeks, then made his first appearance of the season on May 30 after the Senators had pounded Yank starter Al Shealy for five runs. Shocker held Washington scoreless the last two innings.

When the nation celebrated its next holiday — Independence Day, five weeks later, Shocker received his independence in the form of an unconditional release. By then, the Yanks had realized that the former star, who hadn't appeared in a game since his Memorial Day outing, was suffering from an irreversible heart condition and no longer capable of helping the ballclub. Shocker moved to Denver, hoping the high altitude and clean air would cure, but he died in September just prior to his former team's taking their second-straight pennant and World Series.

Veteran pitcher Hal Carlson was in his 14th season by 1930. The year began optimistically for the Cub right-hander, winning four of his first five decisions before taking the mound in Pittsburgh on May 23. The Bucs struck quickly with a pair in the first and one in the second before Carlson was struck on the pitching hand by a line drive in the third and forced to leave the game. Though the Cubs lost to the Pirates, Manager Joe McCarthy's main concern afterwards was the possible temporary loss of one of his starters. Unfortunately, Carlson's absence from the rotation would be permanent.

On May 28, Hal awoke with severe stomach pains. Hearing his

screams from the adjacent hotel room, teammates Kiki Cuyler and Riggs Stephenson rushed to his aid, then notified the team doctor who vainly attempted to treat the stricken 38-year-old. Carlson's death was attributed to "stomach hemorrhages" brought about by ulcers, from which the World War I veteran had intermittently suffered since being exposed to poison gas in 1918.

The Cubs were battling the Cardinals for first when they hosted the Dodgers on September 15, 1935. The Brooklynites cooperated by surrendering four runs in the first two innings and trailed by three in the ninth. Hoping to spark a rally, Dodger skipper Casey Stengel sent in the dangerous lefty Len Koenecke as a pinch hitter.

Koenecke had been a rather old prospect when signed by Brooklyn in 1932 at the age of 28. He batted an unimpressive .255 that year and was sent to Buffalo the following season. Len returned to Brooklyn in 1934 and batted .320, but when he struggled with the bat in '35, Stengel sat him.

In what would be his final at bat on earth, Koenecke grounded to second. Two outs later, the Cubs won their twelfth straight, and Koenecke won a ticket back to Brooklyn where he was told to remain until the Dodgers returned from their road trip. Len had other plans. He hired a private plane shuttle and shuffled off to Buffalo to visit some old buddies. Unfortunately, Koenecke became intoxicated on the plane, tried to take over the controls from the pilot, and was struck on the head with a fire extinguisher and killed by the copilot. It was later alleged that Koenecke's irrational behavior was actually an attempt at suicide, though the assertion was made by the pilot's lawyer.

Willard Hersberger was another old rookie when he signed with the Reds in 1938 at the age of 27. He platooned at backstop for two seasons, gaining a reputation as a solid batter and good handler of pitchers. He was hitting a healthy .322 when the first-place Reds entered Beantown to take on the struggling Boston Braves (or Bees as they were alternately called), in the midst of a nine-game losing streak. Hershberger watched from the bench as Cincy was crushed 10-3 in the opener. He started behind the plate in the nightcap, went hitless in five trips, and gazed helplessly as Chet Ross's bases-loaded single fell into left field to give Boston a twelve-inning 4-3 victory.

As the Reds prepared to play another two at Braves Field the following afternoon, Hershberger remained in his hotel room, having complained of illness. Wanting to check on his friend, Cincinnati businessman Dan Cohen went to the hotel, only to learn that Hershberger's throat had been cut. His death was labeled a suicide, and since the moody catcher had been blaming himself for recent losses and had previously blurted out suicidal threats, it probably was. Still, his success with the stick that year, along with his club's holding a 6 1/2 game bulge after dropping the double-dip to Boston, casts some suspicion as to why Hershberger would become excessively distraught over a few off-games.

Former Yank hurler Ernie Bonham couldn't complain of lack of support from Pirate teammates on August 27, 1949, as the Bucs pounded four Phils's hurlers for nine hits and eight runs. The 6-foot, 2-inch, 200-pound Bonham, paradoxically nicknamed "Tiny," threw effectively, allowing eight hits and two runs in coasting to his seventh victory in eleven decisions. After the game, the 36-year-old righty complained of pains in his side and was taken to the hospital. He was diagnosed with appendicitis and given an appendectomy the next day. The normally routine operation caused severe complications, and Bonham remained in the hospital. His condition deteriorated, and Tiny passed away on September 15.

Thurman Munson batted over .300 in his first full season in 1970, earning him the Rookie-of-the-Year award. By 1979, the 32-year-old catcher had three Gold Glove awards, one MVP, five seasons of batting over .300, three 100-RBI seasons, and the distinction of being named the first Yankee captain since Lou Gehrig.

On August 1 of that year, Munson and the Yankees were in Chicago hoping to cut into a substantial lead held by Baltimore. After Reggie Jackson and Lou Piniella crushed homers in the first inning, Munson drew a walk, then fanned in the fourth frame. While striking out, he strained his right knee and was removed from the game by recently rehired manager Billy Martin.

With no game scheduled the following day, Munson, a licensed pilot, flew to his home town of Canton to be with his family. While he was practicing landings at the airport, the plane crashed and Munson died in the burning wreckage. Grief-stricken teammate Bobby Murcer eulogized at the funeral, "The life of a soul on Earth lasts longer than his departure. He lives on in your life and the life of all others who knew him."

Other instances of players dying during the season have occurred, still more of active players dying during the off-season. Some were preventable, others unforeseen and unavoidable. All were morbid reminders of life's unpredictability and our lack of immunity to tragedy, even among heroes.

HOOKS WHO?

C y Young. Christy Mathewson. Grover Cleveland Alexander. Walter Johnson. Kid Nichols. Rube Marquard. Hooks Wiltse.

Hooks Wiltse?

It may be that he doesn't belong on the elite list of the game's greatest early-era pitchers, but considering his career accomplishments, George "Hooks" Wiltse was one of the outstanding left-handers nonetheless. His retirement following the 1915 season left him with an ERA of 2.47 and 139 wins, most of them gathered in nine seasons as a starter for the Giants. He had back-to-back 20-win seasons in 1908 and 1909. He rates among the top 20 all-time pitchers in fewest runners allowed per nine innings. In 1904, he won 12 consecutive games, one fewer than Mathewson's best streak, one more than Alexander's, with four of them helping the Giants string together 18-straight wins. In a game in 1906, he fanned seven-consecutive batters, including four in one frame. In 1907, he again had four victories in a Giant win streak, this one stretching to 17 games. In 1908, Wiltse pitched 330 innings and had 31 complete games, one of which would be his most incomparable accomplishment.

The Giants were a game-and-a-half out in third place on the Fourth of July when they hosted the Phillies in the first of a morning-afternoon doubleheader, a then-common strategy by owners to double gate receipts. New York's John Brush did well in disposing of 20,000 tickets at two bits apiece, most of which were sold for the second game, won by the Giants 9-3. The high number of tallies was unusual for a pre-20s contest, but as delighted as the spectators were with the action, most undoubtedly wished they had awaken early enough that Saturday to catch the 1-0 opener.

Having used his ace Mathewson the day before, New York skipper John McGraw chose Wiltse as his first-game starter, hoping a win would take pressure off the less reliable Luther "Dummy" Taylor in the second. Wiltse was opposed by the Phillies' George McQuillan who, despite an erratic career, was the club's best pitcher that year in winning 23 games.

McQuillan was tough for the Giants that morning, shutting them out on only six hits through eight innings, but Wiltse did more than match him. He was invincible heading into the ninth, not one Philly batter having reached base. Fans had begun speculating about the league's first perfect game of the century by the sixth inning, with heightened enthusiasm manifested by increasingly louder ovations after Wiltse completed the seventh and eighth. When Hooks set aside Doolin and Dooin in the ninth, then easily threw two by McQuillan, a shaky hitter even for a pitcher if his .117 lifetime average is an indication, hands reached for brims in anticipation of a straw-flinging celebration.

Some hats may have indeed touched grass when McQuillan looked at an apparent third strike. Apparent to all except the one who counted. Charles Rigler would distinguish himself as a National League umpire with nearly 30 years service, but in 1908 he had completed but one year's duty. With the intimidating McGraw at earshot's distance and the knowledge that a ball call would instigate an angry, if not violent, fan reaction, it took courage for the sophomore ump to refrain from throwing his right arm up.

If the fans were upset with Rigler, they became furious when Wiltse's next pitch hit McQuillan, spoiling the perfecto. Instead of hats, bottles might have been sent flying had a victory, and possible no-hitter, not remained within reach. Wiltse retired the next batter, and the side in order in the 10th. In the home half,

Art Devlin singled and scored the winning run a few minutes later. Hooks had the first 10-inning, no-hit victory in history, a feat since matched by only two others (the Reds' Fred Toney and Jim Maloney).

Did George Wiltse become known as "Hooks" for his sharp curve or for his crooked nose? Perhaps this photo gives us a clue. (National Baseball Library, Cooperstown, NY)

It must have irked Hooks that he lost the perfect game by hitting the 27th man he faced, the only pitcher in history to lose one in that manner, while aware that a controversial call preceded his nailing the opposition's weakest hitter (McQuillan admitted afterwards the pitch was a strike). Still, with the possible exception of a game-saving appearance in the 1913 World Series when he threw out two runners at the plate, allowing New York to win game two in the tenth, it's likely the no-hitter was the most memorable thrill for Wiltse.

The 6-foot native of Hamilton, New York, had his share of bad memories. Like the time he was nearly arrested in 1906 when teammates caused a ruckus on a train ride from New York to Albany. Or in 1913 when, prior to relieving in an exhibition game in Tulsa (which featured the first and only confrontation between Walter Johnson and Christy Mathewson), the ballpark's bleacher section collapsed, killing one and injuring 50. Or later that year, when on a voyage to the Far East with other Giant stars (which included Jim Thorpe), stormy seas furiously rocked the boat, upsetting both his stomach and a trunk full of clothes which smashed against his pitching hand.

He wasn't the most dominant hurler of his day, certainly not the most renowned, but Hooks could delight his grandchildren with many tales prior to his death in 1959 at the age of 78. He could joke about the origin of his nickname, derived both from an uncommon curveball and an uncommonly-shaped nose. Wiltse could describe with delight his rookie season of 1904 when, after the opportunistic McGraw, ever-watchful for new talent, snatched him from the Eastern League, he responded with a 13-3 record.

But was it with sheer fondness that Hooks related the story of his Independence Day pitching gem of 1908? Or was there a hint of regret, even bitterness, in his voice when explaining how he came within an inch, or an umpire's misjudgment, of hurling a masterpiece?

OLD MR. YOUNG

From the sidelines, paunchy 44-year-old Denton Young took his 12th warmup toss, then trodded to the mound. A dozen before a game was all he needed, all he had ever needed for the past 21 seasons, 900 games, 7,300 innings, and 510 victories. Few warmups. Few walks. Few wasted pitches. That's why his fastball still had some giddyap, why he never had a sore arm, even after once pitching nine games in 18 days.

If the opener of the twin bill was an indication, the Phillies figured to be difficult opponents, having tallied 13 times off four different Braves' hurlers. Young's mound opponent that afternoon of September 7, 1911, wouldn't make victory any easier. Sure, he was a rookie, but Grover Alexander already had over 20 wins, with another month to go. Still, the crowd at the South End Grounds was on Young's side, and maybe he'd get a few more of the close calls from home plate ump Bill Klem than would the 24-year-old Alexander.

The 6-foot, 2-inch right-hander disposed of the first three Philly hitters and set aside the remainder of the lineup in the next two innings with an ease reminiscent of his first major-league start in 1890, when as a Cleveland Spider he defeated Cap Anson's cocky Chicago Colts on a three-hitter. The arrogant player-manager had ridiculed the rookie prior to the game, and Young made

Cap pay by muscling three fastballs past him in their first encounter. It wasn't much later that everyone was calling him Cy — short for Cyclone.

The Philly batters, so formidable in game one, did little better against Young in their second go-around. Father Time, that most dreaded enemy of athletes, seemed to be ignoring this Buckeye, whose arms and legs still had the look of one who had swung an axe for hours and chased rabbits for miles as a youth on his father's farm. Wasn't it only three years ago in 1908 that he had become a 20-game winner for the 15th time? And now, despite lackluster seasons in 1909, 1910, and most of 1911, Cy was again exhibiting power and prowess not dissimilar to the hurler who'd won 30 games five times, pitched two no-hitters and one perfect game, strung together 44 consecutive scoreless innings and 23 consecutive hitless innings, and on one occasion fanned three-straight on nine swinging strikes.

Another inning, another goose egg for the Phillies. Seven frames and only four harmless singles and a walk permitted by Young. He should have been pleased, but was instead concerned, for Alexander was even more miserly in allowing no runs and only one baserunner — an infield hit by Doc Miller. This classic confrontation between living legend and young phenom was as competitive as could be expected. Which of the two warriors would waver first?

Young began the eighth by retiring Alexander and Dutch Knabe, but Dode Paskert pushed a single through the infield, then put himself in scoring position with a theft of second. Hans Lobert, the next Philly batter, was skilled enough with the stick to have received an intentional pass but Sherry Magee would follow and, as the reigning batting champ, posed a more serious threat. Young went right at Lobert who drilled a single, chasing home Paskert with the game's first run.

Cy retired the Phils in the ninth, but his one mistake proved fatal. Alexander breezed by the final two frames, which offered some excitement for the partisan Boston crowd when the Braves' spirited Mike Donlin and the autocratic Klem squared off in a face-to-face confrontation. The Old Arbiter, as Klem was referred in later years, was only in his seventh of what would be a record 37 seasons, but wasted little time in ejecting Donlin. Teammate

Hank Gowdy's attempt to intervene resulted in Klem's giving him the boot as well.

Legend has it that after the game, Young declared, "When the rookies can beat you, it's time to quit," then did. If 1911 was indeed his final year, the September loss to Alex wasn't his swan song. On the 12th in Boston, he opposed another difficult moundsman, Christy Mathewson, in the second of a double-dip and didn't last three innings in losing to the pennant-bound Giants. (Mike Donlin again earned an early shower after shaking his fists in the face of umpire Jim Johnstone, delighting the 11,000 in attendance.) A week later, Young was at three-year-old Forbes Field in Pittsburgh pitching a nine-hit, 1-0 masterpiece over the Pirates. Fittingly, the shutout would be the final victory of his career. On the 24th at the West Side Grounds in Chicago (Wrigley Field was three years away), Young lost a heartbreaker to the Cubs on an unearned run in the ninth and fell in another well-pitched, complete game at Cincinnati's Palace-of-the-Fans at the end of the month (the Reds would move to Crosley Field the following season). At Washington Park in Brooklyn on October 6 (two years before Ebbets Field), Cy made his farewell appearance and pitched masterfully until the seventh when he was bombed from the box on an eight-run explosion by the Superbas, or Dodgers.

Yet, Young wasn't resigned to retirement following the season. He attended Boston's 1912 spring training camp and became convinced that he was through only when his pot belly prevented fielding slow grounders and bunts. His 511 victories, nearly 100 more than runner-up Walter Johnson's total, remains an unreachable major-league mark.

Those cynical of the abilities of old-time ballplayers would point out that during the early part of Young's career, the pitching distance from home plate was only 50 feet; that he pitched during a time of dead balls and heavy bats when pitchers didn't need to throw hard to retire batters; that ballparks were more spacious then, resulting in fewer homers; that comfortable train travel between cities often only a few hours away made life less hectic for early-era ballplayers.

What they often don't mention is that ballparks were generally in terrible shape, with bad hops in the infield and outfield testing fielders' reflexes more often than they do today; that gloves and catcher's mitts were nonexistent during part of Young's career and ridiculously small later, necessitating sure hands and intense concentration; that playing doubleheaders in 90-degree heat, a nearly-extinct phenomenon today, was fairly common then; that regular pitchers hadn't the luxury of relief specialists to rescue them when a specified pitch count had been reached, but were required instead to finish what they started; and that cramped hotel rooms lacking air-conditioning made life on the road at times unbearable.

In 1893, the pitching mound was moved further back to the current distance of 60 feet, 6 inches. There were two reasons for the change. One was a flamethrowing righty named Amos Rusie who in two of his first four seasons fanned over 300 batters. The other reason was Cy Young.

CHAPTER 12

DOUBLE DOSE OF ALEX

The Young-Alexander pitching duel of September 1911 symbolized age yielding to youth, a champion giving way to the challenger, a magnificent career ending and another just beginning. Grover Cleveland Alexander finished the season with 28 victories which not only led the National League, but remains a major-league record for rookies. His 31 complete games were also a league-high as were his 367 innings-pitched. Alex held opposing batters to a meager .219 average, another league best.

There have been hurlers in baseball history who've begun brilliantly only to fade quickly. The Tigers' rookie right-hander, Mark "The Bird" Fidrych, entertained fans in 1976 with a lively fastball and peculiar mannerisms (talking to the ball; kneeling on the mound while smoothing its surface). He ended the season with 19 wins and as the league-leader in ERA (2.34) and complete games (24). In the next four seasons, Fidrych won a total of 10 games, then quit.

Alexander would prove no flash-in-the-pan, amassing 373 victories (tied for third with Mathewson on the all-time list), 90 shutouts (second), and a 2.56 ERA (second) in his 20-year career which ended in 1930. Old Pete was a 20-game winner in nine seasons, a 30-game winner three times. The right-hander led the league in shutouts seven times, in victories and strikeouts six times, in ERA four times. His still-standing major-league record of 16 blanks in 1916 is arguably the game's greatest seasonal pitching feat.

If having to face the lanky 6-foot, 1-inch, hard-throwing, side-wheeler with pinpoint control was an arduous task for opposing clubs, imagine their plight in seeing him twice in one day. Such was the case with the Reds on September 23, 1916, in a late-season doubleheader at Philadelphia's Baker Bowl. They creamed the Cornhusker for a dozen hits in the opener, but managed merely three runs, as Alex coasted to a 7-3 victory, his 30th of the season.

Embroiled in a three-way fight for the flag with one week re-maining, Philly Manager Pat Moran gambled. He started Alex in the nightcap, hoping his ace's arm could at least last until the late innings. It would do better. Alexander conquered the Reds on an eight-hit, 4-0 whitewash. The master of efficiency threw few that weren't strikes in allowing one walk and completing the game in 1-hour, 7-minutes. The double-victory was the first of his career. It wouldn't be his last.

Though Moran's strategy was successful that day, it went for naught as the Phils failed to defend their pennant of 1915. The following September, Moran's boys were again challenging for the flag, when they visited Brooklyn for a Labor Day doubleheader in front of 19,000 fans. Alexander shut out the opposition in the first game, keeping batters off balance with fastballs and sweep-ing curves which caught the corners of the plate. He fanned five while walking one and surrendered four hits in defeating three-time, 20-game winner and holder of baseball's longest seasonal winning streak (19 in 1912), Rube Marquard.

With the victory, the Phils remained in second place, but were still eight games behind the front-running Giants. As was the case a year earlier, Moran knew that time was running out. Losses weren't an affordable luxury if there was a chance that New York could be caught. Alex had won the opener in under 1 hour and 20 minutes and was willing to work again. The desperate manager let him.

Grover's pitches were slightly more hittable in the second game, but his concentration and control remained. No Brooklyn batter received a free pass, so that the team's nine hits brought only three runs, one of which resulted from a lost ball in the low sun by the Phils' slugging outfielder, Gavvy Cravath. Alexander's mates, meanwhile, bombarded another three-time, 20-game winner and seasonal record-holder (13 shutouts in 1912, most in A.L.), Jack Coombs, in coasting to a 9-3 victory.

Only a score of ballplayers in the century have won two complete-games in one day. Alex and the Giants' Joe McGinnity are the only hurlers who've done it more than once. In 1926, the Indians' Dutch Levson became the last to win a complete game doubleheader, Boston being the victim. With the scarcity of twin bills in today's game and the decline in the number of complete games thrown, a repeat of the feat isn't forthcoming.

It's a team sport, but in no other are individual achievements recognized, even cherished, to the extent that they are in baseball. Literally thousands of player statistics have been diligently recorded by baseball officials and independent researchers, enabling fans to scrutinize, or in extreme cases, memorize the accomplishments of past and present performers. Particular attention is paid to records, so that few fall today without the news being instantly disseminated.

The Phils were again unsuccessful in capturing the flag in 1917, as the Giants outdistanced them by 10 games. Though their quest for the ultimate achievement resulted in consecutive-season failures, it provided the opportunity for a player to maximize his talents. If his team's efforts in 1916 and 1917 have been forgotten, Alexander's accomplishments in those seasons are legendary.

HISTORY OF ABUSE

It was a hot, sunny, Thursday afternoon in late-July of 1994 when an impromptu family meeting with my wife, Lola, and 12-year-old daughter, Jackie, resulted in a drive to Yankee Stadium. Despite it being a mid-week game, we left early in anticipation of a struggle for tickets, with New York in first place and the best pitcher in the league that year, Jimmy Key, scheduled to start. In the parking lot, we were approached by a ticket scalper, who enticed us with three boxes in the shaded third-base ground-level section. Naturally, we ignored him.

New York's opponents were the California Angels, who had righty-swinging Bo Jackson as their designated hitter against southpaw Key. The Bronx ballpark had long been a favorite of Jackson's, once belting three-consecutive homers in a 1990 game. Yankee Stadium, and Key, wouldn't be kind to him on this day.

Bo had been a star in football and baseball until a gridiron injury in '90 ended his play with the pigskin and condemned him to mediocrity on the diamond. If the grit he showed in pursuing his hardball career was to be admired, Jackson still played for the visiting ballclub, and Yankee fans aren't known for showing mercy. The catcalls began as he kneeled in the on-deck circle in the second inning, growing in intensity as he approached the batter's box. When Key threw strike three past him, the crowd erupted with delight. Jackson said nothing as he walked, with head down, back to the dugout on the third-base side.

It was a scene to be repeated three more times that day. The crowd roared with approval after Bo's fourth whiff, many shouting insults as the former superstar walked dejectedly toward the bench for the final time. Unbeknownst to Jackson, that afternoon would be his final appearance at Yankee Stadium. Three weeks later, club owners and players would fail to come to a labor agreement, resulting in the cancellation of the remainder of the season, post-season play, and World Series. When the season belatedly began in 1995, Jackson was already officially retired, the hip replacement surgery of '92 having failed to extend his career much further.

Bo knows that verbal abuse by fans is as much a part of baseball tradition as the National Anthem and the 7th-inning stretch. In fact, there have been times when the wrath of spectators hasn't been limited to hoots and hisses. During the seventh game of the 1934 World Series, fans at Tiger Stadium became so enraged at the rough play of the Gas House Gang's Ducky Medwick that they began throwing fruits and vegetables at him as he helplessly held his position in left field, forcing Commissioner Landis to remove Medwick from the game. In June of 1963, outfielder Frank Howard ran toward the left-field bleachers to retrieve a drive. As he leaned down to pick up the ball, several members of Wrigley Field's bleacher bums showered Howard with so many peanuts that the dumbfounded Dodger delayed in returning the ball to the infield, allowing the runner an extra base. In June of 1970 at Yankee Stadium, a simple-minded spectator chucked a cherry bomb toward the home-plate umpire, injuring instead the Indians' backstop.

On some occasions, players and fans have reversed roles of abuser and abused. In 1912, a heckling New York spectator got the worst of it when the target of his tormenting climbed over the railing. Told that the man he was badly beating was missing a hand and four fingers from the other, the cold Ty Cobb continued pounding nonetheless.

The Cubs' hefty hitter of the '20s and '30s, Hack Wilson, was a sight to behold at 5-feet, 6-inches and 200 pounds. Often the object of ridicule from opponents and fans alike, the good-natured

Wilson usually took the insults in stride. Not so in a 1929 game when constant badgering from a spectator sent Hack diving into the stands after him. The battered fan, a milkman by profession, tried to milk $20,000 from Wilson in court, but failed to get a dime.

In 1961, Rocky Colavito belted 45 into the seats, and in a game at Yankee Stadium in May, he went into the seats to belt a fan. Noticing Rocky's wife being harassed by an inebriated spectator, Colavito's father had tried to intervene and was met with flying fists. Spotting the trouble, Rocky raced to the rescue, followed by several teammates, and nearly got his hands on the troublemaker before finally being pulled out of the stands. Colavito was ejected from the game, but promised afterwards to "do it again" if his family was pestered at the stadium the next day. They weren't.

A spectator once made the mistake of running onto the field to shake the hand of center fielder Jimmy Piersall. As the intruder raced toward him, Piersall ran to meet him. The now-nervous fan decided to forgo any handshake and began running for his

Rocky Colavito is escorted from the field after diving into the stands to reach a fan in a 1961 Tiger-Yankee battle. (UPI/Bettmann)

63

life. Piersall chased him around the outfield, the pursuit ending with a well-placed boot to the fan's rear-end just prior to his apprehension by ballpark security.

Naturally, in today's world of intelligent and sophisticated athletes, instances of ballplayers abusing fans are nonexistent, right? Think again. In April of 1991, Cincinnati's hard-throwing right-hander Rob Dibble angrily fired a ball into the stands. One month later, Cleveland's Albert Belle did the same, injuring a spectator. The Mets' Vince Coleman was in the back seat of a car in the parking lot at Dodger Stadium in June of 1993 when he threw a firecracker towards some fans, injuring a young girl. In July of 1995, Chili Davis' reaction to taunting was to charge into the stands and slap the alleged heckler.

Umpires have traditionally been the main object of abuse from fans. Shouts of "Kill the umpire!" were sometimes accompanied by attempts to do so before pop bottles were finally barred from ballparks in the middle of the century. Instances of attacks on umps on the field or outside the ballpark were frequent in the early decades, though rare today.

On occasion, even umpires have become the aggressor. In 1916 at Ebbetts Field, Bill Byron used his face mask to smash the heads of several fans who had stormed the field in protest of his decisions during the game. After the final out of a game in August of 1945, the 6-foot, 3-inch, 200 pound George Magerkurth ran to the seat of a complaining loudmouth and leveled him with a one-two punch.

Yessir, there's nothing like a peaceful day at the ballpark.

CHAPTER 14

ONE STRIKE FOR COBB

C obb's 1912 attack on the disabled spectator in New York, which included strikes with his fists and kicks with his spikes, did not go unnoticed by American League President Ban Johnson, who proclaimed that Cobb would be suspended indefinitely until "the matter was fully investigated." Cobb's typically defiant reaction was to denounce the autocratic Johnson for "always believing himself to be infallible."

Not as predictable was the reaction to Ban's ban by Ty's Tiger teammates. Never known for being popular with his peers, the Georgia Peach nevertheless became the beneficiary of overwhelming support from Detroit players who, though not admirers of Cobb's gruff, sometimes hostile attitude, were sufficiently cognizant of their slim chances of winning without him. They agreed that drastic measures were necessary to pressure Johnson into reconsidering.

On the morning of May 18 in Philadelphia, the belligerent Bengals met with Manager Hugh Jennings at the Aldine Hotel and declared their intention to walk off the field prior to the start of the scheduled A's-Tiger game that afternoon. Jennings tried diplomacy, stating he sympathized with their belief that the spectator's abusive language warranted Cobb's violent reaction, but that they were under contract with owner Frank Navin and would be putting their jobs in jeopardy with a walkout. Failing to dissuade them, Jennings telegraphed Johnson, hoping for a temporary reprieve for Cobb. Johnson's immediate response was a firm "Cobb's suspension stands."

A frantic Jennings then went on a talent search throughout Philadelphia, hoping to assemble a halfway decent bunch who would replace his regulars should they follow through on their threat. One hour before game time, they did. The crowd of 20,000, somehow aware of the players' motives, cheered as the Tigers walked off. Most did so to show their support, others in anticipation of an easy Philly victory.

Jennings' substitutes consisted of two retired ballplayers, Deacon McGuire and Joe Sugden, both catchers and both in their 40s, McGuire a year away from the half-century mark; Joe Travers, a former St. Joseph's College star; former Georgetown players Dan McGarvey and Reds McGarr; former Philly boxer Billy Maharg; and an assortment of other unknowns feeling slightly insecure in their new, and soon to be former profession.

Today's Hollywood might have Detroit's inept nine reaching for that something extra and defeating the defending world champions. In reality, they were routed. Some of the striking Motowners laughingly observed from the stands. "I wouldn't have missed it for a minute," said second baseman Jim Delahanty. Shortstop Donie Bush remarked, "It's a circus. I'm glad I'm here."

And despite skipper Connie Mack's inclusion of a couple of reserve players in his lineup, the A's thoroughly embarrassed the Tiger pretenders, scoring two dozen runs on 25 hits, while limiting the opposition to a mere four safeties. Many in the crowd weren't amused and by the third inning rushed from the bleachers in a futile effort to obtain a refund.

Following the farce, it remained to be seen if the strike would continue. The Tigers insisted it would and were confident that players from other clubs could be persuaded to join in the protest. Telegrams were sent to such stars as Boston's Smoky Joe Wood and Chicago's Harry Lord, suggesting that a barnstorming trip could compensate for lost salaries.

Player support was not forthcoming. Cobb's chief rival, Boston's Tris Speaker, reported "no talk of any strike or the starting of any trouble on our club." Christy Mathewson, while pointing out that security at ballparks was insufficient and that fans are too often permitted to provoke players, labeled Cobb a "high-strung individual, more likely to resent remarks made from the stands than most players." Many sided with Cobb, but most gave no thought of jeopardizing their salaries to help him.

Cobb's character wasn't lovable, but his undeniable batting and baserunning skills made him an indispensable Tiger teammate. (National Baseball Library, Cooperstown, NY)

Upon hearing of the walkout and possibility of a continued and broadened strike, Johnson rushed to Philadelphia from Cincinnati where he had attended dedication ceremonies that afternoon for the Reds' Crosley Field. Before boarding the train, Johnson professed amazement at the attitudes of the rebellious Tigers. "A player who is abused by a patron has only to appeal to the umpire for protection," hinting that Cobb didn't attempt that recourse.

67

Meanwhile, the victim of the assault was claiming innocence of any inciting. Claude Lueker had been a pressman before losing a hand and some fingers from the other in a work-related accident. He was then able to obtain a minor position in a respected New York law office. Not surprisingly, his comments to reporters bespoke some legal assistance. Lueker maintained he had been mistaken for other bleacher spectators who had been riding Cobb throughout the game. (In fact, Cobb recognized Lueker as the same culprit of previous verbal assaults at New York's Hilltop Park.) While being beaten, Lueker claimed to have heard Cobb answer, "I don't care if he has no feet" when informed of his handicap.

The Tigers were prepared to sit out another in Philly when Cobb met with them prior to gametime. He urged his teammates to forego any further protest, lest they be suspended as well. They agreed. Johnson fined them one hundred bucks apiece for their one-game insurrection, twice the amount the better-paid Cobb was obligated to pay, though Ty was also given a 10-day suspension for his fisticuffs.

"The stormiest single episode in the history of the American League up to then," as labeled by Cobb biographer Charles Alexander, did little to mar the Georgian's reputation as the game's greatest star. That wouldn't be realized until the next decade when another lefty swinger with more fire in his bat if not in his heart made fans forget about Ty Cobb.

WHAT A WAY
TO START

Not every member of Manager Jennings' laughable bunch was hanging his head after the embarrassing Tiger walk-out game of May 18, 1912, nor was the player strike the only precedent established that day. Of the four hits collected by Detroit, Ed Irwin had half (former big-leaguers Sugden and McGuire had the others). Both hits by the local amateur were triples, making Irwin the first of three players in history to hit a pair of three baggers in his first major-league game. Since it would be his only appearance, he simultaneously became the first player to gather two triples in his last major-league game.

The Padres' John Sipin got off to a similar start on May 24, 1969. While baseball owners were officially recognizing Bowie Kuhn as their new commissioner, Sipin was in San Diego banging a triple in his first at bat in the big leagues. Sipin's blow drove in a run and snapped a string of 33 consecutive scoreless innings by the Cubs' prize lefty, Ken Holtzman. Like Irwin, Sipin finished with two triples in his debut. Also like Irwin, they were the only triples of a very brief career, as the 22-year-old Californian played in 68 games in 1969, his only season of big-league ball.

Willie McCovey was in his 11th season, belting his league-leading 11th homer on the same day Sipin was debuting. Willie's career would be the antithesis of Sipin's in regards to longevity and production, yet his major-league opener also featured a pair of triples. Brought up by the Giants on July 30, 1959, from the Pacific Coast League where he was hitting a hefty .377, McCovey faced famed Philly fireballer Robin Roberts and punished the future Hall-of-Famer by becoming the first National Leaguer to smash two triples in his first game, while adding a pair of singles, two RBIs and three runs-scored for good measure.

Four hits in a rookie's debut is also a record, but McCovey wasn't the first to do it. On September 17, 1912, four months after the Detroit debacle, a 22-year-old southpaw by the name of Casey Stengel was purchased from Montgomery of the Southern League by the Brooklyn Superbas and inserted in the starting lineup in center field. He responded with a solid single to center which set up a run in the first inning off Pirate right-hander and 20-game winner Claude Hendrix. The next inning, Stengel delighted the 2,000 fans at Washington Park with another hit, this time driv-

Karl Spooner wants to hear it after his debut performance for the Dodgers. (AP/ Wide World Photos)

ing in a run. Casey gave his club a lead in the fourth with another RBI single off Hendrix, then stole second. With Brooklyn ahead by three in the sixth, Casey lashed a single off reliever Jack Ferry for his fourth hit. In the eighth, the mighty Missourian was greeted with an ovation, then ended his perfect day with a walk off Sherry Smith and another nifty steal of second, sliding under the waiting tag of shortstop Honus Wagner. By game's end, Pittsburgh had its 12-game winning streak broken, and Brooklyn had itself a new star. Amazing!

Sixteen years later, Art Shires was equally amazing, although the boastful boxer preferred the adjective "Great" beside his surname. On August 20, 1928, the White Sox's wacko from Waco roughed up the Red Sox's Red Ruffing with three singles and a triple. Besides the four safeties, Shires scored twice and drove in a run in his debut, while handling a dozen putouts at first. Unfortunately, the Texan's baseball career was far from great, as were his occasional fighting exhibitions.

Four hits is splendid, but what could be better than belting a homer in your first game? Hitting two, of course, a thrill experienced by the Browns' Bob Nieman in 1951. St. Louis fans didn't have much to cheer about in the final month of the pennant race that year, the team in its all too familiar, last place position by September 14. The rookie outfielder aroused them that day with homers off Boston starter Mickey McDermott at Fenway Park -- in his first two major-league at bats. He added a bunt single in the ninth and finished the game with four RBIs. The Browns lost.

And what could top hitting homers in your first two tries in the big leagues? Hitting them on your first two swings, naturally. It's never been done, but Bert Campaneris came close. An injury to A's shortstop Wayne Causey necessitated Campy's being brought up from Birmingham for a July 23 game in 1964. Facing Twins starter Jim Kaat, Bert lifted the first delivery thrown to him in the majors over the left-field fence. Campy didn't connect in his next at bat, but homered again in the seventh. The diminutive dynamo would reach the seats only 77 more times before quitting, but his otherwise distinguished career included leading the league in stolen bases six seasons, four of them consecutively, and in hits and triples once. Remarkably versatile, Campaneris once played a different position in every inning of a game.

The Giants' Bobby Bonds went downtown only once in his major-league debut, yet that one swing earned him a place in history. Facing the Dodgers' John Purdin on June 25, 1968, the 22-year-old, who had been the leading batter in the Pacific Coast League before being brought up the day before, brought the 17,000 at Candlestick Park to their feet in the sixth with a grand slam. No player before or since has hit a bases-clearing homer in his debut. It was his only hit of the game, typical of an all-or-nothing batting style which would result in 332 homers but a mere .268 career batting mark, along with an average 147 strikeouts per season (in his 10 seasons of playing in more than 100 games).

Sensational starts haven't been limited to batters. On September 22, 1954, as Joe Garagiola was contemplating retirement for a broadcasting career, and a young college football back by the name of Jim Brown prepared to start for Syracuse for the first time, rookie hurler Karl Spooner was making his first appearance for Brooklyn against pennant-bound New York. The 23-year-old lefty slew the Giants on three scratch hits, while striking out the side in the fifth, seventh and eighth innings enroute to a record-breaking total for first-time starts of 15 whiffs, all save one coming on swinging strikes. As if that wasn't enough, Spooner doubled in the third — his first plate appearance in the majors, then came around to score his first run.

The Giants were the victims of another September slaying by a rookie in 1971. Despite his fanning 11 in the opener of the twin bill on the fifth, Jack Billingham might have seemed like a piece of cake to the Giants after the towering J. R. Richard disposed of them in the nightcap. The 6-foot, 8-inch, right-hander matched Spooner's K mark for first-timers by notching 15 strikeouts. Unlike Spooner, who was out of baseball after two seasons, Richard was hardly a flash-in-the-pan. He won 18 or more games for four consecutive seasons, led the league with over 300 strikeouts in two consecutive seasons, and led the league in ERA in 1979, one year before collapsing with a stroke at the age of 30 and being forced to retire.

McCovey and Richard may have lived up to the expectations of others, but most with glorious beginnings went on to confirm what George Elliot had written in *Silas Marner*: "Nothing is so good as it seems beforehand."

CHAPTER 16

BENNY KAUFF

I n the winter of 1913, James Gilmore, president of the newly formed Federal League, asked that the organization be permitted to compete in the majors. Speaking on behalf of the National and American Leagues, Ban Johnson refused. Gilmore, whose league was composed of semipro players, responded to Johnson's rebuff by luring major leaguers with high contract offers during the 1914 and 1915 seasons. Though he was relatively unsuccessful in attracting them, some did switch including star first baseman Hal Chase and famed infielder Joe Tinker. The most renowned Federal Leaguer would be a brash, speedy outfielder who became a mediocre major-leaguer and whose career came to an involuntary end in 1921.

Benny Kauff was born in 1890 and spent much of his youth playing ball in the coal town of Middleport, which is located in southeastern Ohio. In 1912 at age 22, Kauff made his debut in the majors, but was used sparsely by the New York Highlanders (they became the New York Yankees a year later). He joined the Federal League in 1914, performing with such brilliance that he was billed "The Ty Cobb of the Federal League," a resplendent title considering Cobb's supreme status.

Kauff's numbers show the claim to have been justified. His .370 average, 211 hits, 120 runs scored, 44 doubles and 75 stolen bases in 1914 led the league and led his Indianapolis club to the pennant. Kauff jumped to McGraw's Giants in the spring of '15, but after National League president John Tener barred him from playing, Benny returned to lead the Federal League in batting (.342), slugging (.509) and stolen bases (55).

When two Fed club owners were given permission to purchase major-league teams, and a cash settlement of over half a million was finalized, the Federal League folded in 1916, though one dissatisfied Federal franchise filed an antitrust law suit against major-league baseball. Five years later, Justice Oliver Wendell Holmes spoke for the majority in the Supreme Court, claiming baseball to be a sport and therefore not subject to antitrust laws. Despite the "sport" making millions for today's owners and players, baseball continues to be protected by the "not-a-business" umbrella.

Former Federals were invited to join the big boys in 1916, and McGraw was quick to snatch Kauff, whom he regarded as a player of the old school. "He thinks and lives baseball, the way I did when I was a youngster." McGraw also liked Kauff's cocky character and comments, such as "I'll make Cobb look like a bush leaguer," which he stated in the spring of '16.

Benny's preseason boast may have been inspired as much from animosity felt towards the irascible Cobb as from his being a consummate braggart. During an exhibition game in 1913, Cobb slid, with spikes-high, into Kauff's second-base teammate. Afterwards, Benny and others decided to pit their fisticuff skills against the Georgia Peach. The plan was to enter Ty's hotel room one at a time. As the first brawl was taking place, Kauff pleaded to be next in turn. Judging from the results of the first encounter (Cobb badly beat his adversary) and their prefight stats — Kauff was 5-feet, 8-inches, 157 pounds; Cobb six-feet, one inch, 175 pounds — it's probably fortunate for Kauff their confrontation never materialized.

For someone who was supposed to be the major's newest sensation, the 1916 season began poorly for Kauff. The bags were loaded when he fanned against Grover Alexander in his first at bat of the season, and he went hitless the rest of the game. His stats at season's end were hardly noticeable: .264 average, 71 runs scored and 40 steals, especially when compared with Cobb's .371, 113 runs scored and 68 stolen bases.

Benny Kauff's major-league career ended prematurely in 1920. (National Baseball Library, Cooperstown, NY)

Still, Benny had his moments. He pulled off an unassisted double play against Chicago in July, becoming only the third outfielder of the century to do it. He excelled during the Giants' late-season winning streak of 26 games, a still-standing record, by hitting

75

four homers. One accounted for his team's sole run in a 1-1 tie, enabling the streak to continue, another coming on a full count with the bases loaded to help win the next-to-last game of the streak, eliminating the Boston Braves from the tight pennant race.

Kauff improved in 1917, batting over .300 with 89 runs scored, but his frequent fanning frustrated McGraw (he once struck out five times in a game). Wartime action limited his play in 1918, though he did hit .315 in 67 games. He returned to full-time activity in '19, but after another ordinary year, and a so-so beginning in 1920, many were wondering when this 30-year-old, once labeled by a sarcastic sportswriter as "modest little Benny-on-the-job," would ever reach the stardom he had so vociferously predicted.

An ill-advised auto business and an autocratic commissioner prevented Kauff from any further attempts at distinguishing himself. Kauff owned a used-car dealership with his brother and in the winter of 1920 was indicted for auto theft and receiving stolen vehicles. By the end of the 1920 season, the matter reached the attention of commissioner Kenesaw Mountain Landis, who had enough troubles dealing with the Black Sox mess. Landis immediately suspended Kauff from further play, making the ban permanent not long afterwards. Kauff filed a lawsuit in 1921 claiming the interdiction illegal. He lost.

Did Kauff deserve banishment? Perhaps not, but at least Landis's decision was consistent with another. Prosecutors in the Black Sox trial may have needed to show proof beyond a reasonable doubt. Kenesaw didn't. Even as they walked out of the courtroom free men, the eight who conspired to lose a Series were fixed by Landis. He was also convinced of Kauff's guilt and, despite his acquittal which Kenesaw called "one of the worst miscarriages of justice," Kauff was kicked out of the game as well.

In spite of Landis's prematurely concluding his career, it's doubtful the flashy, fiery Buckeye would have added greatly to his career numbers. In two years with the Federal League, Kauff averaged 106 runs scored, 65 stolen bases and a .357 batting mark per season, compared with a six-season big-league rate of 52 runs scored, 17 stolen bases and .287 batting average. Still, the "funny little guy who could swing a bat," as described by a former teammate decades later, was a well-known player for a few years and one of the best paid. As his hometown paper described in 1916, "Kauff has made enough money to start a bank."

THE DODGERS'
FIRST PENNANT

One of the most beloved teams in baseball history was the Brooklyn Dodgers. From the late 1800s, when their National League stint began in the town where pedestrians dodged trolley cars (thus the name "Dodgers") to their abrupt exit from New York's most populous borough in 1957, Dem Bums delighted and frustrated loyal fans with sometimes wonderful, but often disappointing performances. Nine pennants were won by Brooklyn in the 20th century, an accomplishment bettered by only six other major-league franchises (Yankees, Giants, A's, Cubs, Red Sox, and Cardinals). Yet, they took the World Series once, and finished no better than fifth in 30 of their 57 seasons.

After 15 years of failure, the Dodgers captured their first flag of the century in 1916. Manager Wilbert Robinson, a rough and tough old Oriole as a player, became a winner in only his third year at the helm and was so popular with players and fans that the team soon became known as the Robins. Unfortunately, Uncle Robbie's success was transitory, winning only one other pennant during his 18-year tenure. In addition, the first one may have been tainted, not unlike the Reds' victory over the notorious White Sox in the Series of 1919.

Ebbetts Field was three years old in 1916. The sounds of clanging cowbells and off-key band music emanating from the stands

The cantankerous John McGraw accused his Giant players of deliberately dogging it in a late-season game of 1916. (National Baseball Library, Cooperstown, NY)

were still decades away, but the Dodgers had a cast of characters that was interesting enough for Brooklynites. There was the gifted gloveman and slugger Jake Daubert, who had become the league's third MVP winner in 1913. Zack Wheat had hit better than .300 in four of his first seven seasons, no mean feat during the dead-ball era. And there was Wheat's zany buddy from K.C., Charles "Casey" Stengel who, when not hiding in crates in the outfield or releasing birds from beneath his cap at home plate, played an above-average brand of ball.

It should have surprised no one, therefore, that the Dodgers were tied for first going into the next to last game of the season. Facing them that day were the red-hot New York Giants, who only recently had a record 26-game winning streak snapped. Meanwhile, the defending-champion Phillies shared the top spot and were playing a pair against the Boston Braves, that miracle team of two years past.

Philly hurler Grover Alexander had completed his greatest season the day before by recording his record 16th shutout. With Alex unable to help, the Phillies dropped both games to the Braves. But New York had been the best club for the past two months. If they could beat the Dodgers, the Phils' hopes would remain alive going into the final day.

It was not to be. The Dodgers survived a 9-6 slugfest, capturing their first pennant. The contest was characterized by sloppy Giant fielding, and when New York manager John McGraw deserted the bench during the game, then complained afterwards about "what was going on," charges of the Giants "laying down" for their cross-town buddies appeared in the headlines. As one Philly writer wrote after the Phils won their final game, "No human agency or criminal collusion can now dislodge us from the runner-up honors anyway." The matter reached Commissioner John Heydler's office, but after some thought, Heydler decided not to investigate further.

Was Brooklyn's first pennant handed to them? Baseball was not devoid of game-fixing before the Black Sox made it a national news story, but money, not camaraderie, was the usual motive. The cantankerous McGraw often criticized players for miscues, but his desire to defeat former teammate and coach Robinson perhaps made careless play seem suspicious. And even if the Dodgers had been unwittingly aided, which today's baseball historians are unable to verify, the Phils could blame no one but themselves for dropping two to the Braves.

The old Orioles weren't known for genteelness. Upon hearing McGraw's accusation, Uncle Robbie's typically crude but frank retort was, "Tell McGraw to stop pissing on my pennant." Nevertheless, in the minds of some, Brooklyn's first flag was clouded. One skeptic was Philly manager Pat Moran who felt he had been cheated. He went on to win it all with the Reds in 1919, but when revelations of Black Sox shenanigans proved the Series a farce, Moran felt cheated again.

CHAPTER 18

CAPTAIN EDDIE GRANT

I
n October of 1918, General Blackjack Pershing gave orders for American troops to advance against the enemy entrenched in an area of the Western Front known as the Argonne Forest. With the aid of British and French forces, the plan was to trap the bulk of the Kaiser's army, but the doughboys were met with a barrage of machine-gun and artillery fire which left many dead. Nevertheless, this last major battle of World War I would put sufficient pressure on the Germans to make them sue for peace.

On October 5, a company of American troops were under heavy attack by enemy fire and in need of reinforcements. Captain Eddie Grant led Company H of the 307th Infantry towards the besieged area. Some of his men made it. Grant did not, becoming one of over 53,000 Americans killed in action in the "war to end all wars." The armistice of November 8 came less than a month after Grant's death.

What makes the Grant casualty significant, from a historical perspective, is that he may have been the first professional ballplayer to die in action, given the fact that organized pro ball began following the Civil War, and assuming that none of the 385 Americans to die in the Spanish-American War were pro players. He certainly was the first major-leaguer to fall in battle, the only one to die "over there."

Grant was a Harvard graduate who studied law and became a practicing attorney before playing second base briefly for the Indians in 1905. The lean six-footer played the infield for the Phils in his first full year in 1907 then was traded to the Reds four years later. Harvard Eddie became a Giant in 1913 and played two seasons for the less cerebral John McGraw.

Grant was never better-than-average on the field, playing full-time in only four of his 10 big-league seasons. In the lefty swinger's best season, he batted .277, and he finished his career with a modest .249 average. The barrister-ballplayer was more skilled during salary squabbles. After a disgruntled owner expressed shock with Grant's refusal to accept the wages offered, Eddie retorted, "Baseball is a business proposition. We're in it for what we can get out of it."

Grant did have his occasional flashes of brilliance on the field. Prior to a doubleheader against the Giants, Eddie predicted he'd get a total of seven hits. The opposing starters were Christy Mathewson and Rube Marquard, two of the top hurlers of their day. He stroked four off Rube, three off Matty. Grant also holds the distinction of becoming the 100th major-leaguer in the century to belt a grand-slam.

In a doubleheader at the Polo Grounds on Memorial Day of 1918 (which the Giants would sweep, then go on to win the flag), Captain Grant was honored in ceremonies between games. Veterans of Company H marched onto the field. Speeches were delivered from a platform in center field by his two sisters, a member of the Harvard club, officers of the 307th Infantry, McGraw, and baseball's rookie commissioner, Judge Kenesaw Mountain Landis. A five-foot-high monument erected by the Giants was unveiled which acknowledged Grant's service for baseball and his country. When the Polo Grounds was demolished in 1964, the Grant Memorial went down with it, adding to the tragedy of that inglorious event. Yet Eddie is still remembered today, a highway in New York having been named in his honor.

Grant wasn't the only player to die as a result of World War I. Mathewson, Eddie's teammate during his Giant days, became exposed to poison gas and died of tuberculosis in 1925 at the age of 45. Hal Carlson was only 38 when he too succumbed to a sickness most likely caused by after-effects of the lethal gas. If some players weren't killed by the war, many were left forever impaired,

Major-leaguer Eddie Grant died "over there" in 1918. (National Baseball Library, Cooperstown, NY)

Grover Alexander being the most notable. Alex lost the hearing in one ear, and battle memories haunted him to the point of pushing him to the bottle. He died a near-pauper.

Governments are formed to serve the people. Governments start wars. Wars kill people. Why doesn't that make sense?

85

CHAPTER 19

THE TRAIN VS. THE EXPRESS

Many consider Walter Johnson and Nolan Ryan to be the two hardest throwers in history. Both dominated their respective eras in strikeouts and threw fastballs so overwhelming to batters that they were given nicknames.

Johnson's "Train" was thrown from the side, and though his reputation for never deliberately aiming at batters made swingers a little less nervous in the box, they weren't helped much by the knowledge, as indicated by their .227 lifetime average against him. The Kansas right-hander's long arms and effortless motion made more formidable a fastball which, though never timed, must have exceeded 90 mph, perhaps even approaching the 100 mph mark. So overpowering was Barney (his nickname) that he finished his 21-year career, spanning from 1907 to 1927, with a major-league record 110 shutouts. He also accumulated 417 wins, second behind Young's all-time total, despite playing for a second-division club most of the time. He won 20 games for 10-straight seasons, including two with more than 30, and led the league six times. Johnson was league-leader in ERA five times, finishing the 1913 season with a minuscule 1.14.

Nolan Ryan delivered his "Express" with an overhand motion, the force of which was propelled by powerful legs built up by daily running and exercise. The Texan's explosive 100-mph fastball was complemented by occasional and, at times, intentional wildness, making hitters wary of digging deep for footholds. Unlike Johnson, who relied almost exclusively on heaters throughout his career, Ryan gradually developed mastery of a curve, making the task of previously unsuccessful batters even more difficult. No wonder, then, that Ryan finished his 27-year career (1966-1993) with a record seven no-hitters and dozen one-hitters. He also led the league in shutouts three times and in ERA twice, and he piled up over 300 victories despite often pitching for unsuccessful ballclubs (though not nearly as unsuccessful as were Johnson's).

Since most of their fame came from their success as strikeout artists, one can't help wondering which of the two was the harder thrower. Johnson led the league in strikeouts in 12 of 21 major-league seasons, Ryan in only 11 of 27. Yet, Ryan fanned more than 300 batters in six seasons, Johnson in only two. Walter's highest total for one year was 313 in 1910. Ryan's 383 in 1973 is a major-league mark to this day. Ryan's career total of 5,714 Ks (also a major-league record) in 5,387 innings computes to an average of 9.5 per-nine-innings. Johnson's 3,509 whiffs in 5,924 frames leaves him with a 5.3 per-game-average. It would appear that Ryan should get the nod as being more overpowering.

But not so fast. The pair of K-kings hurled in different eras. To ascertain whose heater had more fire, additional insight would be gained by comparing their stats with that of respective contemporary pitchers. Listed on the following page are the strikeout totals of Johnson and Ryan for each of their league-leading seasons, along with the runner-up total for each year. Ryan's outdistancing his closest competitor by an average 59 strikeouts was 23 better than Johnson's average, more evidence that Ryan was the harder thrower.

The following table contains the strikeout rate per-nine-innings of Johnson and Ryan during their league-leading seasons, along with the average rate of the league's opposing hurlers for the same years:

STRIKEOUT-LEADING SEASONS OF JOHNSON AND RYAN ALONG WITH RUNNER-UP TOTALS

Walter Johnson					**Nolan Ryan**			
		Runner-up					Runner-up	
Year	Ks	Total	Diff.		Year	Ks	Total	Diff.
1910	313	258	55		1972	329	250	79
1912	303	258	45		1973	383	258	125
1913	243	166	77		1974	367	249	118
1914	225	179	46		1976	327	261	66
1915	203	182	21		1977	341	244	97
1916	228	182	46		1978	260	248	12
1917	188	150	38		1979	223	201	22
1918	162	129	33		1987	270	233	37
1919	147	128	19		1988	228	213	15
1921	143	132	11		1989	301	230	71
1923	130	125	5		1990	232	221	11
1924	158	119	39					
Average Difference 36.3					Average Difference 59.4			

STRIKEOUT RATE (PER-NINE-INNINGS) OF JOHNSON AND RYAN DURING LEAGUE-LEADING SEASONS ALONG WITH RATE OF OPPOSING HURLERS

Walter Johnson					**Nolan Ryan**			
		K-rate					K-rate	
Year	K-rate	Opnts.	Diff.		Year	K-rate	Opnts.	Diff.
1910	7.5	4.1	2.4		1972	10.4	5.4	5.0
1912	7.4	4.1	3.3		1973	10.6	5.0	5.6
1913	6.3	3.8	2.5		1974	9.9	4.8	5.1
1914	5.4	4.0	1.4		1976	10.4	4.6	5.8
1915	5.4	3.9	1.5		1977	10.3	4.9	5.4
1916	5.5	3.7	1.8		1978	10.0	4.5	5.5
1917	5.2	3.3	1.9		1979	9.0	4.5	4.5
1918	4.5	2.9	1.6		1987	11.5	5.9	5.6
1919	4.6	3.1	1.5		1988	9.3	5.5	3.8
1921	4.9	2.9	2.0		1989	11.3	5.4	5.9
1923	4.5	2.9	1.6		1990	10.3	5.6	4.7
1924	5.1	2.6	2.5					
Average Difference 2.0					Average Difference 5.2			

89

As you can see Ryan's per-game-average was more than five strikeouts higher than the league's other pitchers, compared with Johnson's two-strikeout differential. Long live Nolan, King of the Fastball, right?

Nolan Ryan had his fastball clocked at over 100 mph in 1974. Radar guns weren't available during Walter Johnson's playing days. (National Baseball Library, Cooperstown, NY)

Not quite. Stats are meaningful, but don't always reveal the complete truth. Johnson pitched during a time when amassing strikeouts was more difficult. Yes, bats were heavier and bulkier, but they were held high up the handle by most hitters, who used a short swing in order to meet the ball squarely. Ryan had the advantage of pitching in a free-swinging era, when batters like Willie McCovey, Reggie Jackson and Mike Schmidt thought nothing of 100-strikeout seasons as long as they were accompanied by 30-homer totals. During the teens and '20s, Johnson faced only one batter who finished a season with 100 or more whiffs — Gus Williams in 1914, and he was out of baseball the following season.

Also not shown in stats are the two distinctly different pitching strategies of Johnson and Ryan. Unlike Ryan, who'd try to throw three by a batter, Johnson didn't always go for the strikeout. Smoky Joe Wood, known for "bringing it" until a sore arm finished him, was Johnson's chief rival for a couple of seasons, and he once pointed out, "Johnson doesn't exert himself, and when he wants to cut loose, he has all his power at his command." His throwing at full speed "only in a pinch," as Walter once stated, makes plausible the assumption that, had he tried, his strikeout totals could have been higher. But Johnson hadn't the luxury of firing at full speed from the get-go, knowing each time he took the mound he'd be throwing nine innings or more. His lifetime completion percentage of 80 percent stands in stark contrast to Ryan's finishing only 29 percent of his career starts. Ryan was blessed with a strong arm and body, but was also unconcerned with pacing himself. He let her rip from the first inning until the final out, or the club's bullpen, ended his day's work. His averaging fewer innings per game than Johnson made it easier for Ryan to compile a higher strikeout rate, since most of his Ks usually came during the first five frames.

Two other factors to be considered when comparing the velocity of the two moundsmen have already been touched upon. During the second half of Ryan's career, his control of the curve enabled him to catch as many batters looking as were swinging at third strikes. For Johnson to be as successful as he was with only a fastball adds belief to the legend that it was virtually untouchable at full speed. Ryan's was too, until late in his career when his slants set up strikeouts. Johnson lacked that advantage, yet he still managed to lead the league in Ks three of his final six full seasons. The final element is that batters facing Johnson knew he'd abstain from any knockdown pitches. Those hitting against Ryan felt no such comfort, and their tentativeness made them easier victims.

Who was the better strikeout artist? Ryan. Who threw harder? It's anyone's guess.

BABE'S PITCHING
HELPED HIS
SLUGGING

Babe Ruth a singles hitter? Were it not for his pitching career, that description might have been appropriate.

Ruth began playing ball as a catcher for St. Mary's Reform School, using a right-hander's mitt despite being left-handed. His coach, Brother Matthias, gave him a chance to pitch, whereupon Babe found his niche. He was spotted and signed by Jack Dunn, owner of the minor-league Baltimore club. Ruth hurled effectively, but Dunn needed cash and accepted $20,000 from the Red Sox for his budding star and two other Orioles. The player who would become the greatest Yankee in history made his major-league debut in midsummer of 1914 with Boston, the team that would become New York's greatest rival. His victory at age 19 that day was the prelude to several years of pitching prominence.

Babe won 18 in 1915, his first full season, had the fourth highest winning percentage, and allowed the second fewest hits-per-inning. He won 23 the following season, led the league in ERA and shutouts, had the second best winning percentage, was third in strikeouts, and fourth in number of games finished. He was first in complete games in 1917 while improving to 24 victories, and had two of the four Red Sox wins in the Series. By 1918, Ruth was, next to Walter Johnson, arguably the best pitcher in the league.

By then his other talent had also become evident. From 1914-1917, Babe's combined average was .300. He had hit nine homers in only 350 at bats. How could such an obvious offensive force continue to be regularly excluded from the lineup? Of course, if Ruth played daily he'd be unable to pitch as often, and his striking out an average of once every five tries was another problem. Nevertheless, the possibilities justified experimenting. Ruth became a part-time pitcher, part-time outfielder in 1918, initiating the inevitable battle for dominance between arm and bat, won by the latter. Ruth started 19 games in 1918, 15 in 1919, and only four the remainder of his career which ended in 1935 with 94 lifetime victories — and 714 homers.

Ruth's batting philosophy was the same throughout his career — to "swing big with everything I've got." It was a strange style during the dead-ball era of the pre-20s when batters choked up on the bat, hoping to make contact. Skippers during Babe's early years had little patience, not likely to be forgiving of fellows fanning frequently. Even if a hitter showed exceptional power, the manager would suggest cutting down on the swing, and expect results. If none were forthcoming, the player was sent packing.

Then why was Babe left alone? Ruth was a pitcher. His swinging from the heels was of little consequence to Boston manager Bill Carrigan. He struck out often, but that's why he batted ninth in the lineup like other moundsmen. Ruth was expected to pitch, not hit.

Thus ignored, Babe continued his unorthodox approach, punishing the horsehide with everything he had. Eventually, it became evident to even the most uncompromising skippers that the home run was a new and effective weapon. No longer were batters discouraged from going downtown. The '20s were characterized by an increasing number of Ruth imitators, marking the first decade of homer hitters.

What if Ruth hadn't been converted by Brother Matthias, remaining a catcher instead or becoming an outfielder? Assuming he made it to the big leagues, one look at his swing would have prompted a managerial lecture on the advantages of short-line drives, hitting to the opposite field, and hitting ground balls on poorly groomed infields. As a rookie, Babe would have felt compelled to acquiesce.

Babe Ruth, shown here in 1921, was an outstanding pitcher. His hitting, however, transformed baseball into a free-swinging sport. (National Baseball Library, Cooperstown, NY)

Ruth's rebellious nature is legendary, and after a few inhibiting years he might have begun uppercutting the ball anyway. But his singles style would have been difficult to abandon. Boston skipper Ed Barrow stated in 1919 that Ruth would be a .400 batter if he shortened his swing.

Players can be as conservative as managers. Amidst the batting revolution, Ty Cobb refused to change his style. Had Babe been content with hits rather than homers from the start, he might have felt the same way, especially after leading the league in batting every year.

Such a gifted athlete was Ruth that, with a more compact swing, he could have become the game's first .500 hitter. Then again, think of all those missed home runs!

BABE'S 715TH HOMER

I t was a glorious moment, as Henry Aaron unleashed a drive towards the left-center-field fence at 9:07 p.m. on April 8, 1974, Opening Day in Atlanta. Never was there a more anticipated event in sport's history than the surpassing of Ruth's lifetime homer mark by Hammerin' Hank. Few in the record crowd of 53,775 at Fulton County Stadium, a.k.a. "The Launching Pad," remained in their seats, or were fooled by Bill Buckner's vain attempt to scale the fence and catch the ball prior to its landing in the bullpen. (Said Buckner afterwards, "I was trying to jump over and get it. They were offering $30,000 for it.")

A glorious moment for all, save one. It couldn't have been a pretty sight for the Dodgers' Al Downing, the victim of Aaron's dinger. His fastball had helped him limit batting opponents in 1963 to a .184 average, a league best, gather a league-leading 217 strikeouts the following season, and win 20 with a league-high five shutouts in 1971, but the fastball they'll remember would be the one not sufficiently rapid to sneak past Henry's quick wrists. "Why me?," Downing must have asked himself as Hank circled the bases for the 715th time. The record-breaking blast was inevitable, but why had fate chosen him as its donor? If only Ruth had hit just one more homer, the dubious distinction would belong to the next casualty of Aaron's assault, not him.

Actually, Ruth did hit 715 homers. The one that didn't count occurred in the first game of a twin bill at Fenway Park on July 8, 1918. The Red Sox, the eventual pennant winners, held a game and a half edge over the second-place Indians, their opponents that day. The opener featured two superb pitchers in Boston's Sad Sam Jones, a former Tribesman who would lead the league that year with a .762 winning percentage (16-5), and future Hall-of-Famer Stan Coveleski, in the middle of his first of four-consecutive 20-win seasons.

The hard-throwing, right-handers were in top form that afternoon as both allowed no runs in nine innings, with Jones nearly untouchable in allowing four harmless singles, while Coveleski scattered six, one being a triple by shortstop Deacon Scott, the only extra-base hit to that point. Jones set down the side in the top of the 10th and watched from the dugout as Coveleski attempted to do the same.

Ruth, held to a single thus far, was due to bat third that inning. If Coveleski could retire the first two hitters, he'd be able to pitch more carefully to the dangerous power hitter. Stan disposed of veteran Dave Shean for the first out, but lefty-swinging Amos Strunk then tagged him for a single. Unable to pitch around Ruth, Coveleski challenged him with a fastball. Babe's blow landed in the right-field bleachers.

Final score, 2-0, right? Not in 1918. Ruth would lead the league in homers for the first time that year, but the ball that left the park that day wasn't one of his 11. Since Strunk scored the winning run ahead of Ruth, Babe was credited with a triple and the score went in the books as a 1-0 Boston victory. As far as anyone knows, it's the only instance in which Ruth hit one out and was not credited with a homer.

Under today's rules, of course, the homer would count. Some might therefore argue that Ruth technically had 715 homers after quitting in 1935. Some did. Fifty years after Ruth's nonhomer, a records committee ruled the wallop should have counted and put his career total at 715. The decision was reversed in 1969 when members of the committee, principally researcher Joseph Reichler, who authored *The Great All-Time Baseball Record Book* a dozen years later, and Jack Lang of the Baseball Writers' Association, correctly maintained that if modern rules were made

Babe Ruth connects, one of 54 he'd lose in 1920. (National Baseball Library, Cooperstown, NY)

retroactive, that is, made to apply to past accomplishments, nearly every player's stats would be affected. We might judge a long-abandoned rule to be unfair, even ridiculous, but it wouldn't change the fact that it existed, and that the rule applied equally to all at the time. (A case could be made that the old rule regarding game-ending wallops was more logical; a sudden-death victory results the moment the winning run scores, making any additional runs uncalled-for.)

Aaron finished his career 41 homers ahead of Ruth, making the Babe's lost round tripper inconsequential. Unimportant, at least, to everyone except Al Downing.

NICKNAMES

George Ruth had just turned 19 when he hopped aboard a sleeper destined for Fayetteville, North Carolina, and his first spring training. Sensing a childish naiveté in their new teammate, the Orioles began calling him Babe. The name stuck, and years later in New York, he became "The Bambino" to numerous Italian immigrants. After Jimmie Foxx's surname was misspelled on a scorecard, he was labeled "Double X," though pitchers still thought "The Beast" a more apt title for the muscular slugger. Tall Ted Williams was all of 146 pounds his first year of pro ball, but was still "The Splendid Splinter" even after beefing up. Charles Stengel was "Dutch" to teammates until his jocular jabbering about hometown Kansas City (K.C.) made him Casey.

It may no longer be America's most popular spectator sport, but in regards to a proud tradition baseball is supreme. For proof, one need only look at its wealth in nicknames. Yes, football has its Broadway Joe and Steel Curtain, basketball its Wilt the Stilt and Magic Johnson, hockey its Rocket Richard and The Cat Francis. But the most avid follower of those games would strain to name more than a dozen.

Not so with hardball fans. Who hasn't heard of that monstrous but affable "Gentle Giant," Ted Kluszewski? Or "The Barber," Sal Maglie, who enjoyed shaving batters' whiskers with inside fastballs? And what about the rebellious Billy "The Kid" Martin? In fact, the frequency of ballplayers acquiring nicknames has resulted in many being reused. Greenberg and Bauer were known as "Hammerin' Hank" before Aaron popularized it later.

Not surprisingly, many nicknames suggest royalty. Babe Ruth was the "Sultan of Swat," indicating his supremacy in belting homers, and Lou Gehrig was "The Crown Prince," the next in line to the throne. Gehrig shared his regal title with Prince Hal Schumacher. Rogers Hornsby's hitting made him "The Rajah," and lefty Carl Hubbell's 24-game winning streak elevated him from "The Meal Ticket" to "King Carl." Charlie Keller's strength and looks made him "King Kong."

Nicknames weren't reserved exclusively for players. Dictatorial manager John McGraw was "Little Napoleon," and the diminutive but volatile Gene Mauch, who reacted to heartbreaking defeats by throwing players' food off the clubhouse table, was "The Little General." Ralph Houk, once described by Umpire Jim McKean as a maniac, was "The Major," the crew-cutted, ex-Marine Hank Bauer, "The Sarge," and the distinguished coach Jim Turner, "The Colonel."

Other titles, though simpler, suggested equal eminence, the most common being "Mister." Ernie Banks played in more games, and accumulated more at bats, hits, doubles, homers and RBIs than any other Chicago player, thus becoming "Mr. Cub." "Mr. Impossible" suited Brooks Robinson, whose miraculous glovework made Oriole pitchers better than they were. Reggie Jackson was a fearsome hitter, but "Mr. October" saved his best for World Series play. Of course, not all "Misters" reflected admiration. Gaylord Perry wasn't shy about loading one up to gain advantages over batters, but would laugh rather than be scornful of the unflattering appellation "Mr. Moist." Equally derisive but accurate was Hornsby's other nickname, "Mr. Blunt," signifying a propensity for telling it like it is.

Adjectives were frequently included in nicknames. Walter Johnson's fastball was a "Big Train" to batters, Paul Waner's hitting was "Big Poison" to pitchers, and Dominican Rico Carty's skills and accent made him a "Big Mon" with teammates. Art Shires had pugilistic ambitions and promoted himself as "Shires the Great." Pitcher Dizzy Dean called himself "The Great Dean," but unlike Shires, had the talent to justify the claim. Like Shires, Billy Martin enjoyed scrapping and was called "The Great Agitator." George Scott's size and power made him "Great Scott."

In baseball, veteran players and managers are respected, so that "Old" nicknames had positive connotations. Pete Alexander was "Old Pete," Tommy Henrich "Old Reliable," and, when he wasn't "Country" Slaughter, Enos was the "Old Workhorse." Longtime skipper Stengel became recognized as the "Old Professor," and Connie Mack's seniority was reflected in his nickname "Old Man River," until he stopped rolling along after half a century as the A's helmsman.

There may be an affinity between baseball and animals, judging from some nicknames. Loony Mark Fidrych was "The Bird," agile Johnny Mize moved like a "Big Cat," and Frank Thomas was as stubborn as a "Donkey." Speedy Walt Maranville and Ralph Garr were "The Rabbit" and "Road Runner" respectively, and Ron Cey walked like a "Penguin." Dave Parker uncoiled like a "Cobra" when hitting. Bill Skowron was as strong as a "Moose," or just looked like one, according to teammate Joe Pepitone.

Some nicknames were misnomers. Honus Wagner was "The Flying Dutchman," despite being German. Frank "Home Run" Baker never hit more than a dozen in a season and finished his career with fewer than a hundred. Willie Mays was the "Say Hey Kid," though he infrequently used the phrase.

Famous duos have at times been honored. Dizzy Dean was goofier than brother Paul but both were known as "The Daffiness Boys." Mickey Mantle and Roger Maris were tagged "The M & M Boys" while pursuing Ruth in '61. All-American Steve Garvey and his wife were the "Ken and Barbie" of baseball, until marital problems rendered the nickname obsolete.

Then there are the team nicknames. The "Miracle Braves" were world champions in 1914 after being in the cellar in mid-July, and the "Miracle Mets" were no less spectacular in taking the Series in '69 following basement berths in five of their first seven seasons. The rough tactics of the Cardinals of the '30s made them the "Gas House Gang." Mention of "Murderers Row" usually brings to mind the 1927 Yankee lineup, though the nickname originally applied to the 1919 batting order. Slightly less formidable in the '70s was Cincinnati, the "Big Red Machine."

In *Baseball's Greatest Quotations*, author Paul Dickson offers nearly 500 "noms de press and sobriquets." His list is fascinating, though far from complete.

THE LONGEST
GAME

O n May 1, 1920, Ruth launched a missile over the grandstand at the Polo Grounds. *The New York Times* reported
the blow to be not only Babe's first of the year, but 50th
career homer, a significant statistic then considering the home
run era of the '20s and beyond had yet to unfold. How insignifi-
cant the observation would seem after Babe more than doubled
his career output that year by amassing 54 four baggers.

A more noteworthy event took place in Braves Field that day as
Boston hosted the eventual pennant-winners, the Brooklyn Robins. Starter Leon Cadore hadn't impressed in five seasons with
Brooklyn, other than to show an adeptness at card tricks and in
doctoring baseballs. The humorous hurler developed a close friendship with Casey Stengel while the two were teammates, and was
the main culprit in what would become Casey's most notorious
stunt. In 1919, Cadore used his quick hands to catch a sparrow
in the Dodger bullpen. Prankster Stengel, now a Pirate, grabbed
it, and in his first plate appearance turned raucous catcalls from
the partisan crowd to hilarious cheers by lifting his cap and releasing the bewildered bird.

Boston's Joe Oeschger hadn't distinguished either after six seasons, accumulating a 32-44 record with the Phils before being
traded in 1919. He had shown flashes of brilliance, exemplified

by a complete-game, 20-inning tie in '19. That feat would seem ordinary following the May Day of 1920.

Both right-handers set down the opposition through the first four innings, but Oeschger wavered in the fifth. Lead-off batter Ernie Krueger drew a walk and took second when Cadore, after failing to sacrifice, hit a slow roller to the mound. Ivy Olsen brought Krueger home with a drive over shortstop Rabbit Maranville's head.

Boston quickly tied the score. With one out, slugger Walton Cruise cruised into third after a long blast to the scoreboard in center. Cadore appeared headed out of trouble after inducing a pop-up, but Tony Boeckel lined a single to center, tallying Cruise. Maranville then tomahawked a double, but Cadore helped his own cause by taking the cutoff throw from center fielder Wally Hood and firing to the plate, nipping Boeckel.

Hood's assist, ironically the only one of the part-timer's major-league career, made possible what would become a record for longevity. Had he not retrieved Maranville's drive and relayed the ball to Cadore in time, Boston would have had the lead and eventually the game. Instead, the contest remain knotted until its conclusion, when either darkness or "an appointment with a succulent steak" (if one imaginative reporter is to be believed) forced umpire Barry McCormick to call a deadlock. The 26-inning game is a still-standing major-league mark.

It will be argued later that Carl Hubbell's 18-inning shutout of 1933 was the greatest pitched game, but the efforts of Oeschger and Cadore in the 1920 duel were close. Incredibly, both went the distance. Cadore pitched 20 consecutive scoreless innings after yielding the run in the sixth, matching Joe Harris's record set in a game in 1906, but Oeschger's 21-straight, scoreless frames set a record still held to this day. Cadore walked five and fanned eight, Oeschger three and four. Though Cadore surrendered 15 hits, only twice did more than one come in the same frame, while Oeschger's nine allowed were spread out through eight innings. Neither yielded any in the final six frames. And despite its length in innings equivalent to nearly three games, the fast-working firemen finished in 3 1/2 hours.

There were a couple of close calls. The Braves loaded the bags with one out, but lefty-swinging Charlie Pick pulled a wormburner to second where Robin second sacker Ivy Olsen grabbed it, tagged the runner, and fired to first to end the inning. For Pick, the frustration of having stranded the winning run in the ninth was compounded by seven hitless at bats thereafter, his zero-for-eleven still a major-league record for futility.

Brooklyn had the same chance in the 17th but was done in by a doubleplay as well, albeit an unorthodox one. Oeschger snatched a comebacker and threw to the plate for the force, but the wide return toss to first couldn't be handled. When Ed Konetchy tried to score from third, catcher Hank Gowdy made amends for his errant throw with a headlong, barehanded dive at the sliding Konetchy. McCormick's shriek of "You're Out!" must have ignited a hearty cheer from the remnants of the 2,000 who had paid to get in.

Only three baseballs were used in the contest, a fact slightly less amazing when aware that balls hit into the stands were returned, and scuffed or discolored ones weren't barred. When Indian infielder Ray Chapman was killed by a pitch a few months later, some felt the accident was partly due to Chapman's inability to see the soiled sphere. A rule prohibiting the use of spitballs and damaged balls was adopted the following season. The new edict, complemented by a livelier ball, helped batters gain a noticeable advantage. As author William Curran points out in *Big Sticks*, the Boston-Brooklyn battle "symbolically rang down the curtain on two decades of low-scoring games. In the 1920s, hits and runs would be plentiful regardless of how close the contests."

Perhaps for this reason, Cadore floundered in four more years with Brooklyn, finishing 25-31 from 1921-1924 before quitting the game, but not before one other noteworthy effort. Four months following the Boston marathon, Cadore blanked the Braves on a dozen hits, two shy of Larry Cheney's league record for most hits allowed in a shutout.

Boston's Oeschger had some success in the '20s, but his failures were more abundant. In 1921, he won twenty games, led the league with three shutouts, and in one game hurled a perfect inning, a rarity in hardball, by striking out three batters on nine pitches. But he lost 21 the next year, including a stretch of 13-straight, and strung together ten-consecutive losses enroute to a 5-15 record in 1923. He retired in 1925 after starting only three games that year — pitching for Brooklyn.

If the Robins felt battered following 26 useless innings, there were worse times just ahead. The next day they played the Phils and lost in 13 frames, then returned to Boston and took 19 innings to lose to the Braves. Their two losses and one tie in 58 innings' work is an unofficial record for futility by a major-league club. It could only happen to Brooklyn.

What did Paine know of pain when he wrote, "These are the times that try men's souls."

THE KNOCKDOWN

The afternoon before his last day on earth, Ray Chapman told Cleveland teammates, "(Carl) Mays is pitching for the Yankees today, so I'll do the fielding and you fellows do the hitting."

In the fifth inning, leadoff batter Chapman froze on Mays' first pitch as it sailed toward his head. A dreadful thud could be heard throughout the Polo Grounds, but the submarine pitcher thought the ball, which actually rebounded off Chapman's temple and dribbled toward him, had hit the bat. He fielded it and threw to first baseman Wally Pipp.

Chapman was sitting semiconscious at home plate, with blood rushing from his left ear. With some assistance, he was able to stand and actually began walking on his own toward the clubhouse located in center field. By the time he reached second base, he dropped. Two teammates assisted him the rest of the way. In the clubhouse, physicians called for an ambulance to take Chapman to a nearby hospital while the injured second baseman moved his lips in a vain attempt to speak. A one-hour brain operation at midnight appeared at first to have saved his life, but four hours later he was dead.

The chilling tale of the only fatal beaning in major-league history doesn't end with Chapman's death, as there were several consequences. The moody, unpopular Mays became even more detested by peers, who suspected him of deliberately nailing the likable Indian infielder, though he was exonerated in court of any intent to harm. Immediate changes in the rules were also forthcoming. Scuffed or soiled baseballs which previously had been kept in play, were no longer allowed. Deliberately defacing the ball and using spitballs, also permitted in the past, were declared illegal.

One rule that wasn't added was prohibiting pitchers from using the brushback or knockdown pitch. For many decades afterwards, hurlers would continue to protect their turf (strike zone) by firing at a batter's feet, legs, chest or head. Not until 1978 were pitchers inhibited with warnings and ejections by umpires, who were instructed to "act without hesitation" in enforcing the new no-knockdown rule. The rule was amended 10 years later, enabling a pitcher to be expelled even without a prior warning.

It's not surprising, then, that several other instances of batters being beaned followed the Chapman tragedy. The most notable occurred in 1937 when the Tigers' player/manager Mickey Cochrane was struck on the head by another Yank right-hander, Bump Hadley. Cochrane was hospitalized and although his life was spared, Mickey's playing career ended. Boston's star outfielder Tony Conigliaro was hit in the face by the Angels' (but not angelic) Jack Hamilton in 1967. He missed the remainder of the season and all of the next, and returned in 1969 with permanent damage to his eyesight.

Equally understandable have been the instances in which batters attempted retaliation. In June of 1924, the Yankees were playing the Tigers in Motown when one of Bengal Bert Cole's fastballs came perilously close to Babe Ruth's noggin. When the next batter, Bob Meusel, was hit on the back, he went after Cole. Ruth came to help his teammate and was met by a charging Ty Cobb. They were separated, and Meusel and Ruth were ejected. While entering the dugout, the Babe screamed insults at Cobb and the pair again nearly came to blows.

Perhaps the game's greatest headhunter was Dizzy Dean, who wouldn't think twice about making a hitter hit the deck, then do it again on the next pitch. In a May game of 1937, Dean became so infuriated with a balk call that he sent sprawling one Giant hitter after another. The batter abuse continued for several innings until Jimmy Ripple retaliated in the ninth. He pushed a bunt down the first-base line and when Diz covered at first, Ripple ripped into him. A free-for-all followed, with the principle instigator, Dean doing little of the actual fighting.

Numerous confrontations occurred during the '60s. Only two years after being fined for brawling, the Indians' Jimmy Piersall charged at Tiger hurler Jim Bunning in a June game of 1961 at Cleveland Stadium. Missing a left hook, Piersall fell to the ground but resumed the offensive by kicking at Bunning. No one was injured in the ensuing melee, but Piersall's bruised wrist, resulting from Bunning's wild (or accurate) fastball, forced him to miss the second game of the twin bill. In the clubhouse afterwards, Bunning denied intentionally throwing at Piersall, but Jimmy complained of being previously hit by Bunning a half dozen times and that he was "tired of it."

In a doubleheader in New York in August of 1963, the young Yank Joe Pepitone displayed for the first time a temper which would reappear often during his career. After stroking three hits

Jimmy Piersall takes a swing at hurler Jim Bunning (right) in a game at Cleveland in 1961. (UPI/Corbis-Bettmann)

in the opener, Pepi became a target for Cleveland starter Gary Bell in the nightcap. He was hit by a pitch in his first at bat and was nailed again in his second appearance. Joe charged the mound but before reaching Bell, was met by Indian first baseman Fred Whitfield. The two exchanged lefts and rights, Whitfield getting the worst of the exchange. The fight led to what one newspaper described as "one of the wildest free-for-alls in Yankee Stadium history," resulting in several spike wounds, muscle pulls and other injuries on both sides. Yankee manager Ralph Houk later complained that Bell and other Indian pitchers had been picking on his hottest hitter, but Tribe skipper Birdie Tebbetts countered, "When I played ball the only ones we threw at were .300 hitters. They don't have any." Both Pepitone and Bell received $50 fines.

One of the most famous confrontations occurred in a 1965 late-

Joe Pepitone is in the midst of this fracas which he instigated in an Indian-Yankee game in August of 1963. Cleveland fans, try to locate Joe Adcock; Yankee fans, Mickey Mantle. (UPI/Bettmann)

season battle for first between the Giants and Dodgers which followed two hard-fought, spirited games, won by Los Angeles. The finale of the three-game set at Candlestick featured the clubs' best hurlers — L.A.'s Sandy Koufax and Frisco's Juan Marichal. Early in the game, the Dodgers' Maury Wills was decked by Marichal, possibly in retaliation for Wills' reaching base in the series opener by intentionally getting nicked with a pitch. The mild-mannered Koufax refused to retaliate on his first pitch to Marichal in the third (in a 1995 interview, Marichal stated that Koufax later told him he had been ordered to knock him down), but catcher John Roseboro fired a return throw that nearly hit Marichal in the head. Juan's reaction, which was to strike the backstop with his bat, would appear in sports pages of newspapers across the country. He was fined $1,750, given a nine-day

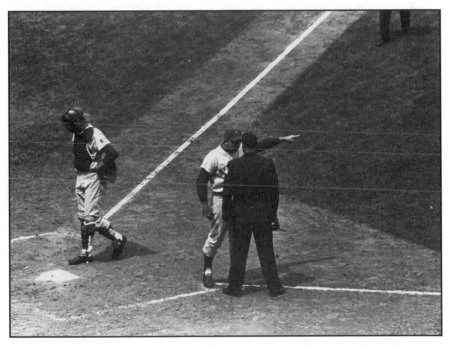

"What about the other guy?" asks Manager Gil Hodges after home plate ump Frank Secory warned Met hurler Tom Seaver about throwing at Cub batters. (UPI/ Corbis-Bettmann)

113

suspension which resulted in his missing two crucial starts, and received death threats from Dodger fans warning him to stay away from Los Angeles.

Reggie Jackson often responded to a dusting by picking himself up and homering on the next pitch. Not so on April 24, 1969, in Minnesota when Twins reliever Dick Woodson threw consecutive high-inside pitches. Having homered in his previous two at bats, Reggie's not-irrational notion that Woodson was sending a message led to his charging and tackling the right-hander. Jackson was ejected. Woodson remained in the game.

Two weeks later, the Mets and Cubs battled in a game at Wrigley Field. Believing that his teammates had been targets of Cub hurlers in the first two games of the series, Tom Seaver took it upon himself to aim a fastball "between the helmet and the head" of Ron Santo in the second inning. Chicago's Bill Hands retaliated in the third with a heater off Seaver's back. Hands came to bat in the same frame and felt a fastball bounce off his breadbasket. Both managers, first the Cubs' Leo Durocher, then Gil Hodges, rushed to protest to umpire Frank Secory, but neither pitcher was ejected. The Mets took the game, later the pennant, from the Cubs.

With the rule changes of the '70s and '80s, the brushback and knockdown are rarely used today. Batters, already profiting from a reduced strike zone, have a huge advantage knowing they can "dig in" close to the inside edge of the plate without fear of being hit. This benefit, not the increased average size and strength of hitters, is most likely the chief cause of homers being hit by more players than in the past.

If the near extinction of the knockdown has given batters an edge, perhaps it's the way it should be. Even with batting helmets, the use of which became mandatory in 1971, the sight and sound of an accelerating fastball zooming toward the temple should be experienced by hitters as infrequently as possible. Baseball offers enough entertainment for fans. Knockdowns and fistfights aren't needed.

THAT RASCALLY
RABBIT

C arl Mays took his windup, leaned to the right, and fired a
knee-high pitch. The batter, amazed at the sight of the
umpire's raised right hand, complained for a few moments
before again approaching the plate, only to have the submarine
hurler throw another low fastball that was called a strike. The
flabbergasted batsman protested, but was warned to return to
the box. He complied by assuming his stance in a kneeling position, then hollered to the pitcher to throw the ball. The normally
sullen and somber Mays laughed uncontrollably. The umpire, finding no humor in the antic, warned the hitter to get up or be thrown
out. Satisfied that he had made his point, the batter arose and
promptly singled to left on the next pitch. While skipping to first,
he took out a handkerchief and waved it to the crowd.

Such clowning with umpires was nothing new for Rabbit
Maranville. Once, after an umpire emerged from the middle of a
free-for-all, Maranville convinced him he was badly bruised, then
painted his uncut face with iodine. In another instance, Rabbit
objected to an ump's call by taking out a pair of glasses, conscien-
tiously wiping them with his shirttail, and handing them to the
embarrassed arbiter.

Walter Maranville, who acquired the nickname Rabbit when a
young girl observed that he looked like one hopping around the

basepaths, was never an outstanding hitter, but was one of the greatest fielding shortstops in history. The Hall-of-Famer's still-standing shortstop records include six years leading the league in putouts, 5,133 lifetime assists, and 12,471 lifetime chances. He still holds the record for playing the most innings in one game without an error (26 on May 1, 1920).

Though not known for his batting, as shown by a .258 lifetime batting average, Maranville did sparkle with the stick on occasion. In his first game as a starter in 1913, he drilled three hits to help the Braves beat Christy Mathewson. Probably his greatest game came during the twilight of his career. Facing the Cardinals on June 10, 1931, Rabbit stroked a triple and three singles, walked twice, scored five runs, and dazzled fans in the second inning when he sprinted into the medium-left field to make a basket catch of a fly ball.

But then, basket catches were Rabbit's trademark long before Willie Mays made them famous. He was equally adept at "turning two," and covered the left side of the infield better than most. When second baseman Johnny Evers, middleman in the famed Tinkers-to-Evers-to-Chance double play trio, left the White Sox to team with Maranville in 1914, "it was like Death Valley for whoever hit a ball down our way," to use Rabbit's words.

Nineteen hundred fourteen was the year the Boston Braves battled from last place in mid-season to capture their first flag. As Rabbit recalled years later, the turnabout began when George Stallings, whom Maranville considered "one of the greatest managers in baseball," insulted the Braves players after a humiliating defeat by likening them to a bunch of females. From then on, the inspired ballclub couldn't do anything wrong, typified by a ninth-inning, game-winning homer socked by a besotted Rabbit, who had to be reminded to circle the bases after the blast.

Not that the Springfield, Massachusetts native wasn't normally a "heady" ballplayer, as he once proved while trying to reach base against the formidable right-hander, Babe Adams. Aware that the odds were against his getting a hit, Maranville moved up on the plate in an effort to get nicked on the shirt with a pitch, a plan not too far-fetched considering the baggy jerseys worn at the time. Adams's first toss came within a few inches of Rabbit's elbow, the next hit him squarely on the head. After a few minutes unconsciousness, Maranville walked to first, satisfied that he had achieved his goal, though not in the preferred method.

The son of German-Irish immigrants, Walter fought for Uncle Sam's navy in 1918 and survived World War I unscathed, but had countless close calls as a civilian. While training with the Pirates at Hot Springs in the early '20s, Maranville was tricked by a teammate into believing he had a date with a beautiful blonde they had seen at the hotel lobby. After knocking on her apartment door that evening, the patsy became aware of the setup when pistol shots from an irate husband went whizzing past him.

Rabbit attracted more bullets than any of his animal namesakes. A woman once ran into his hotel room pleading for help, followed thereafter by a heavy pounding on the door, then a gunshot. Maranville escaped injury. During spring training with the Brooklyn club in 1926, a soused Brave, Bernie Neis, pointed a loaded gun at Maranville in his hotel room in Clearwater, then pulled the trigger. The only empty chamber in the gun spared the life of the lucky Rabbit, as another teammate rushed to grab the revolver before Neis could try again.

Trouble seemed to follow Maranville. His wife (whom he called "Mrs. Rabbit") once forgot her luggage containing valuable jewelry on a subway car. Rabbit raced alongside the moving subway and jumped in through the window. Spotting the suitcase under a seat he reached to pull it out, ignoring the woman sitting there, who misconstrued Walter's intentions and belted him in the mouth.

Maranville once got into a fistfight with a cab driver when he and his friend refused to pay the exorbitant fare. He was taken to the police station where he almost enjoyed municipal hospitality, but the judge recognized him in court and sent him to the ballpark instead. While being chased by cops on another occasion, Rabbit gave them the slip by ducking into a Salvation Army band, grabbing a tambourine, and joining the march.

Maranville was once nearly choked to death in a "friendly" wrestling match with pitcher Jack Scott. Walter got even by pretending he had died. Scott was distraught as Rabbit's teammates played along with the gag, and only when Scott threatened to cut his own throat with a razor blade did Maranville rise from the dead.

Jim Thorpe was a great athlete, but never made it big in the big leagues. His best season was his last in 1919 when he batted .327 in 60 games with the Braves. Maranville was Thorpe's roommate that year. One day, a drunken Thorpe demanded a drink from his roomie and threatened violence if not accommodated. The puny Rabbit (5-foot, 5 inch, 155 pounds) would have gladly given a bottle to the bigger, more muscular Thorpe, but reminded the Native American that none was available. Unconvinced, Thorpe asked again, this time while clutching Maranville, who was hanging halfway out the hotel window. When Walter stuck with his denial even at the risk of death, Thorpe realized he was telling the truth and finally let go, after first pulling the Rabbit inside.

A master at clowning, Maranville made Casey Stengel seem like a stuffed shirt. Rather than joining a mid-game brawl between the Cubs and Braves in the late 1920s, Rabbit stepped to the side and began shadowboxing, dishing out left uppercuts and

Maranville poses for pitcher-photographer Wilbur Cooper, succeeding in his attempt to look even goofier by reversing his cap, a popular fashion nowadays. (National Baseball Library, Cooperstown, NY)

right crosses, while feinting being hit with them, and even pretending to being knocked out. The crowd turned their attention from the brawl to the burlesque, transforming their potentially-violent mood to one of hilarity, for which Commissioner Kenesaw Landis thanked Maranville the next morning.

Maranville's pranks and antics were countless. At a restaurant with a friend, Rabbit accepted a dare and stuck his fork into a fish tank, speared a goldfish, and ate it. Another time, Walter decided that rather than walking 10 blocks to get to the other side of a river, it would be better to swim across, which he did, clothes and all, an act slightly less ridiculous than his once crawling onto a high-story hotel ledge to try to grab some pigeons. But Rabbit had a good reason. He wanted to fill his hotel closet with them.

Teammates could never guess what Maranville would do next. Posing in a prone position for a photographer one afternoon, Pirate Charlie Grimm clenched a golf tee with ball atop between his teeth, while Rabbit pretended to swing. Except that Rabbit didn't pretend. Fortunately for Grimm, Maranville hit nothing but ball. George Stallings once opened his hotel room door for room service and found Maranville clad as a bellhop, demanding a tip. In his only year as manager in 1925, Maranville was canned by Cub owner Bill Veeck for a supposed inability to control his players (in particular, a heavy-drinking Grover Alexander). Rabbit reacted minutes later by rushing outside Wrigley Field, grabbing newspapers from the newsboy, and shouting, "Extra! Extra! Maranville fired!"

A rare Rabbit, indeed!

THE MOST FEARED BATTER

F ive centuries ago, Leonardi Da Vinci advised, "Courage im-
perils life, fear protects it." It's a philosophy embraced often
by pitchers forced to gaze at sinewy sluggers menacingly
waving two pounds of lumber in their direction. Consequently,
more than a handful of history's hardball hitters have been hallowed by hurlers who avoided the strike zone, rationalizing that
less harm would result from a freebie to first than a wallop over
the wall.

But which of baseball's batters has been most feared? Was it
Stretch McCovey, whose 200 pounds was evenly distributed over
a 6-foot, 4-inch frame, and who swung the bat in a deliberate,
pendulum motion prior to propelling pellets, like the one which
ended the '62 Series, when Yankee second baseman Bobby
Richardson's glove prevented his head from being knocked into
the right-field seats? Or perhaps the brawny Willie Stargell's
windmill warmup was more ominous, once prompting Cincinnati
skipper Sparky Anderson to remark, "He's got power enough to
hit home runs in any park, including Yellowstone." How many
dozens of other mighty mashers have frightened hurlers?

Baseball is not a science and cannot be made into one despite
efforts by some researchers and statisticians to do so. Rating hitters and pitchers involves innumerable variables, and conclusions

inevitably are a matter of opinion, not fact. However, it's fun trying, and wondering which batter wobbled pitchers' knees most frequently and effectively is too tantalizing not to attempt an answer.

Knowing the rate in which hitters accumulated walks won't solve the mystery, but it will give us somewhere to start. Listed below are the top 20 hitters in walk percentage, according to the reliable source, *Total Baseball*:

1. Ted Williams
2. Max Bishop
3. Babe Ruth
4. Eddie Stanky
5. Ferris Fain
6. Gene Tenace
7. Roy Cullenbine
8. Eddie Yost
9. Mickey Mantle
10. Charlie Keller
11. Joe Morgan
12. Earl Torgeson
13. Bernie Carbo
14. Roy Thomas
15. Ralph Kiner
16. Harmon Killebrew
17. Lou Gehrig
18. Elmer Valo
19. Joe Ferguson
20. Rickey Henderson

In selecting the most feared hitter, 13 of the 20 listed can be eliminated "right off the bat" for not having sufficient power to frighten pitchers. None of these 13 ever hit 30 or more homers in one season, or accumulated (or, in the case of still-active Rickey Henderson, will accumulate) as many as 300 homers. Bases-on-balls by many were a tribute to their keen batting eye and selectiveness, not their instilling fear. Eight of the 13 players measured under 6 feet (Morgan's height is 5-feet, 7 inches), and some, like Henderson, further diminished the strike zone by crouching at the plate. Ferguson and Carbo were legitimate home run threats, but played much of their careers as part-timers. Roy Thomas led the league in walks seven times, but never had more than three homers while playing during the dead-ball era. Of the 13, only Joe Morgan became a Hall-of-Famer, though Henderson will undoubtedly make it as well. Both, however, are known for their basestealing, not homerun hitting.

Of the 20 only Williams, Ruth, Mantle, Keller, Kiner, Killebrew and Gehrig can be considered fearsome. Since Williams had the highest walk percentage, it's logical he be given the nod as most feared, correct? Not necessarily.

That Terrible Ted terrorized moundsmen is inarguable. In 1946, Red Sox Manager Joe Cronin acquired heavy-hitting Rudy York and placed him in the cleanup spot so that third place batter

Pitchers feared Ted Williams, but his walks resulted as much from his discerning eye as from their antipathy to throwing anything hittable. (National Baseball Library, Cooperstown, NY)

Williams would have some protection. Williams still led the league in walks, and his 156 that year was the highest total since Ruth's still-standing record 170 in 1923.

Williams hit over 521 homers in his career and combined with his .344 batting average and reputation for hating hurlers, presented a substantial threat. But his refusal to swing at anything but a strike was also widely known, often taking pitches a fraction of an inch off the plate. Indeed, Williams' knowledge of the strike zone was so respected that many walks might have been strikeouts had the umpires not been reluctant to call "Strike Three!" Base-on-balls resulted as much from Ted's patience as from pitchers' wariness. He saw more hittable balls than did some other sluggers.

In addition, Williams' lanky appearance didn't help to terrorize, even late in his career after adding pounds to his body, and homers to his career total. His swing was pretty to watch, perfectly timed and with little wasted motion, but, though that made him a highly efficient hitter, it made him less frightening than some powerhouses who did swing with all their might. His four baggers were generally hit in the same area — right field, and though he could hit them a long way, few were tape-measure jobs. Williams must be given his due as the second-greatest hitter in history, next to Ruth, but he wasn't the most feared batter. (It can be argued that Hornsby and Gehrig were Ted's equal as hitters.)

Gehrig's swing was as superb as Williams, equally polished and controlled, but unlike Ted, Larrupin' Lou would hit them out in any direction, and wouldn't settle for walks by taking close pitches. Lefty Carl Hubbell once tried to intentionally pass Gehrig and threw a ball too close to the plate. Lou hit it over the left-field fence. Gehrig's legs looked powerful, his entire body muscular. Any pitchers not made fidgety by Gehrig, should have been.

But Lou's strategy was to hit the ball hard, not necessarily for distance. When teammate Ruth, and later Mantle, swung at a pitch, their intent was always obvious — to hit it as far as they could. A sphere disappearing on its 500 foot journey to parts unknown would make a lasting impression on any pitcher. Like Williams, Gehrig was a fierce hitter with a picture-perfect swing, but that controlled swing made him slightly less frightening to pitchers.

Charlie Keller was a strong, lefty-hitting Yank who hit 30 or more homers three times, and led the league in home run percentage in 1943. Staring at the King Kong look-alike at home plate while aware of Yankee Stadium's short porch in right made any pitcher tentative in his delivery. Yet, Keller played in more than 100 games in only six of his 13 years in the majors. He was a solid, reliable power-hitter, but didn't play long enough to deserve consideration.

Kiner, too, had a somewhat limited big-league tenure, but his home run production during his 10-year career was impressive enough to warrant closer examination of the Hall-of-Famer. After all, Ralph's lifetime home run percentage is the best in baseball history except for Ruth, his leading the league in homers for seven-consecutive seasons unmatched. But Kiner didn't hit them especially far either, and, as indicated by his lifetime average of .279, he was an easier out than were Gehrig and Williams. Pitchers exercised caution with Kiner, but realized, too, that the right pitch would send him back to the bench.

So it was with Harmon Killebrew (.256 career average), but his bulging biceps also made him one of the best-built batters in history. He wasn't an extremely gifted gloveman at third, but what he couldn't field with his mitt, he often blocked with his body, with the baseball invariably suffering heavier damage from the collision. Killebrew would inflict more serious punishment with his bat if moundsmen were careless, often crippling baseballs with enough force to drive them not a few feet, but a hundred feet beyond the fence, not into the third row, but the third deck in left field. His surname helped to form his nickname, but "Killer" would have been an appropriate sobriquet had his last name been Goldilocks. (In fact, Killebrew is quite bald.)

Like Kiner, Killebrew had a high career homer percentage, third best in history, and accumulated over 200 more homers than Ralph. His belligerent stance, powerful swing and explosive blasts were sufficient to penetrate the psyche of the most confident of pitchers. It's difficult to bypass Killebrew, but there are two others who were slightly more feared by more hurlers.

Mantle could hit them as far as Killebrew, or anyone before or since. Though he struck out often, he was not as easy an out as Killebrew or Kiner, hitting .300 in 10 seasons and winning the batting crown in 1956. Though lefty swingers Williams and Gehrig made all pitchers uneasy, southpaws may have felt slightly more comfortable. Hurlers found no reprieve with the switch-hitting Mick, whose power was equally lethal from both sides of the plate. Mantle's broad back would widen, his muscular legs and arms bulge larger as each pitch approached, leading to a mighty, rarely inhibited swing. Despite his being surrounded in the lineup by such redoubtable hitters as Yogi Berra, Hank Bauer, Ellie Howard, Moose Skowron, Enos Slaughter and Roger Maris, pitchers shunned the strike zone with Mantle, and even late in his career when legendary leg problems worsened, the Oklahoman's walk percentage remained high. Mick's taking runner-up honors in the American League with over 100 base-on-balls in 1967 and 1968, while attaining the worst offensive stats of his career, is a testament to the respect shown him by hurlers. To quote the Commerce Comet, "The stats will show that I struck out a lot. What it doesn't reflect is me trying to hit all those bad pitches. As long as I had a bat in my hands, I wanted to be boss." Long before Steinbrenner or Springsteen, Mantle was "The Boss."

But so was Babe Ruth, the originator of long-distance service. Like Williams, Gehrig and Mantle, Ruth hit for a high average while maintaining exceptional power. Like Mantle, he could hit them farther than any contemporary. But Ruth was slightly more appalling for pitchers than Mickey because his blasts were unprecedented. The 6-foot, 2-inch, 200 pounder's huge hitch and long stride which preceded a swing mighty enough to spin him to the ground when missing must have been an awesome sight for moundsmen of the '20s who had become accustomed to the singles hitters of the previous two decades. Mantle frightened pitchers, but only after Ruth, Gehrig, Foxx, Greenberg, Mize, Williams and other sluggers' powerful pokes had done the same. Mickey's wallops may have traveled as far as Ruth's, but the Babe terrified pitchers more because his were unique at the time.

The most feared batter? Ruth. But remember, that's just one opinion.

COBB LETS LOOSE

O n May 5, 1925, Rabbit Maranville was swapping crutches for a cane in Chicago more than a month after breaking an ankle in an exhibition game in Los Angeles. Babe Ruth was out of a St. Vincent Hospital bed for the first time since his famed "bellyache heard round the world" necessitated an operation three weeks earlier. And Ty Cobb was considering a transformation in hitting style while preparing for a game in St. Louis.

By then, it was clear that Ruth had displaced him as the game's greatest star. Disgusted with the superior press coverage given his rival, even when inactive, Cobb told a veteran sportswriter in the clubhouse, "I'm going for home runs for the first time in my career."

The first victim of the Tiger changing his swipes was the Browns' 33-year-old Joe Bush, whose bullets had decreased in velocity since winning 26 of 33 with the Yankees in 1922. Ty laced into a Bush heater in the first, the ball comfortably clearing the right-field barrier. The next inning, Cobb found the same section of the bleachers, with veteran right-hander Elam Vangilder a somewhat surprised eyewitness from the mound. Cobb doubled and singled twice, then literally went downtown in the eighth off sophomore righty Milt Gaston, the ball bouncing across the street adjacent to the bleachers.

Six hits in a game was extraordinary, even for Cobb. He did it for the first and only time that day, becoming the fourth American Leaguer to stroke half a dozen since the league became an official member of the majors in 1903. The hits accounted for a still-standing, major-league record of 16 total bases, a mark matched by only five others since.

Yet, three homers in a game was the real story, a feat worthy of media coverage today but even more so in 1925. Only two American and three National Leaguers had accomplished it by then, and that Ruth wasn't among them made the achievement even sweeter for the Georgia Peach. (Babe would hit a trio of round trippers in a 1930 contest and would repeat the feat with the Braves in his final season of 1935.)

A first-inning single the next day gave Cobb nine-consecutive hits but he was retired in his next try, leaving him two shy of Speaker's record (Pinky Higgins and Walt Dropo own the current major-league mark with 12-straight hits). Ty then turned on the power, blasting two drives off a pair of southpaws, thus setting a record with five homers in two games.

Knocking the ball out of the park more than once in a game was an unprecedented experience for Cobb, although he had hit two inside-the-park homers in a 1909 contest. Now he had done it in consecutive games. In the finale of the St. Louis Series, Cobb nearly parked another, his liner missing the top of the right-field wall by two feet.

Having proven "he could clout with the musclemen when he chose," as noted by biographer Charles Alexander, the conservative Cobb reverted to the slash-bunt-and-spray style which had won him 10 batting titles. He finished his 21st season among the league leaders with a .378 average, but with only a dozen homers, nearly half of his total coming in two games.

Why didn't Cobb continue to go for the fences? Critics might insist that he did, that after his initial success, which may have been a case of beginner's luck, his swings for the seats went in vain. Still, it's difficult to believe that the well-built, 6-footer, whose skill with the bat is undeniable, couldn't have added dozens more than the 23 homers he accumulated from the time of his two-game explosion to his retirement following the '28 season.

Cobb's cessation of power was voluntary, yet at the same time uncontrollable. Much has already been written regarding Cobb's driving personality being manifested on the field — his refusal to accept defeat, his belief that baseball wasn't a game, but a war. This passion for winning made each pitcher-batter confrontation crucial. Knowing big swings and long strides would result in many more strikeouts and pop-ups than home runs, Ty's choice was to either accept increased defeats at the hands of the hated hurlers, or abandon his long-ball quest. For Cobb, the decision came easily enough.

Just as Ruth could have added points to his average with a more controlled swing, Cobb's 117 lifetime homers might have been tripled had he joined in the fun during the fence-clearing frenzy of the '20s. And just as Ruth did well to keep swinging, Cobb's persistent pursuit of perfection left him with a .366 career average. Talk about your unbreakable records!

THE BEAST'S
MONSTER GAMES

H is walk percentage is not among the top 20 lifetime leaders, but Jimmie Foxx rates as one of the most feared
sluggers in history nonetheless. Foxx's feats are ignored
by some today ("His accomplishments have been one of baseball's
best kept secrets," wrote one Foxx biographer), but pitchers paid
particular attention to The Beast during his playing days.

And why wouldn't they? All Foxx did during his 20-year career
was win a Triple Crown in 1933, take four homer titles, and capture three RBI and batting championships. He nearly broke Ruth's
60-homer mark in 1932, but fell two short. The Maryland
muscleman would have easily surpassed 60 had two of his homers not been rained out, a screen hadn't been placed atop the
right-field wall at Sportsman's Park in St. Louis prior to the season, a barrier which Jimmie hit five times in 1932, and a fall
from a ladder hadn't left him with an injury which hampered his
swing in the final two months. His first Triple Crown should have
come that year, but Dale Alexander took the batting title with a
.367 average, three points better than Foxx's, despite Alexander
only gathering 392 at bats.

Like Mantle, Foxx's accomplishments have been supplanted by
a reputation for unimaginable strength. The son of an Irish-Ameri-
can farmer, the youthful Jimmie milked cows, worked in the wheat

fields, baled hay, and lifted heavy phosphorus bags, acquiring more muscles than most modern athletes do in weight rooms. As a major-leaguer, the 6-foot, 200 pounder cut short the sleeves on his uniform, exposing Herculean biceps capable of powering baseballs improbable distances, like the time in '32 when he rocketed a 500-foot drive out of Philadelphia's Shibe Park and completely over a factory building across the street. For those of us denied by time the chance to see Foxx at work, we have former hurler Ted Lyons's words, "No matter what story you hear about Foxx's power, believe it!"

Among Jimmie's incredible achievements were his record-setting performances. Except for Ruth, probably no other hitter exceeded Foxx's number of explosive games. His best still ranks as one of the most awsome in history.

On July 10, 1932, Foxx's A's were battling the Indians at League Park. The Beast's day began humbly enough, a first frame single off the Tribes' Clint Brown. With his team trailing by a run in the third, Foxx smashed a homer into the left-field bleachers to tie the score. Jimmie capped a seven-run seventh with another homer off reliever Wes Ferrell, then doubled off the same hurler to drive in two in the ninth. Philadelphia's 15 runs weren't quite enough as Cleveland tallied in the bottom half, forcing extra innings. In the 16th, Foxx broke the deadlock with a two-run blast, but the stubborn Indians squared it with a pair in the home half. In the 18th, Double X singled and scored the eventual winning run, ending the four-hour shoot-out. In all, Foxx collected three homers, a double, two singles, and eight ribbies that day, and his 16 total bases remains an American-League record shared by five others.

By stroking six hits in a game, Foxx duplicated a feat of two years earlier. In a 1930 Memorial-Day doubleheader at Philadelphia, Connie Mack's pride-and-joy laced three singles, two doubles and a triple off the Senators' Ad Liska and Firpo Marberry in another extra-inning game which ended after 13 with a 7-6 defeat of Washington. For Foxx, it wasn't as productive a performance as in '32, his safeties producing only two RBIs, but it made him the first A's player in history to get as many as a half-dozen hits in a game. Foxx added a pair of doubles and RBIs in the nightcap.

Nor was the '32 affair at League Park the only occasion Foxx would belt three homers. On June 8, 1933, almost exactly one year later, Foxx whistled three drives in consecutive innings off the Yanks' Lefty Gomez, negating homers by Gehrig and Ruth, giving Philadelphia a 14-10 victory. (Babe's drive was described as "landing on a housetop across the street and being the mightiest of the day.") Having reached the seats in his last at bat the day before, Foxx thus tied a still-standing record of four consecutive homers.

Foxx's most productive game of his career occurred a couple of months later. Playing at League Park on August 14, he ambushed the Indians' Ace Hudlin with a two-run triple in the first and a bases-loaded homer in the second. He drove in another with a double in the fourth off Bill Bean and plated two more off Bean with a single in the sixth. In his final try Foxx was fanned, but his nine RBIs were a junior-circuit record until broken by Tony Lazzeri's 11 in 1936. Foxx also became the second Athletic in a week to hit for the cycle, Pinky Higgins having done it on August 6.

Foxx might have surpassed Lazzeri's ribby record while playing for the Red Sox in a 1938 contest, had weather not interfered. After Boston skipper Joe Cronin was presented with a set of silver in pregame ceremonies on September 7, his veteran first baseman single-handedly presented him with a victory. The Beast was slain by Yankee ace Red Ruffing in the first inning, but Foxx punished the future Hall-of-Famer with a three-run wallop onto the screen atop the Green Monster in the third. The next inning, Foxx chased Ruffing from the box with another three-run blast to left and nearly had another homer in the fifth when his bases-loaded drive off reliever Poison Andrews resulted in a double and two more RBIs. Having knocked in eight runs in five innings, it appeared Jimmie would have at least one, probably two more cracks at New York's shaky bullpen (Johnny Murphy was the best in the league that year, but McCarthy wasn't about to use him trailing 11-4). As the Yanks batted in the sixth the rains came, and perhaps the pinstripers weren't the only disappointed losers when the umpire called the game a half hour later, as Foxx's shot at the record book was lost as well.

Sometimes, the best way to pitch to Foxx was not to pitch to him. That was the strategy employed by the St. Louis Browns in 1938. On June 16, the day after Cincy's Johnny Vander Meer threw his record second-straight no-hitter in Brooklyn, Jimmie set a record by going to the plate six times and accumulating no official at bats. Browns' pitchers Toots Tietje, Ed Linke and Sheriff Van Atta completely avoided him, but their strategy backfired in a 12-8 St. Louis setback, poetic justice for such cowardly conduct. Foxx's six walks in a game remains the major-league mark today. (Montreal's Andre Thornton faced comparable chicken-hearted hurlers in a 1984 game, but his half dozen walks were acquired in 16 innings.)

A rather friendly-looking beast was Jimmie Foxx — until he stood at the plate that is. (National Baseball Library, Cooperstown, NY)

Foxx was known for his skill in driving home baserunners, but in 1939 Jimmie matched a record for runs-scored in a game. After homering in the first of a twin bill on June 9 at Sportsman's Park, the Sox superstar reached base in all five plate appearances in the nightcap and scored each time, once on another homer. His American League mark was bettered by two future Boston infielders, Johnny Pesky in '46 and Spike Owen in '86, both tallying six times.

Foxx could not only set records in games, he could set them within the span of one inning, as he did in his first season as a regular in 1928. Facing the Tigers' Vic Sorrell in the second inning at Shibe Park on August 16, Jimmie drilled a double and scored, and smacked a double and scored again off reliever Josh Billings 10 minutes later, becoming the first Athletic and only the ninth American Leaguer to belt a pair of two-baggers in the same frame. Not satisfied, Foxx blasted a homer over the right-field wall in the fourth.

Foxx chose one game, rather than a seasonal or career achievement, as his choice for greatest thrill. Facing Burleigh Grimes in Game Five of the 1930 World Series, The Beast looked for a breaking ball and got it, driving the ball out of Shibe Park while driving in the only two runs of the game. When the Series ended in an Athletic victory a few days later, Foxx and two other teammates became the first players to give a live radio interview from the clubhouse.

Foxx retired from the game in 1945 and was inducted into the Hall of Fame six years later. In 1967, while eating dinner, Jimmie choked on a piece of steak and died at age 59. His remarkable lifetime stats include a .325 average, .609 slugging percentage, 534 homers and nearly 2,000 RBIs, making him the second-greatest righty batter in baseball history, behind Rogers Hornsby. Yet, with all his single game, seasonal and career achievements, Foxx's fame faded fast. Relatively little mention is made today of the Sudlersville slugger who, in the '30s, replaced an aging Ruth as baseball's new home run king.

HOT DOGS AT
THE BALLPARK

"I'm not a conformist. I'm a showman. Call me a hot dog."
So boasts Rickey Henderson in his book, *Off Base*.

Hot dogs, or players who perform in a manner which
could be described as showing off, have been spilling
mustard on the field for as long as vendors have been dressing
dogs in the stands. Their shenanigans have at times spurred
laughter and cheers, other times catcalls and boos, but never have
hot dogs been ignored.

Babe Ruth was known for his excesses. He drove cars faster,
spent more money, tipped more lavishly, and had a larger appetite than most people, so it's not surprising he was a hot dog on
the field. He waved to spectators, bantered with opponents, and
predicted home runs. His most famous "called shot" occurred in
the '32 Series, though many believe he was pointing at Cubs'
pitcher Charlie Root, not at the center-field stands where the
ball landed on the next pitch.

In *Babe*, biographer Robert Creamer mentions two less-famil-
iar occasions when the phenomenal slugger with the flamboyant
style made a "point" with homers. In Boston, a loudmouth taunted
him while batting. Rather than react angrily, Ruth turned toward the fan, his right arm extended, index finger pointing to
right field. After knocking the ball over the fence, Ruth laughed

while circling the bases, then bowed to the disgruntled spectator after crossing home plate. In a 1928 game in St. Louis, Babe again pointed to where in a few seconds he would hit it, waving to the opposing bench and crowd while circling the bases.

When Ruth retired in the '30s, Dizzy Dean became baseball's champion of show-offs (or showmen, as Monsieur Henderson prefers). The Cardinal Hall-of-Famer's lively fastball matched a demeanor which exuded confidence. Diz would sometimes inform hitters when his heater was coming, then strike them out. He'd intimidate the opposition with insults before games, like the time he walked behind Elden Auker while the Tiger starter was warming up for Game Seven of the '34 Series and asked, "You don't expect to get anyone out with that stuff, do you?"

Dean often was unsatisfied with merely retiring batters, once yelling for his teammate to drop a foul pop-up so that he could strike out the batter, which, naturally he did. Like Ruth, Dizzy often played to the crowd, tipping his hat to heckling fans after a wild pitch, or when making an appearance as a pinch-runner. If things weren't going his way, he wouldn't be afraid of showing defiance. In a 1937 game, Dean protested an umpire's ruling by staging a "sit-down" strike on the mound, not resuming with his pitching for about 10 minutes.

Perhaps the spiciest hot dog in history was Jim Piersall. The talented center fielder, who played most of his career during the '50s, was probably a decade ahead of his time in terms of nonconformity. It's a shame that the two-time All-Star, who was one of the best defensive players of his day and skillful enough with the stick to once lead the league in doubles and to bang out six hits in as many at bats in a game, is not known today as much for his skills as for his antics. Piersall would wear a football helmet while batting, carry bug spray to the outfield, or dance the hula between innings. He'd bow after making catches, mock his teammates, or purposely make routine plays more difficult.

Piersall liked to taunt opposing batters from the dugout in an attempt to distract them, not always successfully. In a game in the '60s, Piersall was badgering the Yanks' Joe Pepitone, another hot dog who is usually credited with being the first to bring a hairdryer to the locker room. Pepi had been bothered by a bad wrist and during his at bat, Jimmy mocked the injury by wrapping a towel around his wrist. Pepitone hit one into the right-field stands and while rounding third, nodded and pointed to his wrist as he gazed at Piersall, now sitting quietly in the corner of the dugout.

Jimmy didn't hit many homers, but would make the most out of the few times he did. In a game with Cleveland in 1960, he made like Ruth and pointed to the left-field seats, surprising everyone (probably including himself) by connecting. His home run trot was anything but constrained, as he laughed and clowned all the way around the diamond.

It's appropriate that Piersall was with the laughable Mets in 1963 when he reached the seats for the 100th time. To celebrate the momentous career homer (momentous for him at least, since he only hit four more), Jim ran the bases backwards, proving his prediction made to Duke Snider that his 100th dinger would draw more attention than the Duke's 400th had a couple weeks before. Unlike the appreciative applauding New York fans, Philly hurler Dallas Green didn't see the humor in it all, vowing afterward to get even. He never did, unless his managing the Mets to a last place divisional finish in '93 was his method of revenge.

Jimmy didn't like it when opposing players hit the long ball. In a game against the White Sox in the '60s, Piersall became annoyed with Bill Veeck's exploding scoreboard, which proceeded each Chicago homer with ear-shattering fireworks. He reacted by throwing a baseball at it which, according to an outraged Veeck, could have short-circuited his latest innovation, a circumstance which would have delighted others besides Piersall.

Jimmy retired in 1967, the same year another famous hot dog began broiling. Reggie Jackson retired 20 years later with 563 homers, many of them the tape-measure variety, but is best remembered for his bragging, proficiency in attracting attention, and style of play which made former hurler Darold Knowles once remark, "There isn't enough mustard in the world to cover that hot dog." It wasn't a coincidence that Jackson's concentration at the plate enhanced during the World Series (thus the nickname Mr. October), or when facing Nolan Ryan in the ninth with a chance to break up a no-hitter (which he did in 1979), or when performing in front of a large crowd or television audience.

If he wasn't hitting on a particular day, Reggie would do other things to become noticed, like "dogging it" on the field, as he did during a nationally televised game in June of 1977, when the Yank's casual fielding turned a single into a double. Manager Billy Martin removed him from the game immediately, prompting a shouting match between the two proud adversaries in the dugout.

Many admired Jackson's power, none as much as the power-hitter himself. If the brawny lefty wasn't the first to stare in marvel at his homers, he deserves credit, or blame, for making it fashionable. After launching a long one, Reggie would drop the bat at the plate and stand motionless, watching the flight of the ball until its descent into an upper deck. Only then would his home run trot begin. If the pretentious pose disgusted old-timers, it inspired Reggie's contemporaries to copy the act with increasing frequency to the point where few of today's batters refrain from taking at least a peek at a long one before leaving the box.

Home run, cha-cha-cha, That's Ruben Sierra's unique method of celebrating long-distance homers. Hey, Yankee fans. How many of the pinstripers in the dugout can you identify? (National Baseball Library, Cooperstown, NY)

The home run stare has evolved, with some modern artists adding even more color to their masterpieces. During the 1995 American League Divisional Series between New York and Seattle, the Yanks' Ruben Sierra belted a drive, the destination of which was obvious to all. As the sphere sped toward the back rows of the bleachers, Sierra, with head down, danced sideways toward the dugout, looked up to watch the splashdown, then began his jubilant journey around the basepaths. Now that's art!

One of Jackson's admirers was the still-active Rickey Henderson, whose home run stares have been less frequent only because his home runs haven't been as numerous. Rickey has other ways of drawing attention. The talented basestealer holds records for the most thefts in a season — 130 in 1982 and in a career — 1,117 as of 1994. (He boasted after breaking Lou Brock's mark in '91, "I am the greatest!") He also has a keen eye and bats in a crouch, thereby drawing many walks. After taking ball four, Henderson drops the bat on the plate before slowly treading toward first. When he successfully swipes a base, Rickey applauds his effort or points toward the catcher or pitcher.

Henderson plays the outfield with panache, highlighted by "snatch catches." With glove up, he grabs at falling fly balls with a sweeping sideways motion, finishing with the flourish of a matador, then victoriously tosses the corralled horsehide from glove to throwing hand. Opponents accuse him of showboating, but Rickey proudly defends the peculiar putouts by declaring, "The snatch catch isn't for everybody. Not everybody can be a hot dog."

Hot dogs. Some find them appetizing. For others, they're totally disagreeable.

CHAPTER
30

THE GREATEST
GAME EVER
PITCHED

A merica's oldest sport has produced hundreds of amazing pitching performances. The A's Jack Coombs once hurled for 24 frames before prevailing over the Boston Pilgrims, still a record for most innings by a winning pitcher. Cub Zip Zabel entered a 1915 game with one out in the opening inning and went the rest of the way in winning 4-3, his 19-inning stint the most by any reliever. Roger Clemens blew away 20 Seattle batters in a Red Sox victory in late April of '86, one less than Tom Cheney's still-standing record 21 in 1962, though the Senator star had 16 innings with which to accumulate Ks. For several seasons, Sandy Koufax may have been the closest thing to a perfect pitcher, and on September 9, 1965, he was, setting down 27 consecutive Cubs in a 1-0 masterpiece, his 14 whiffs the most by any of the 11 perfect games of the century. Nolan Ryan's no-hitter against Toronto on May Day of 1991 was perhaps baseball's most overpowering performance, allowing only two baserunners via walks, while fanning 16. He was 44 years old at the time. The fact that Ryan was able to dispose of hitters as effectively late in his career as he had three decades earlier adds little credence to the "superiority of modern athletes" theory.

On July 2, 1933, 50,000 fans gathered at the Polo Grounds to watch their Giants twice take on the Cardinals. New York skipper Bill Terry selected lefty screwballer Carl Hubbell to start the opener, and though Hub was clearly the ace of the staff following five winning seasons and a 1928 no-hitter, he hadn't yet shown the consistent greatness that would lead to five-straight, 20-win seasons, a record 24-game winning streak, and a 1934 All-Star effort in which he struck out five-consecutive future Hall-of-Famers.

The Cards' skipper Frankie Frisch would often pit his top hurler against King Carl, but because Dizzy Dean had pitched two days earlier, the matchup was avoided that day. Tex Carleton opposed Hubbell, and though the fireballer from the Lone Star State wasn't Dean's equal in ability, he was a fierce competitor who would never have a losing season in his eight full years in the majors. Carleton had defeated New York in the series' opener and requested the assignment despite only two days rest.

Hubbell and Carleton were close to untouchable as the game remained scoreless through nine innings. In the 11th, the Giants loaded the bases with one out, but Carleton escaped by inducing a force-out and pop-up. Terry teased the home crowd with a long triple to the wide open spaces in center in the 15th, but was stranded.

Carleton left for a pinch-hitter in the 16th, and the veteran Jesse Haines set down New York in the next frame. In the 18th, two walks put the winning run in scoring position. With two outs, Haines had a two-strike count when Hughie Critz cracked his next pitch for a hit to center. Carleton's valiant effort was wasted, as Hubbell was victorious in what amounted to a double-shutout victory.

Hub allowed only six hits, four of them being infield singles. In no inning did more than one Cardinal reach base, only once did a runner reach third. Known for his exceptional control, Carl was perfect in yielding no walks, while whiffing a dozen. An 18-inning shutout is impressive, but more so when it's known that the moundsman hurled 12 perfect innings and was never in real danger of being scored upon.

Hubbell's long blank must rank as the greatest single-game pitching performance of the century. There have been players who've allowed fewer hits, pitched more innings, or struck out more batters in one contest. But consider that a pitcher's job is to win, and to do that he must prevent the opposition from scoring. On July 2, 1933, Carl needed to do that for 18 innings.

Only two others have matched the feat. The Senators' Walter Johnson defeated the White Sox in a May game of 1918, but the Big Train was slightly less overpowering in his 18-inning whitewash, allowing 10 hits and one walk, while gathering nine strikeouts. Ed Summers blanked the opposing club for 18 innings in 1909, but also yielded more hits and walks, collected fewer Ks, and the game ended in a tie, not a victory.

Perhaps inspired by his rival, Dean demanded to pitch the second game, despite only one day's rest. He allowed a solo homer to Johnny Vergez and lost 1-0 to Tarzan Parmalee. The clubhouse comments from the top two hurlers in the league were characteristic of their personalities. Said the modest Hubbell, "The boys were really behind me and didn't make an error." Dean drawled, "Tell Tarzan I said he pitched a good game. He'll like hearing that coming from me."

HORNSBY HANGS 'EM UP

O n July 23, 1937, a group of reporters gathered at a late-night press conference in a downtown St. Louis law office where it was announced that Rogers Hornsby had been fired as manager for the fourth time. For $10,000, St. Louis Browns' President Donald Barnes bought out his contract, which ran through the '38 season. In acknowledging the reason for his dismissal, Hornsby stated, "While my contract did not forbid betting on races, Mr. Barnes objected to my doing so." Previous protests of his gambling excesses had been raised by other owners, even by Commissioner Landis, but aside from baseball, the track was Hornsby's greatest passion.

Moreover, Hornsby was not one to be told what to do. Conversely, he often told others. Wrote sportswriter John Kieran after Hornsby's firing, "The Rajah is a man of one idea, and that idea is that Hornsby is always right. Which mightn't have hurt him much if he hadn't so often made a point of telling his club owners where they were wrong."

Present-day critics of Hornsby often elaborate on his autocratic attitude as skipper. Players were barred from drinking or smoking and forced to sleep at early hours. Mr. Blunt verbally abused players for mental mistakes and was quick to bench those who weren't performing.

But historians quick to label Hornsby as an ineffective, over-bearing manager should think again. If his bans on tobacco and alcohol were strict, those players who complied were probably better off. If he criticized players for amateurish blunders, per-haps modern professionals should hear it more often when failing to lay down a bunt, hit the cutoff man, or stay alert on the basepaths. And if his success was limited (actually, Hornsby won a World Series, which is more than most skippers have accom-plished), it wasn't entirely his fault. In fact, only once did a team finish higher in the standings in a year following a Hornsby dis-missal.

The July news conference in St. Louis held further significance. Hornsby was released as a player as well, and though he'd man-age again for the Browns and once more for Cincinnati, he would never again swing a bat in major-league competition. The year had begun optimistically for Rogers, who was anticipating a pro-ductive season with the help of 30-minute salt baths and 15-minute rubdowns which he hoped would rejuvenate a 41-year-old body beleaguered with foot and ankle problems. The therapy was sufficient to enable his banging out two singles and his 301st career homer on Opening Day. By the end of April, Hornsby was confident enough to predict he'd get his 3,000th hit before season's end. But despite a .321 batting average by midseason, Hornsby's defiance was such that Barnes felt he had to go. The Opening-Day homer was his last, and it's one of the tragedies in baseball that the greatest right-handed hitter in history fell 70 short of the 3,000-hit milestone.

Rogers may not have been the ideal manager, but critics lack ammunition when attempting an assault on his playing career. Few stars have accomplished more. From his rookie year in 1915 when Cardinal skipper Miller Huggins, who would become Hornsby's only idol, convinced the tall, skinny Texan to add weight and change his batting style, to his final injury-plagued seasons, the Rajah accumulated stats matched by no National League player before or since: two Triple Crowns; a .359 career batting average; three seasons batting over .400 including a still-stand-ing major-league mark of .424 in 1924; six-consecutive batting and slugging titles; and six-straight years leading in on-base per-centage.

Don't let that big smile fool you. Rogers Hornsby ordinarily wasn't extremely friendly. (National Baseball Library, Cooperstown, NY)

When a 1930 foot operation put an end to his full-time play, Hornsby continued to produce as a part-timer. From 1930-1937, he batted .313 in 719 at bats. He was a reliable pinch-hitter, and in 1933 stroked a homer, two doubles and three singles for six-straight pinch safeties, two shy of the major-league mark.

Ted Williams was known for his keen batting eye. Not surprisingly, his mentor was Hornsby who warned Williams to always "get a good ball to hit." Hornsby, too, would swing only at strikes.

In a television interview in 1959, Hall-of-Famer Gabby Hartnett claimed that because umpires respected Rogers' knowledge of the strike zone, he "got more fourth strikes than anyone in baseball."

In a popularity contest among his peers, Hornsby might have finished last. Unperturbed, he would have countered that popularity doesn't produce base hits.

THE GREAT
DEAN DEAL

On April 16, 1938, Charles Drake, an assistant to Cubs'
owner Phil Wrigley, announced the trading of the Cards'
ace right-hander Dizzy Dean for pitchers Curt Davis and
Clyde Shoun, part-time outfielder Tuck Stainback and a lot of
cash. Dean and Cardinal teammates were in the clubhouse following an exhibition game when news of the trade arrived. "I'll
bet they give me $10,000 more than I'm making here," Diz boasted.
Said a depressed Pepper Martin, "There goes our pennant and
World Series money."

Martin's pessimism was justified. From 1932-1937 Dean had
been the winningest pitcher in baseball, accumulating 133 victories for St. Louis's rowdy Gang House Gang and was tops in the
National League in complete games (140) and strikeouts (1090)
for that same period. He led the league in complete games and
strikeouts four times, in victories and shutouts twice, and even
led in saves one year.

Still, with all Dean's heroics St. Louis had taken but one pennant, that being in 1934 when Dizzy dazzled opponents for 30
wins. They finished a distant fourth in 1937. Furthermore, there
was reason to believe Dean's best days were behind him.

During the All-Star Game of '37, Dean was struck in the foot by
an Earl Averill comebacker. Despite warnings to give his cracked

toe time to heal, Dizzy returned to pitch two weeks later. As he admitted afterwards, "I shouldn't have been out there." By favoring his left foot, Dean threw out his arm. His pitching was so lackluster thereafter that by season's end, Cardinal executive Branch Rickey suggested he sit out the entire 1938 season (with no pay, of course).

When Diz refused, the club's most valuable pitcher for six straight seasons suddenly became expendable. Rickey and Cardinal owner Sam Breadon would have jumped at the Cubs' offer of $185,000 even without any players thrown in. Wrigley was gambling, hoping Dean's winter prediction that "the old wing's gonna be fine again" would come true.

Charlie Grimm was anything but grim when he heard of the deal. "I'm tickled to death we got him," the Cub skipper told reporters. "I know he'll be a big help to us." As if to prove Grimm correct, Dean won his first start on April 20 and afterwards bestowed praise upon his new boss and teammates. "He's the greatest manager in the game," said the self-proclaimed Great One, unaware that Grimm would be replaced by catcher Gabby Hartnett in July. "And what a ballclub these Cubs are. They're the greatest bunch I've ever been with." When he shutout his former team four days later, it was "two down and 28 to go."

Actually, it was five to go as Dizzy finished with seven victories, his sore arm enabling him to start only 10 games. But was the Dean deal a dud for the Cubs? Not when you consider he dizzied batters with junk on days he was able to pitch, resulting in only one loss and a 1.81 ERA. It's not preposterous to suggest that Chicago's narrow pennant victory that year, highlighted by Hartnett's late-season "homer in the gloamin'," would have been thwarted had it not been for Dean's superb, though somewhat limited, contribution. (Many historians, recalling Hartnett's game-winning blast, fail to point out that it followed an inspiring 2-1 victory by Dean the day before.)

In contrast, Curt Davis pitched in 40 games for the Cards, but was mediocre at best in winning only 12, and his ERA of 3.63 was only slightly lower than the league average. Perhaps he would have done better with the Cubs, but not much better. Shoun and Stainbach weren't a big help either. And if the reputedly wise Rickey, nicknamed the Mahatma, was correct in his assessment

The sore-winged Dean in Cub locker room in 1938. (National Baseball Library, Cooperstown, NY)

of Dean's damaged arm, he may have underestimated Dizzy's influence on team attitude. Dean had been well-liked by most teammates and was a morale booster. His presence on the bench was welcomed by the Cubs, missed by the Cards. St. Louis dropped from fourth in '37 to sixth in '38.

153

Davis rebounded with 22 wins in 1939. Coupled with the fact that Dean won only 16 games in his four seasons with Chicago, the trade, in retrospect, appears to have favored St. Louis. But the Cubs got a pennant out of it and, after several more seasons of failures, all Rickey got was fired. In 1942, Breaden turned on him as quickly as Rickey had with his Arkansas ace, in the Great Dean Deal of '38.

CHAPTER 33

SATCHEL

There were several aspects of Leroy Satchel Paige's life which may not be regarded as meritorious. As a child, he was thrown into reform school after a shoplifting escapade, although his repeatedly ricocheting stones off kids' noggins and habitual hooky-playing would have eventually landed him there anyway.

Pitching skills acquired from the reformatory earned him a position with the Chattanooga Lookouts, but he quickly jumped to Birmingham of the Negro Leagues the following season. Self-interest over team-loyalty would be a Paige characteristic throughout his career, made evident by his record of having hurled for over 250 teams.

Besides possessing a blistering fastball and unorthodox hesitation pitch, both made more unhittable by a distracting high-kick delivery, the skinny 6-foot, 3-inch superstar is best remembered for his show-off demeanor. Prior to starting assignments, the maverick from Mobile would deliberately arrive late to the park, be the last to take the field, and walk to the mound about as quickly as a caterpillar crawls across a limb. To accentuate his superiority over hitters, Paige would occasionally order his outfielders to park their rear ends on the grass prior to delivering. He was as accomplished at pitching gibes as at pitching baseballs, frequently taunting batters with comments similar to the one heard by Cardinal great Pepper Martin when they faced in a 1930s barnstormer: "They tell me you can hit. Then hit this!" He often issued challenges, like the time he set up a duel with former teammate Josh Gibson, considered by many to be the greatest of the Negro League batters, purposely loading the bases with two outs in the ninth by walking the two batters ahead of Gibson.

Satchel, whose nickname derived from carrying suitcases as a boy porter at a railroad station, was as accomplished a boaster as he was a pitcher. His vocabulary was limited, (he once replied to the question of whether he throws fast consistently by stating, "No, I do it all the time") but his articulations were interesting enough. He described his fastball as good enough to "nip frosting off a cake," his control so precise that all a catcher need do is "hold the glove still. I'll hit it," and that on occasion he'd throw one that "ain't never been seen by this generation." He claimed that other Negro Leaguers benefited from his fame, saying, "Those other players ate lean meat. If it wasn't for me, they'd have been eating side meat." Hooked up in a scoreless, extra-inning mound duel with his boastful, talented white counterpart Dizzy Dean one afternoon, Paige announced he'd pitch shutout ball "if we have to stay here all night." Satch was equally hostile toward baserunners, once advising a fidgety Phil Rizzuto at third base to "calm down, Sonny. You ain't going nowhere."

A juvenile delinquent. A braggart. Self-centered. Not exactly attributes which enhanced a sports professional's popularity, especially when his color already gave some in the country an excuse not to like him. Yet, aside from humble Joe Louis, Satchel Paige was the most popular black sports figure of the '30s and '40s, renowned not only among blacks, but whites as well.

His being well-liked by other players is not incomprehensible. Paige's assessment of his value in drawing large Negro League crowds was undoubtedly accurate and explains the rarity of criticism which emanated from teammates and opponents, who realized the foolishness of biting the hand that was feeding them. Barnstorming exhibitions between Negro Leaguers and major-leaguers were certain to attract fewer paying customers without Paige. And though Satchel was an expert showman, he was genuinely liked by most players who knew him well.

Satchel Paige relaxes near the dugout of the Negro League ballclub, the Kansas City Monarchs. (National Baseball Library, Cooperstown, NY)

But what accounts for the public's admiration of a haughty athlete whose boldness and egotism differed dramatically from the qualities of humility and selflessness expected of Americans (especially black Americans) until the '60s, when Muhammed Ali and forthcoming sports figures rendered those qualities passé? Why did over 51,000 pay their way into Comiskey Park in July of 1948 to witness Paige's first start in the majors, with additional thousands entering by barging past police barricades? Why was a record 73,000 in attendance in Cleveland a week later in his next start?

The chief explanation is that, like Ali, Paige's talent proved worthy of his boasting. Satchel would say he'd fire the ball past a batter, then do it. He would predict a no-hitter, then throw one. He would dare a Josh Gibson to hit his fastball, then blow three by him. He would order outfielders to lie down, then show why he didn't need them. He would mock big league batters like Pepper Martin, Joe DiMaggio and Hack Wilson, then show he could handle them.

Ali's arrogant attitude antagonized many at first. His switching from the Christian to Muslim faith and refusal to be inducted into the armed forces didn't help his popularity. Yet many sports enthusiasts embraced him. The turnabout came partly as a result of increasing tolerance during the '60s and '70s, partly a result of the public's recognition of his superior skills.

Satchel didn't have the advantage of performing for an enlightened society, which marveled at his skills yet did nothing to prevent a sport touted as the "national pastime" from barring him because of his race. Unfortunately, we can only speculate today as to what might have been had Paige been allowed to compete in the majors, not at the age of 42 as was the case in 1948, but in his prime when still in command of Long Tom, Trouble Ball, Midnight Rider, Four-Day Creeper and other assorted pitches.

Unfortunate, too, is the effect Ali and Paige had on American sports. Following them came a multitude of obnoxious imitators who mimicked their idols' bluster and rebelliousness despite obvious shortcomings, so that it's now difficult to find any professional athlete whose actions speak louder than their words. Even those currently regarded as outstanding would have inspired hysterical laughter from Paige had he heard their vain pronouncements. Reggie Jackson was one of the game's accomplished home run hitters but his vaunting comments, like the one in 1977 claiming to be "the straw that stirred the drink" for the Yankees, snubbing teammate and captain Thurman Munson, seem misplaced coming from a .262 lifetime hitter.

For all his crowing, it was Paige's ability and hard work that were ultimately responsible for his success and fame. If only more ballplayers understood that today.

THE GREAT
DiMAGGIO HOLD-OUT

I t's customary nowadays for ambitious ballplayers to demand salary increases from budget-conscious owners, yet pay squabbles have always been a part of baseball economics. Rogers Hornsby was as great a bargainer as he was a batsman. Dizzy Dean was famous for his holdouts, though unlike Rajah, usually fared poorly in financial confrontations with the sharp, tightfisted Branch Rickey. Babe Ruth did little better in dealings with Yankee owner Jake Ruppert, who thought ballplayers ungrateful for asking for more than was offered. In 1938, another of Ruppert's stars had the audacity to reject his generous offer.

Joe DiMaggio, entering only his third season, had already earned quite a reputation. As a minor-leaguer in San Francisco, DiMaggio hit safely in 61-consecutive games in 1933 and batted .398 in 1935 before Ruppert purchased him for $25,000. His rookie season in '36 was anything but disappointing, finishing with 29 homers, 125 RBIs, and a .323 average. Nor did he suffer from a sophomore jinx in '37, belting what would be career-high stats of 46 homers and 167 ribbies, along with an average of .346. He had been paid $15,000 in '37. When the spring of '38 arrived, Joe was ready to talk money.

Through frugal General Manager Ed Barrow, Ruppert offered DiMaggio $25,000, the same amount Joe had requested and was denied in '37. DiMaggio now wanted more. He returned the contract unsigned, asking for $40,000 instead.

Ruppert was furious, but reacted shrewdly. He publicly accused DiMaggio of being unfair and greedy, asking for an enormous salary while other Americans were struggling to survive in a Depression year. He was quick to remind everyone of veteran Lou Gehrig's $40,000 salary, that it was outrageous a third-year man should demand equal pay with the Iron Horse.

The ploy of Ruppert and Barrow was to make DiMaggio appear to be the villain. It worked. The press was critical of Joe's holdout, even more so when he failed to return at the start of the regular season. The fans felt no sympathy for someone asking for more money than many would make in a lifetime.

By the second week of the season, Joe relented. On April 20, he contacted Ruppert from his San Francisco home and announced he had accepted the $25,000. Not so fast, retorted Ruppert. The center fielder hadn't played in several games and would be docked for the time missed. Furthermore, it would depend on the discretion of Manager Joe McCarthy as to when DiMaggio would be ready to play, with his pay further cut accordingly.

"I hope this young man has learned his lesson," the victorious Ruppert admonished in front of the press. For his part, DiMaggio was relieved that his first prolonged dispute with Ruppert had ended. "Naturally, I thought I was worth more," Joe admitted to reporters, "but I'd rather play ball than hold out."

DiMaggio had a superb season in 1938, followed by equally astounding years in '39 and '40. His season of 1941, which included the record 56-game hitting streak, is legendary. Yet, after four-consecutive super seasons, Joe was "rewarded" with a $2,500 pay-cut offer, Barrow's excuse being that it was a war year. DiMaggio refused to accept, this time winning the bargaining battle and obtaining a $6,000 increase to over $40,000 a year.

In his debut in '38, DiMaggio was booed. He heard many more that year, as fans reacted to what they believed was an ungrateful athlete who should consider himself lucky to be playing a kid's game for a living. Yet, few gave much thought to the greediness of owners, who made more than enough while dealing in an unscrupulous manner with players.

Joe DiMaggio crosses home plate after third-inning homer in Game Five of the 1937 World Series. That's Lou Gehrig talking with the home plate umpire. (UPI/ Bettmann)

Owners' attitudes haven't changed much since, only the rules. With the reserve clause extinct and free agency very much alive, modern players enjoy a much more comfortable negotiating position. Some would say the pendulum has swung too far in the players' direction. With an intimidating union, competent attorneys, collusion laws and mediators protecting them, players have become too formidable off the field and too lackadaisical on. Many also believe that with the major-league minimum salary being far greater than most salaries of Americans, every player, instead of griping as some do, should indeed consider himself lucky to be playing a kid's game for a very lucrative living.

One writer in 1939 erroneously predicted, "Solidarity among baseball players is impossible since rival teams are supposed to hate each other and any cooperation between them would remove their reason for existence."

If he could see them now.

A NIGHT TO
REMEMBER

Meeting Babe Ruth for the first time would be a thrill for any young ballplayer. Twenty-three-year-old Johnny Vander Meer was no exception. Ruth had always been his idol. Now, the Reds' gifted hurler was not only shaking hands with the retired superstar, but receiving a congratulatory "nice going kid" as well.

Had it only been four hours since Manager Bill McKechnie informed him in the clubhouse that he'd be starting in Brooklyn that night of June 15, 1938? Quite an honor, considering it was the first game played under the lights at Ebbetts Field with a crowd of over 38,000 in attendance. The belated news might have induced either a rush of adrenaline or rush to the bathroom for other hurlers, but the sophomore southpaw merely decided to "go out and pitch my own natural game."

That "natural game" would take him to the ninth inning with more than just a 6-0 lead. Not one Dodger batter had come close to getting a hit, and as Vander Meer took the mound for the final time, he began thinking no-hitter for the first time. It almost cost him. His eagerness led to three wild pitches before finally disposing of the first Dodger, then consecutive walks to Babe Phelps, Cookie Lavagetto and Doug Camilli. Just when it appeared his well-known wildness would be his ruin, Johnny's control returned.

He retired Ernie Koy on a force-out at home, leaving Leo Durocher as Brooklyn's last hope. After home plate umpire Bill Stewart missed an apparent third-strike pitch, Leo the Lip's attempt at playing spoiler ended futilely on a can-of-corn to center.

It was dejá-vu for Vander Meer. Only four days earlier, he had thrown baseball's first no-hitter of the season in shutting down the Braves 3-0 in Cincy. Known for his rapid fastball, Johnny had a particularly effective sinker that afternoon, with only a handful of putouts coming on fly balls. The no-hitter was nearly prevented when Boston's Vince DiMaggio, the eldest of three ballplaying brothers, hit a liner that caromed off Vander Meer. DiMaggio was thrown out on a close play.

The first no-hitter had been exciting, but couldn't match the thrill of the second. True, the first was played at home, but there had been only 10,000 spectators that day and half of them had been youthful guests of the Reds. The second came in front of a packed stadium and with extraordinary media attention for Brooklyn's inaugural game under the stars. Furthermore, though his Brave no-hitter was the first by a Red in nearly 20 years, pitching a second consecutive no-hitter was unprecedented in baseball history.

It had only been two years since minor-league owner Fay Murray had spurned offers from the Red Sox and Giants and sold his prize lefty to Reds executive Larry MacPhail for $15,000. After an unimpressive rookie season in 1937, Vander Meer began patterning his pitching style after Lefty Grove in the spring of '38 and improved enough to earn a regular position in the rotation. Now, with back-to-back no-hitters Vander Meer was the talk of baseball.

Could three-in-a-row be possible? Johnny refused to think about it, saying "I'll just start out like I did last night, and we'll see what happens." Four days and a record 21 consecutive, scoreless innings later, the dream ended on a fourth-frame hit by Boston's lefty-swinging Debs Garms.

Yet, his dream season continued. Three weeks later, he was the National League starter and winner in the All-Star Game. Though he won only 15 in 1938, his limiting opponents to a .213 average was a league best. A sore arm resulted in sporadic play in '39 and '40, but he recovered sufficiently to capture three-consecutive strikeout crowns from 1941-1943 and to pitch in two more All-Star Games. After two years of wartime duty, Vander Meer pitched four uneventful seasons with the Reds (uneventful except for a game in 1948 when he walked a dozen batters, still a Cincy record for southpaws), one season as a reliever with the Cubs, and finished his career making a one-time appearance with the Indians in 1951.

Despite more than 200 being thrown in the century, a no-hitter is still regarded as a rare baseball achievement. Vander Meer's pitching consecutive no-hitters may be the closest thing to an unbreakable baseball record, since a hurler would have to throw three in a row to do so. They're still trying to match his two-straight. The Reds' Ewell Blackwell came close in 1947 when he followed a no-hitter against the Braves with eight innings of no-hit pitching against Brooklyn before pesky Eddie Stanky's one-out hit in the ninth disappointed 31,000 Cincinnati fans.

One spectator that day might have had mixed emotions as Blackwell flirted with immortality. From the Reds' dugout, Johnny Vander Meer was pulling for his teammate, but couldn't have been too upset after seeing Stanky's seeing-eye single scooting into center. During the game, perhaps Johnny's thoughts strayed to nine years past when a legendary performance and handshake from a living legend left him with one unforgettable night.

THAT OTHER
STREAK OF '41

J immy Dykes began his playing career in his hometown of
Philadelphia in 1918. Over 2,200 games later on May 15,
1941, almost precisely 23 years following his debut, the 44-
year-old Dykes, then the player-manager for the White Sox,
officially quit as an active player. He was honored that afternoon
with a "Jimmy Dykes Day" at Yankee Stadium. Sportswriter Dan
Daniel, representing the Baseball Writers Association, presented
him with an award and the game began. Dykes' crew were rude
to their hosts, shellacking the Yankees 13-1.

In retrospect, there was more significance to the contest than the
retirement of a long-time big-leaguer or the rare rout of the mighty
Bombers of '41. Joe DiMaggio was robbed of a pair of hits, but
managed to drill an RBI single off Eddie Smith in the first frame.
The safety marked the beginning of what many believe to be the
ultimate baseball achievement — his 56-game hitting streak.

The cleanup batter for the Pale Hose that day was a muscular
lefty-swinging Tarheel by the name of Taffy Wright. When his
single and homer drove in four of Chicago's 13 runs, he lengthened to eight a stretch of games with at least one RBI. Before
Wright's streak would end, he'd own a record which like
DiMaggio's is still-standing, but unlike DiMaggio's is relatively
unknown.

Wright had been injured when the season began, making his first appearance as a pinch hitter in early May. After pinch-hitting again on the third, Wright started for the Sox the next day. It's doubtful many at Comiskey Park remembered his RBI single after 28 runs were scored, but it was the first of 13-consecutive games in which Wright would successfully bring one home.

Who cared about Taft's third-straight RBI game at Comiskey on May 7, when Ted Williams was drilling two homers in that same game? Or who cared about his fourth-and-fifth straight against Detroit when the baseball world was still buzzing over Tiger slugger Hank Greenberg's recent induction into the army? And did anyone care about his sixth in a row in Boston on the 14th, when the beastly Jimmie Foxx launched one over the Green Monster at Fenway?

After Wright's four-ribby contribution in New York, he lengthened the streak to nine at Yankee Stadium the next day, the same game DiMaggio creamed a 415-foot triple and parked a homer into the left-field bleachers which, according to The New York Times, was only the third time in the park's history a ball had landed in the area later labeled "Death Valley" for its notoriety in swallowing long fly balls. DiMaggio managed a single in three at bats off Johnny Rigney in the series finale, extending his then-modest hitting string to three. Wright was held hitless in five tries, but one of his outs scored a run and was vital to the Sox's 3-2 win.

Taffy stretched the streak by driving in three in each of his next two games, then increased it for the final time on May 20 with an RBI double in Washington. The following afternoon, Wright was held hitless and ribbyless by Philadelphia's Phil Marchildon and Lum Harris, while Joltin' Joe was just warming up in hitting for the seventh-consecutive game.

Driving in a run in 13-straight wasn't as difficult as hitting in 56-straight. The Yankee Clipper's major-league mark (Wright's is an American-League record) hasn't been seriously challenged since, with Cincy's Pete Rose coming the closest with a 44-hit streak in 1978. In contrast, Taffy's RBI streak was nearly matched by Ted Williams' 12-straight games in 1942, and has since been approached by four junior-circuit batters with 11-straight, nine others with 10-straight.

Taffy Wright was no Joe DiMaggio, but his record streak of 1941 has lasted as long as Joltin' Joe's. (National Baseball Library, Cooperstown, NY)

The RBI streak wasn't as glamorous a feat as the hitting streak, nor Wright as glamorous a ballplayer as DiMaggio. And since the RBI opportunities had to be there for Wright, it's probably also true that his record required more luck than DiMaggio's, a supposition even more believable knowing he was held hitless in six of the 13 games, making it likely he had the advantage of a runner on third with less than two outs in each of those six contests.

Nevertheless, setting any record means taking advantage of opportunities, which Taffy was able to do. Let's not forget as well that only a formidable record could resist challenges for over half a century. Certainly, it's deserving of some recognition. Wright's received none. In all likelihood, even the record-setter had no knowledge of his accomplishment.

When the nine-year veteran retired in 1949, a career cut short by three years' service during World War II, Wright had many proud memories of his playing days — his rookie season of 1938 when he batted .350, a point better than league-leader Foxx, but was denied the crown due to insufficient plate appearances despite having played in the 100 games then required for eligibility; playing in the Hall-of-Fame All-Star Game in June of 1939, the year Honus Wagner, Ty Cobb, Babe Ruth, Walter Johnson and Christy Mathewson became Cooperstown's first inductees; his pinch-hit grand slam on July 3, 1940, the first in White Sox history; five-consecutive seasons batting over .300 and a career .311 average; the exhibition games played for Pacific GI spectators during the war.

How tragic that when Wright died two months following his 70th birthday in 1981, he was probably unaware of his greatest baseball achievement. With the meticulousness in which modern stats and records are kept, an RBI string similar to Wright's would undoubtedly draw attention today. Taffy happened to do it at the wrong time and for the wrong team. With Ted Williams' batting over .400, the last major-leaguer to do so, it was enough to overshadow a league mark for consecutive RBIs, but to have one of the greatest Yankees in history attain his most renowned accomplishment in the same year makes the subsequent ignoring of Wright's record quite comprehensible.

Nineteen hundred forty-one was a tale of two streaks. One became the most famous in baseball history, the other the most obscure.

TAFFY WRIGHT'S CONSECUTIVE-GAME RBI
STREAK OF 1941

Date	Opponent	Ballpark	AB	H	RBI	Score
5/4	Athletics	Comiskey Pk.	4	1	1	17-11(Phi)
5/5	Athletics	Comiskey Pk.	5	1	1	5-4 (Phi)
5/7	Red Sox	Comiskey Pk.	4	0	1	4-3 (Bos)
5/10	Tigers	Comiskey Pk.	2	0	1	4-3 (Chi)
5/11	Tigers	Comiskey Pk.	2	0	1	2-1 (Chi)
5/13	Red Sox	Fenway Pk.	4	2	2	3-2 (Chi)
5/14	Red Sox	Fenway Pk.	5	0	1	10-7 (Bos)
5/15	Yankees	Yankee Stad.	6	2	4	13-1 (Chi)
5/16	Yankees	Yankee Stad.	4	0	1	6-5 (NY)
5/17	Yankees	Yankee Stad.	5	0	1	3-2 (Chi)
5/18	Senators	Griffith Stad.	5	4	3	10-5 (Chi)
5/19	Senators	Griffith Stad.	4	2	3	8-2 (Chi)
5/20	Senators	Griffith Stad.	2	1	1	5-2 (Chi)

CHAPTER 37

WORKING WITH A HANDICAP

Washington manager Ossie Bluege could recall more grati-
fying hours than the last, as his Senators hopelessly
trailed the Red Sox. With his team still in the pennant
chase (they'd finish second, 11 games behind the Yanks that season of '47), the blue Bluege sought to save moundsmen for more
opportune occasions and called on his pitching coach to hurl the
rest of the way. The chance to watch a 45-year-old in action was
enough to enliven fan interest that August afternoon, but when
Bert Shepard entered the game considerably more drama entered
with him than was induced by his age.

It's widely known how major-leaguers gave up the game to serve
their country during World War II. What's often forgotten is that
many minor-leaguers did the same. Bert Shepard had been one
of them, sacrificing more than most in doing so. While flying a
bomber, Shepard's plane was shot down in May of '44, just one
month before D-Day. The injured pilot was captured by Nazis
and his right leg amputated below the knee.

The Senators hired the wooden-legged veteran in 1945, partly
out of sympathy, partly for publicity. Certainly, no thoughts were
given to his doing any pitching. Yet, there stood the 6-foot southpaw ready to take over in the middle of the fourth inning. The
expectation must have been that the Hoosier hurler with no pre-

vious major-league experience would be bombed from the box as effectively as he had been bombed from the sky a year earlier, and that in doing so, he'd be "taking one for the team." That prospect never materialized. Though the Senators lost, Shepard sewed up the Sox, allowing no runs on only three hits and one walk while fanning two in five-and-a-third innings.

The beginning of Shepard's big-league career was also its end. Despite pitching against the Dodgers in an exhibition game, notching a 4-3 victory, he was never again used in a regular-season game, thus joining a few other little-used pitchers (slugger Rocky Colavito being one of them) to finish with a 0.00 ERA. Unfortunately, his limited service makes the stat ineligible for the record books.

Shepard's one-day duty was made slightly less newsworthy by the American League's "One-Armed Wonder" Pete Gray, who was playing the entire 1945 season as an outfielder for the St. Louis Browns. Born in the coal town of Nanticoke near the Pocono Mountains of Eastern Pennsylvania in 1915, Gray spent his winters ice skating, his summers swimming and playing ball, until the age of six when he hitched a ride from a truck-driving farmer and fell from the rear when the vehicle came to a sudden halt. Pete's right arm became entangled in the wheel's spokes. The farmer drove Gray home and, seeing no one was around, made a hasty retreat leaving the distraught youth bawling on the porch. When finally taken to the hospital by a good-Samaritan passerby, Gray's arm was in bad-enough shape to necessitate an amputation just below the elbow.

The injury made greater Gray's determination to "work damn harder than anyone else to become a good ballplayer." The natural right-hander learned to bat lefty by tossing up rocks, then hitting them for hours daily. He practiced playing the outfield with an intensity that enabled him to eventually catch with his gloved hand, remove it instantaneously, and throw accurately to the infield. His skills and dedication led to semipro and minor-league work, and finally in '45, a chance to play in the majors.

The St. Louis Browns, winners of the American League pennant for the first and what would be only time in their history in 1944, were still the other team in town after their defeat by the more popular and successful Cardinals in the Series. Ownership signed Gray as a public-relations gimmick, ignoring complaints by some players that hiring a handicapped person jeopardized their chance to repeat. Skipper Luke Sewell insisted Pete would be given a starting position based only on merit. Whether due to pressure from the front office or Gray's abilities, Sewell penciled in the 30-year-old rookie on April 17. "Petey" responded with a line single off the Tigers' future Hall-of-Famer Hal Newhouser for his first major-league hit. Unfortunately, forthcoming hits weren't frequent, going zero-for-thirteen following the safety off Prince Hal. Unable to adjust to slow curves and inside fastballs, and with runners too often successfully taking extra bases on hits, Pete was removed from the lineup and used sparingly for the remainder of the season. Argumentative with umpires, unpopular with players for his ill-tempered character and a perceived aloofness, and with the front-office feeling the novelty of a disabled ballplayer had worn off, Gray was sold to the Toledo Mud Hens in 1946. He played in the minors for two more seasons, then quit.

Historians maintain that Gray's chance in '45 arose not only from sentimentality or opportunism on the part of Browns' Owner Donald Barnes but also because many big leaguers were still serving in Europe and the Pacific. With a smaller talent pool from which clubs could choose, Gray could be given serious consideration. Notwithstanding the circumstances, reaching the ultimate level in baseball, a level which even during the war years was more difficult to attain than it is today (due to fewer teams and lack of competition for talent from other sports), was a tribute to Pete's perseverance and athletic abilities. And despite his season average of .218, Gray did occasionally display exceptional skill. In a doubleheader against the Yankees in May, he drilled four hits and two ribbies against a furious Spud Chandler, then had a hit-and-run single and made three shoestring catches in the outfield in the nightcap.

Following the 1945 season, Gray was offered $15,000 by movie moguls to play himself in a baseball flick. Not wanting to have to wear a toupee, as the director was insisting, he turned it down. Monte Stratton wasn't asked to act when he accepted $80,000, allowing Jimmy Stewart to portray him in the '49 flick The Stratton Story.

Named after an uncle, Monte was a 6-foot, 5-inch Texan, one of nine children raised on a 100-acre farm in the county of Celeste, located in the eastern part of the Lone Star State about 50 miles from the Oklahoma border. His father died while he was in high school resulting in a heavier work load for the teenager, but the Texan still found time between tending cattle and working on the cotton field to play baseball. Though his chores made him a frequent absentee in class, he pitched for the school team and later made money hurling in Sunday semipro games. Monte threw in the Texas League in 1933 and was signed by the White Sox the following season. He appeared only once that year, five times in 1935. Stratton became a starter for Chicago in '36, but a tonsil infection and appendicitis attack limited his play. By the middle of the '37 season, the righty hurler with good control and a trick pitch called "The Gander" had recovered sufficiently to become a "ranking member of the Sox staff. He's what is known as a natural", as sportswriter Irving Vaughn wrote in a June Sporting News article. He finished the season completing 21 of 22 starts with a 15-5 record, five shutouts, and ERA of 2.40. He was nearly as good the next year, again winning 15 and completing 22 of 26 starts. Stratton would have begun the '39 season as the recognized top hurler on the club and among the best in the league.

In November of '38, Monte was hunting rabbits when he accidentally shot himself with a pistol. The bullet damaged his right leg so severely that it had to be amputated. His big-league playing career ended, Stratton hung on as a coach for Chicago from 1939-1941. Shepard had pitched but one game in '45, but in 1946 the wooden-legged Stratton made a comeback and threw for an entire season, albeit the Texas League. The 34-year-old won 18 games!

Undeniably, the most successful handicapped player has been Jim Abbott, born without a right hand. The tall, blond Flint native, who played and graduated from the University of Michigan in 1988 and made it to the majors the next year, learned to hold the glove against his body with the stub of his right arm while firing the baseball with his left, then quickly glove his throwing hand. Despite his disability, Abbott became one of the finest fielding moundsmen in the American League.

His pitching has been even more impressive. In his debut season of 1989, Abbott won a dozen games in starting nearly 30 for the California Angels. In 1991, he won 18 with an ERA of 2.89, and though he notched only seven in '92, his ERA was even lower at 2.77. Traded to the Yankees in '93, Abbott scalped the Indians on September 4 at Yankee Stadium, becoming only the sixth pitcher in the proud history of the club, only the third lefty, to throw a no-hitter.

There have been several other instances in which players have ignored physical handicaps. Hugh Daily was probably the first, the one-armed hurler winning 23 games as a National Leaguer in 1883. The Cardinals' Charlie Gelbert nearly lost his leg when he fell from a boulder while carrying a shotgun. The gun went off, hitting him in the leg. Though the limb was saved, the infielder was a near-cripple during the 1935 season when he hit close to .300. The great Grover Alexander had no obvious disability, but epileptic attacks, which became more frequent after nightmarish experiences during World War I, at times occurred while on the mound, but didn't prevent his winning 20 twice during the '20s.

The next time a modern major-leaguer gripes about a minor injury and decides for the manager that the bench is the place to be, someone should remind him of the courage shown by players known for working with a handicap.

THEY COULD HAVE
BEEN GREATER

With the exception of Ruth, and possibly Hornsby and Gehrig, Ted Williams had no equal as a batsman. Had it not been for five years in the military, The Kid might hold indisputable claim to being the game's all-time greatest hitter.

By the end of 1942, the 24-year-old Red Sox slugger had 127 homers in four seasons, an average of 32 per year, and two home run titles ('41 and '42). Following three years' service during World War II, Williams hit another 196 homers from 1946-1951, averaging 33 per season while leading the league in '47 and '49, until military duty again intervened, with the Splendid Splinter serving as a fighter pilot in Korea during most of the 1952 and 1953 seasons. Ted then played for seven more years before retiring in 1961 with 521 career homers, having averaged 30 homers per season in 17 years (excluding his brief '52 and '53 seasons).

How many homers did Williams lose while batting for Uncle Sam? Considering the rate in which he was belting balls out of the park prior to and following his hiatuses, a conservative estimate puts Ted's averaging 32 homers for each of the five missed years, giving him an additional 96 homers from 1943-1945 and another 50 from 1952-1953 (Williams hit one homer in six games in '52 and 13 homers in 37 games in '53). Williams would have ended his career with 667 homers (Mays is third on today's all-time list with 660) and might have added another two or three homer crowns to his career total of four.

Williams wasn't your ordinary power-hitter, winning seven batting titles and finishing with a career mark of .344. He averaged .356 from 1939-1942, leading the league in hitting in the two years preceding his military service, his .406 in 1941 making him the last player to reach the coveted .400 mark. Following World War II, Ted took another two titles prior to his Korean stint and returned in 1954 to win another.

It's probable, therefore, that the war years robbed Williams of another two or three batting championships. Had he won each year, not likely, but a possibility, Ted would have matched Ty Cobb's record dozen crowns. Undeniably, Thumper would have batted over .300 each missed season to give him 20-consecutive .300 seasons (1939-1958), and 21 for his career. Cobb holds the record for both with 23.

Williams was one of the game's greatest run-producers, ending his career with nine seasons of 100+ RBIs. He reached the plateau in each year from 1939-1942, and from 1946-1951 missed the mark only once (97 in 1950). It's not an outrageous assumption that Williams would have produced similarly during each of his World War II years, which would have given him 11-straight 100-RBI seasons from 1939-1949. Since he preceded his service in Korea with 126 ribbies in 1951, it's also probable that Williams missed out on two more 100-RBI seasons in 1952 and 1953. Therefore, he might have retired with a total of 14 such seasons, one more than the current big-league record shared by Ruth, Gehrig and Foxx, if war hadn't interfered.

Had Ted maintained a 1939-1942 rate of 129 RBIs per season while playing from 1943-1945 and a 1946-1951 average of 124 RBIs while playing in 1952 and 1953, he would have accumulated another 598 ribbies. Added to his career total of 1,839 (10th on the all-time list), Ted instead finishes with 2,437 RBIs. Even averaging only 100 per season during the war years, a ridiculously low estimate considering his prior rates, Ted's additional 463 RBIs (500 minus the 37 he gathered in '52 and '53) puts his total at 2,302. Aaron holds the current career mark with 2,297. It's also likely that Williams would have added to his four RBI crowns, challenging Ruth's still-standing major-league record of six. He might have even taken another Triple Crown. Williams and Hornsby are currently the only two-time Crown winners in history.

War robbed Williams of the chance to lead in other career categories. His 2,019 walks, only 37 shy of Ruth's major-league-leading total, would have exceeded 2,500. Averaging 105 runs-scored in 17 full seasons, Ted's career total of 1,798 would have increased to over 2,300 and bypassed Cobb's record 2,245.

Williams' chief rival, Joe DiMaggio, also lost three years of baseball to World War II. Using the same rationale as with Williams, estimates put DiMaggio's producing an additional 90 homers and 390 RBIs , raising his career totals from 361 homers to over 450 (only eight righty batters with more), and from 1,537 RBIs to 1,927 (only Aaron and Ruth with more) had he played from 1943-1945. Driving in runners at a rate of 133 per year prior to the war, a civilian Joe would have had 10-straight 100+ RBI years from 1936-1945, and a career total of 12 such seasons. Had he maintained his prewar rate, DiMaggio's lifetime total of 1,537 ribbies would have risen another 400, putting him tantalizingly close to the 2,000 mark. Like Williams, Joe had already pocketed a pair of batting titles prior to the war and thereby missed three chances for another.

Detroit's Hank Greenberg became the first big-name big leaguer to switch from a player to military uniform when he was inducted into the army in May of 1941, not returning to baseball until midseason of '45. Along with Jimmie Foxx and Lou Gehrig, Hammerin' Hank had been the most productive hitter of the thirties, gathering two home run and RBI crowns. In 1938, he missed matching Ruth's 60-homer mark by two, after having missed by one Lou Gehrig's American League record 184 RBIs the year before. In 1940, Greenberg nearly won the Triple Crown, leading the junior circuit with 41 homers and 150 ribbies, and a dozen points shy of DiMaggio's .352 batting average. Averaging 43 homers and 148 RBIs from 1937-1940, Greenberg would have collected another 200 homers and 670 RBIs had he played full-time from '41 to '45, raising his career numbers from 331 to 531 homers and from 1,276 to 1,944 RBIs. Though the native New Yorker never won a batting title, it's likely he would have continued to challenge for the homer and RBI crowns, considering the fact that the tall, muscular first baseman reached his 30th birthday by 1941. He also served Uncle Sam during what was considered at the time the prime years of most players' careers, and he returned to capture both titles in 1946.

Stan Musial lost merely one year to the Navy (1945), but it was enough to thwart his attaining several cherished career goals. The Cardinal great averaged 23 homers per season in 21 full years, compiling nine seasons of 25+ homers, and was capable of adding another 25 to his career total 475 had he played in '45. Musial finished with 1,951 RBIs, so that his driving in only about half his career rate of 93 per season in 1945 would have made him a member of the elite 2,000-RBI club.

Musial's one missed season cost him a chance at several National League records. Upon retirement, The Man held seven batting titles (second to Wagner's eight), ten 100+ RBI seasons (second to Aaron's 11), and six seasons of leading in hits (second to Pete Rose's seven). Musial led the league in doubles eight times, and in triples five times, both shared major-league records which Musial might own alone today had the opportunity to repeat as champion been available to him in '45.

Few would exclude Cleveland's hard-throwing right-hander Bob Feller from their "All-Time-Greatest-Pitchers" list. Nevertheless, his accomplishments were limited due to four years of World War II service. Rapid Robert began his career in 1936, fanning 76 batters in only 62 innings-pitched. From 1937-1941, the 6-foot Hawkeye averaged 231 strikeouts per season, including four-straight 200+ K crowns before entering the Navy in 1942. He returned to pitch two months of the '45 season, fanning 59. He followed up in 1946 with what baseball writer Tom Meany once described as "in many respects, the greatest season of any modern pitcher," winning 26 and whiffing 348 batters. He went on to average 236 strikeouts from 1946-1948, leading the league each season.

Based upon pre-and-post war performances, Feller would have gathered at least another 700 strikeouts from 1942-1944 (about 233 per year) and another 175 in 1945. The additional 875 Ks raises his career total from 2,581 to 3,456. Walter Johnson is the only American Leaguer with more. Logic dictates Feller's taking the strikeout title each of his four missed seasons, so that he would have led the league for 11-straight years. Johnson holds the current major-league mark with eight-consecutive crowns. And Feller was assured of another four 200+ strikeout seasons had he pitched during the war, which would have given him nine-straight such seasons, matching Tom Seaver's current major-league mark.

Unlike some strikeout specialists, Feller knew how to win. He was a 20-game winner from 1939-1941, 1946-1947 and again in 1951, so that he could have been a ten-timer had he won 20 in each of the war years. Had he averaged 20 wins from 1942-1945, Bob would have accumulated an additional 75 victories, which would have lifted his career total from 266 to 341. Only four pitchers in the century have had more.

Following his rookie season in 1951, Willie Mays missed most of 1952 and all of the '53 season following his military induction. Considering his homer totals of 41 and 51 in the two years following his discharge, the Say-Hey Kid might have belted another 90 homers had he not been drafted. To quote baseball author Donald Honig, "If not for the lost time it would in all probability have been Willie's home run record rather than Ruth's that Henry Aaron broke in 1974."

We become so awed by the strength and skill of modern ballplayers that the accomplishments of past superstars are underrated and overlooked. Take note, however, that many of our heroes of yesteryear could have been even greater had they not abandoned the game to serve their country.

183

CHAPTER 39

THERE GOES
ANOTHER ONE

As popular as is the sight of a ball disappearing over the wall, some would contend that an overabundance of homers can diminish their attraction. When four baggers were on the increase during the '20s, one sportswriter complained, "The jolly home run isn't what it used to be." For others, the more round trippers, the better. On June 23, 1950 at Tiger Stadium (or Briggs Stadium as it was then called), enough baseballs left the ballpark to satisfy the most passionate partisan of the jolly home run.

The setting for the setting of a long-ball record couldn't have been better. Tiger Stadium dimensions were favorable to batters, unless straightaway center was their target, and the weather was clear and warm that afternoon. The Tigers were hosting the world-champion Yankees, with 51,000 optimistic rooters hoping Detroit would extend their lead over New York to two games. Future Hall-of-Famers Hank Greenberg and Charlie Gehringer were retired by then, but the Bengals retained a potent offense with such sluggers as batting champ George Kell, who bettered perennial leader Ted Williams by a fraction of a percentage point in 1949, and venomous Vic Wertz, still four years away from helping Willie Mays establish his place in World Series history. Nor were the Bronx Bombers devoid of power. Joe DiMaggio, among the league leaders in homers, was surrounded in the lineup by musclemen Hank Bauer, Yogi Berra and Johnny Mize.

The game began ominously for the Tigers. Scrappy Phil Rizzuto reached on a single and, one out later, scored on a Bauer blast to left. In the third, Bauer again reached the seats off Ted Gray, as did Berra two batters later. Normally powerless Jerry Coleman joined the fun in the fourth, his tag sending Gray to the showers with a 6-0 deficit.

Yank hurler Tommy Byrne, having shown no signs of vulnerability, successfully started the fourth by retiring Hoot Evers on a fly ball. Two hits and a walk filled the bags, but Byrne breathed easier when Detroit pitcher Dizzy Trout was permitted to bat for himself; not so easily when Trout lifted a 2-2 fastball into the reachable seats in left for a grand-slammer. Having seen his six-run bulge lowered to two with one pitch, the rattled hurler yielded another homer into the same area in left, whereupon Byrne left.

His replacement, Fred Sanford, threw a junk pitch to Kell who lashed it for a single. A Wertz blast to right-center followed which caromed off the top of the grandstand roof 120 feet high and 370 feet from home plate. (The task of estimating the distance had the drive carried unimpeded is best left to mathematicians more qualified than myself.) The next pitch to Gerry Priddy wasn't pretty and was launched into the upper deck in left-center, thus completing Sanford's completely unsuccessful outing, leaving it to reliever Tom Ferrick to finally retire the side. The four Tiger homers, accounting for all eight runs, tied the American League mark for most in one inning, later broken by the Twins of 1966.

But the scent of first place was too near to allow New York to quit. DiMaggio's poke in the seventh brought the Bombers within one, and a pinch two-run homer by reliable Tommy Henrich gave them the lead the next frame. With pellet-throwing Yankee fireman Joe Page on the mound in the ninth, victory seemed certain.

Page killed Kell on a foul pop-up, but Wertz lined a bullet to left-center for two bases. Evers then connected on a fastball which, though not as long as his earlier drive, chased DiMaggio to the base of the wall in center. Joe's relay eluded second baseman Billy Martin and the game ended both appropriately, with a home run, and ironically, the game-winner being the only homer not to leave the park.

The 11 homers that day set a big-league record for most in a game by two teams. The mark was later matched by seven other clubs, and finally broken in 1995 when the White Sox and Tigers combined for a dozen dingers at that same Tiger Stadium. Interestingly, the 11 homers in the 1950 shootout accounted for all runs in the 10-9 Tiger decision, in contrast to the slugfest of '95, where 10 of the 12 homers in the 14-12 Sox win were solo shots.

Alas, for the '50 Tigers the victory still left them three short by season's end, as the pinstripers took the second of what would be a record five-consecutive world championships. Nevertheless, with all their future success the Yanks couldn't prevent 51,000 Motown fans from describing to children and grandchildren how the Bengals bested the Bombers in the most spectacular confrontation between them in their long and proud histories.

GIVING A LITTLE
EXTRA

I t wasn't because the French were celebrating Bastille Day
on July 14, 1946, that Cleveland player-manager Lou
Boudreau decided to unveil his new strategy against Ted
Williams. Rather, it was the three homers which the Splendid
Splinter had hit in leading Boston to an 11-10 win in the first of
two at League Park which helped make up his mind.

Weeks before, Boudreau had thought of the idea to thwart Williams, who was tearing apart junior-circuit hurlers enroute to an
MVP season and his first appearance in a World Series. Using a
tablecloth, the Indian shortstop diagrammed a plan whereby he
and all fielders would be positioned to the right side of second,
with the exception of the third sacker who would be stationed
slightly to the left of the second-base bag and the left fielder who
would play slightly to the left of center. The ploy, intended for use
only with no one on base, would make it virtually impossible for
the consummate pull-hitter to get a hit to right field, forcing Ted
to go the opposite way and thus neutralizing his power.

Williams doubled to right his first time up in the nightcap, and
in his next at bat gazed in bewilderment as the Boudreau defense was employed for the first time. Ted barked at home plate
ump Bill Summers, but was told no rule prohibited such strategy. He took a swing at the next inside pitch and whistled a

grounder between first and second, a sure hit under normal circumstances, but now an easy out for Boudreau. Williams walked his last two times up, and after the game he joked that he'd beat the shift next time by batting from the right side. In fact, Williams continued pulling the ball with success throughout his career despite other teams adopting what was originally labeled the "Boudreau Shift," but later referred to as the "Williams Shift." Maybe Boudreau should have patented the plan.

Described by *The New York Times* as "the most unusual defense against Williams ever seen in Fenway Park," Lou's ruse along with Ted's thumping that day ironically overshadowed the Hall-of-Famer's most productive game. In the opener, Boudreau blasted a home run off Sox right-hander Joe Dobson in the first inning, then belted doubles in his next four at bats. He became the first player of the century to collect as many as five extra-base hits in a game.

Three others have since duplicated the feat. Joe Adcock became the first National Leaguer to do it when he borrowed teammate Charley White's heavy bat during a Braves-Dodgers slugfest in Brooklyn on July 31, 1954, and connected off Don Newcombe in the opening inning, doubled and homered off Erv Palica his next two trips, and reached the seats off Pete Wojey and Johnny Podres his last two times up. Adcock's four homers and double added up to a still-standing major-league record 18 total bases. A photo of Joe appeared on the front pages of two Sunday edition Milwaukee newspapers the next day but the power-hitter, who'd finish with only 23 round trippers, moaned after the game that he'd "hit 35 homers a year" playing for the Dodgers at cozy Ebbetts Field, an amount he reached twice in his career.

Wonderful Willie Stargell's windmill wind-up prior to cocking the bat led to 475 homers during his record 21 seasons as a Pirate. His greatest game occurred on August 1, 1970 in the high altitude and highly hittable Atlanta Stadium, a.k.a. "The Launching Pad," where Brave pitchers were feeling significantly less brave since the franchise's move from Milwaukee's County Stadium in 1966. Following a Braves-Yankees Old-Timer's Game, which featured a ground-rule double by Mickey Mantle which bounced over the left-field fence, Stargell doubled three times and homered twice in leading a 20-10 Buc rout of Atlanta. Besides tying the extra-base marks of Boudreau and Adcock, Willie also scored five and drove in six in a half-dozen trips to the plate.

Dodger star Steve Garvey put together his best power numbers in 1977 with 33 homers and 115 RBIs. Not coincidentally, his best game came that year as well. On August 28 in Los Angeles, Steve punished Cardinal hurlers Bob Forsch, Clay Carroll and Tom Underwood with three doubles and a pair of homers. Garvey's stats that day read: five at bats, five runs scored, five RBIs and, of course, five extra-base hits.

Five long hits in a game isn't the most famous record in the books, but it's rarity affirms the difficulty of the accomplishment. A tip of the hat to the four who did it.

INTERVIEW WITH A HALL-OF-FAMER

---

*G*eorge Kell was a prominent third baseman during the '40s
and '50s, playing 15 seasons, most of them with the Tigers.
Besides winning the batting title in 1949, Kell led the league
in hits and doubles in 1950 and 1951. He batted over .300 ten
times, eight consecutively, and ended his career with a .306 average. He was elected to the Hall of Fame in 1983.

George spoke with me on the phone from his home in Swifton,
Arkansas on an unusually cold morning in late February of 1994,
just prior to his departing for the more appealing climate of Lake-
land, Florida — the training home for the Tigers. He recalled the
final month of the 1949 season when he erased a dozen-point deficit in the batting race, capturing the crown on the final day:

If somebody had told me at the beginning of the '49 season that
I would win a batting title, I wouldn't have believed him. Winning batting championships was reserved for the DiMaggios,
Williams and Musials. I did hit .396 in the minors once, leading
both the majors and minors that year. In fact, Tony Oliva and I
are the only players to ever win a batting title in both the major
and minor leagues.

I was injured during the final month of 1949. I was hit in the
right hand by a pitch, and it became swollen. I missed about five

or six games. When I returned to action, I had to use a piece of foam on the bat to hit. It was a little awkward, and whenever I hit the ball off the end of the bat, it jarred the heck out of me.

I didn't think about beating out Ted (Williams) until the final week of the season. Then I stayed within three points until the final game on Sunday. Before the game, Hoot Evers told me in the clubhouse, "You get two hits today and you win the batting title." And of course, it turned out he was right.

Bob Lemon was starting for the Tribe that day. He was tough for everybody, including me. I'd have to put him on the list of top three pitchers that were toughest for me to hit. But I got a double and single against him my first two times up, and I really began to think I would win it. Then (Bob) Feller came in to relieve. I couldn't believe they brought him in. I would have bet anyone that Feller never relieved in his life before that day. But I saw Bob at the Hall of Fame once, and he told me that he relieved about a dozen times in his career for various reasons. That day, the Indians needed to win the game to finish third and pick up the extra money. That's why they brought in Feller. It didn't really have anything to do with trying to stop me.

Somebody wrote a book about three years ago stating that after I got two hits, I left the game and won the batting title sitting in the clubhouse on a stool. The writer was a law professor, from Princeton if I recall correctly, and he really should have known better. I batted four times that day. After the hits against Lemon, I walked and struck out against Feller, then was due to bat fourth in the ninth. When (Dick) Wakefield pinch-hit a single, I took my place in the on-deck circle, waiting to hit after Eddie Lake. Lake hit the first pitch to Ray Boone, who stepped on second and threw to first for the double play to end the game. I was tickled to death when I saw that twin-killing.

Later, Red Rolfe (Tiger skipper) told me that he would have sent Joe Ginsberg out to hit for me if Lake hadn't been doubled up. He had just got word from Lyle Smith, a sportswriter for the *Detroit Free Press*, that Williams had gone 0-2 in New York. Smith told Rolfe, "Don't send Kell up again because he has the batting title won." But Rolfe would have given me the final say on whether or not to hit. As for what I would have done if the double play hadn't happened, I honestly don't know. I'm just glad I didn't have

Hall-of-Famer and 1949 batting champ, George Kell. (National Baseball Library, Cooperstown, NY)

to make the decision.

After the game, everybody was happy for me. While I was dress-ing near my locker, talking with Hal Newhouser and Evers, all my teammates came over to congratulate me. I guess you could say I was a popular player on the club.

195

I should have won the batting title the following season, and would have if Williams hadn't broken his arm in the All-Star Game at Comiskey Park. He was having a pretty good year until then, but not a great one. He didn't play the rest of the season, but his replacement in left field, Billy Goodman, had a great year. Billy went to bat 424 times and hit .353. You needed 400 at bats to qualify for the batting title so he barely had enough to win it. I hit .340 with 641 at bats as runner-up. No one else was even close to me that year. It's ironic that I beat out Williams for the crown by less than a percentage point one year, and Williams robbed me of a batting title by getting injured the next year.

I had several years that were actually better than the one in 1949. I think 1946 (.322 with the A's and Tigers), 1947 (.320 with 93 RBIs), and 1950 (.340 with 101 RBIs) were better seasons. That 1950 season was probably my greatest. Not only did I hit .340, but I drove in over 100 runs and led the league in doubles with 56. No one has had that many doubles in one season since. (Kell's 56 were only 11 shy of Earl Webb's still-standing major-league mark.) And in 1949, 1950 and 1951, I finished first, second and third in the batting race.

Williams was the best hitter I've ever seen, but not the best ballplayer. DiMaggio, Mantle and Frank Robinson were the greatest ballplayers I've ever seen. I couldn't believe some of the things I saw Robinson do on a baseball field. And Mantle? He could hit, run, throw, field — I don't know what he couldn't do. And he played hurt half the time. If Mantle hadn't been injured so much, this might have been the greatest player of all time.

Winning the batting crown in 1949 rates as one of my top thrills, but being elected to the Hall of Fame was the greatest thrill of my baseball career. That's as high as you can go — the ultimate goal. I've never experienced anything in my life as great as the day they notified me. I thought I had the credentials to get in, but I wasn't voted in by the writers. The Veterans' Committee voted me in.

I was so glad to hear that Phil Rizzuto finally got in the other day. He should have been elected a long time ago. Even with DiMaggio, Mantle and Berra who would destroy you, Rizzuto was the glue for the Yankees. Too many writers who vote for the Hall of Fame candidates have never seen some of them play. A writer traveling with a National League team wouldn't see a Rizzuto except during an All-Star Game or perhaps a World Series. So how could he decide? That's why when I was elected by the Veterans' Committee, I was pleased, because I was voted in by guys I played with, guys I played against, club presidents and general managers — the people who had seen me play. Joe Cronin was on the Committee that voted me in, and he told me afterwards, "Hey, you should have been in there a long time ago. I saw you play every day. I know how valuable you were to the ballclub." (Cronin managed Boston when Kell played there from 1952-1954.)

I've been the play-by-play announcer for the Tigers for the past 33 years, currently working with Al Kaline. My broadcasting career began in 1958, the year after I retired from baseball. Bill McPhail hired me to work with Dizzy Dean and Buddy Bladner doing the Game-of-the-Week for CBS. Dizzy was a great guy and I enjoyed working with him. He had his way of saying things that weren't grammatically correct, but that's what sold him to the listening audience. I think a lot of it was a put on, but it was his trademark and people loved it.

The athletes today are bigger and stronger than in the past, but the talent has become diluted. There are more teams, so more players make it to the majors who might not have been good enough when there were fewer teams. They've got ballplayers today that are every bit as good or better than when we played, but they don't have as many good ones. And I don't think the pitchers today are as tough. For instance, when I played, Cleveland had a staff of Lemon, Feller, (Mike) Garcia, (Early) Wynn and (Herb) Score. That's five starters who were just awesome. The Yankees had just about as good a staff with (Allie) Reynolds, (Vic) Raschi, (Eddie) Lopat and (Whitey) Ford, with Joe Page to relieve. Today, they just don't have teams with those kind of quality pitchers.

I love the game so much, and it bothers me that there is so much animosity between the players and owners today, much more than when we played. I think it turns off a lot of people. And there are other sports like football and basketball competing for attention now, so baseball loses fans when that happens.

LEADER OF THE PACK

I n October of 1948, Joe McCarthy's Red Sox faced Lou Boudreau's Indians in a one-game showdown to decide the pennant. The first playoff in American League history went to the Tribe. The next year, Mac needed one of the final two games of the season to clinch, but again failed as his former club, the Yankees, beat the Sox in both contests and took the flag.

Many managers have endured late-season heartbreaks. A half game separated Nap Lajoie's Indians from the Tigers at season's end in 1908. A rainout had resulted in Detroit playing 153 games rather than the scheduled 154, but no rule yet existed requiring makeups. A joyless Lajoie was left to speculate on what might have been had Cobb and company been obligated to play just one more.

In 1922, the Browns came about as close as they'd ever come to a flag, save for their fluke first-place finish in 1944. Led by George Sisler's .420 average and Ken Williams' league-leading 39 homers, Lee Fohl's crew battled the Yankees throughout the season, but fell a game short.

The picture of Chicago's Gabby Hartnett crossing home plate in virtual darkness after connecting off a hanging curve is a favorite of many baseball aficionados. Not a favorite of Buc skipper Pie Traynor who was an eyewitness to the game-winner in late

September of 1938. The "homer in the gloaming" catapulted Hartnett's Cubs over the Pirates and into the lead. When the race ended a week later, Traynor could boast only that Pittsburgh had come close in finishing two behind.

Detroit stuck it to Cleveland again in 1940. Oscar Vitt's Indians held the top spot most of the way but choked in the final month, allowing the Tigers to take the lead. The final three games would be a battle between the two contenders in Cleveland, with Detroit needing only one victory. Vitt felt confident in game one, with fireballer Bob Feller on the mound against the unknown rookie Floyd Giebell. But slugger Rudy York reached Feller for a round tripper, and Giebell pitched the game of his life in shutting out the Tribe. For Giebell, it would be the final win of his brief major-league career. Cleveland took the next two meaningless games, which would be the last of Vitt's managerial career.

Four years later, it was the Tigers' turn to agonize. World War II had deprived baseball of many of its stars, but despite the missed services of sluggers Hank Greenberg and Charlie Gehringer, Detroit held a substantial lead by September. It must have been startling for Bengal manager Steve O'Neill to see the perennial doormat of the A.L., the Browns, climb to a share of the lead going into the final day. The Tigers were still in good shape. Their opponents were the Senators, only 25 games behind, whereas the Browns had to play the always difficult Yankees. But Washington upset O'Neill's boys 4-1 behind the inspired pitching of knuckleballer Dutch Leonard (the night before, an anonymous phone caller had offered him a $20,000 bribe to lose), while St. Louis fought from behind to sabotage the Bombers 5-2. Was it a coincidence that the Browns' only flag came at a time when Uncle Sam had ravaged the rosters of ballclubs? Probably not.

McCarthy's counterpart in 1949 was Cardinal skipper Eddie Dyer. St. Louis battled to the top by midseason and stayed there until the final week, but their two-game lead over the Dodgers evaporated when they lost four straight. Now down by a game, the Cards won the season closer and it appeared Brooklyn was choking in Philly when their 7-0 lead disappeared. But the Dodgers plated two in the 10th to win it. An exasperated Dyer explained his club's collapse by remarking, "We just ran out of gas."

Brooklyn's Burt Shotten celebrated in the clubhouse on that

pennant-clinching day of '49, but suffered in that same hideaway exactly one year later. His Dodgers had closed a considerable gap to pull within a couple of games of the Whiz Kids, setting up a climactic two-game, pennant-deciding series in Brooklyn. The Dodgers easily beat the Phils in the first game and faced Philly ace Robin Roberts the next day. Roberts, still trying for his 20th victory after four failures, was pitching for the third time in five days. His mates gave him an early 1-0 lead, but when Pee Wee Reese sent a fly ball to right which stuck to the ledge of the screen instead of bouncing off, the freak homer might have given Shotten confidence that luck was on his side. The Phils' Dick Sisler hit a more orthodox four bagger in the top of the 10th with two on, and Roberts sealed his 20th and the pennant with three consecutive outs in the bottom half, permitting Shotten to experience the thrill of victory and agony of defeat within a two-season span.

Fortunately for Shotten, he wasn't around a year later. Chuck Dressen had been a manager for four years with the lackluster Reds of the '30s. In 1951, Dressen ended a 14-year layoff when he replaced Shotten with the hope of his first legitimate shot at a pennant. That hope was eradicated more painfully than any other skippers' when Bobby Thomson made his mark in history by destroying Ralph Branca's misplaced fastball. Branca cried in the clubhouse, but Dressen's grief was made worse by his ill-advised midseason prediction when New York was 13 games behind, "The Giants is dead."

Had Dressen been a student of history, he would have understood the wisdom of allowing sleeping dogs to lie. Bill Terry felt his Giants were sufficiently superior to the Dodgers to tauntingly inquire prior to the opening of the 1934 season, "Is Brooklyn still in the league?" Fate would have it that New York's final two games was with their chief rival, and though Casey's Dodgers had been eliminated by then, the Giants were tied for first with the Cards. The motivated Dodgers defeated the Giants twice, giving St. Louis the flag. Terry later claimed that his quote was taken out of context, but Brooklyn fans never forgave him.

In May of 1956, Fred Haney took control of an unmotivated Milwaukee club, replacing Charlie Grimm who hadn't been sufficiently spirited for Braves owner Lou Perini. The aroused Braves remained in contention with the Dodgers and Reds until the final week. Recently traded Sal Maglie then pitched a no-hitter for Brooklyn and won again four days later, thus changing the hearts of Brooklynites towards the once-hated Giant. The Braves were bounced on the final day. Haney's anguish over the one-game deficit was only slightly more than Birdie Tebbetts's, whose Reds finished two games out. Yet, more misery awaited Haney.

Pittsburgh's ElRoy Face won 17 consecutive games in 1959. When he was finally beaten, Face accepted the defeat stoically, saying, "Well, Walter Johnson lost, too." But for Haney, that lengthy streak wasn't quite long enough. It was snapped in September by the Dodgers, with whom the Braves were again embroiled in a desperate chase. When the season ended with the two clubs deadlocked and the Dodgers prevailed in the best-of-three playoffs, winning the pennant-clincher in 12 innings, Face's late loss to Los Angeles loomed large.

To lose first at the finish is disheartening. To lose it after having a sizable lead down the stretch is devastating. Just ask Gene Mauch. His Phils were comfortably in front by 6 1/2 lengths on September 18, 1964. Two weeks later, they finished one length behind in the place position, the result of a 10-game losing streak coupled with a Cardinal winning string of eight. Said a gallant Mauch after it was over, "I wish I did as well as the players did. They did a great job." Yet, despite not winning a pennant in his 26 years as manager, Gene can take some solace in the fact that he is remembered more than most others, thanks to the one that got away in '64.

It was triple trouble for junior-circuit skippers in 1967. By mid-September, four teams were vying for the number one position, only one game separating them. A week later, Detroit's Mayo Smith, Chicago's Al Lopez, Minnesota's Cal Ermer and Boston's Dick Williams still had hopes of October gladness. By the final day, only Lopez's dream had been shattered. The pennant would perhaps be decided by a Twin-Red Sox brawl in Fenway Park, while the Tigers needed a sweep of two in California to force a playoff. Ermer had his ace Dean Chance on the mound, but the 20-game winner who had pitched a no-hitter six weeks before was destined to lose that day. When Boston shortstop Rico Petrocelli snagged a pop-up in the ninth to nail down a 5-3 victory, Ermer became just another close-finisher, as did Smith when his Bengals failed to win the nightcap of the twin bill. Three heart-breaking setbacks — all within a span of 48 hours!

The reliable source *Total Baseball* lists "the managerial record of every man who ever held the reins of a major-league club." As of 1995, the list totals almost 600. Of those, only about 100 have managed at least one pennant winner. Even those who have won a flag have lost far more frequently. In spite of the odds against success, history shows that relatively few have turned down owners' offers to manage.

Why take a job when it's almost a mathematical certainty you will fail? One possible reason is that a manager likes the idea of being in control. As with a Broadway director, the chances of flopping are greater than succeeding, but it's better to take the blame for a performance than not to direct at all.

A more likely reason is the lure of a possible victory celebration. Few players who have experienced a pennant-clincher will select another moment in their career as being more exciting. Jim Northrup is one of a handful of players in major-league history to wallop two grand slams in one game, yet he told me in 1994 that the Tigers' 1968 pennant clincher was his greatest thrill. To be the leader of the pack in its hour of glory is even more exhilarating.

It's the nature of baseball that individual players can succeed even when the team fails. But for managers, winning isn't everything, it's the only thing. That's why they keep trying.

ENOUGH IS ENOUGH

M any managers have experienced excruciating late-season pennant losses, but McCarthy's two last-second defeats in 1948 and 1949 rank as the most unpalatable consecutive endings in history. After the Yankees beat his Sox off in '49, Mac contemplated retirement, refraining from renewing his contract with Boston for another two months. However, the emotional effects of the demoralizing defeats were cushioned by a managerial career marked with unusual success. McCarthy would give it another try.

Statistics point to Mac as being one of the greatest managers, if not the best. In 24 years, Marse Joe accumulated a winning percentage of .615, a still-standing, major-league record. He managed seven world championship ballclubs, his nine pennant-winners are one shy of the mark held by McGraw and Stengel, and he twice came within a game of winning another.

With all his accomplishments, McCarthy never got the credit he deserved. From the beginning, he was resented by players for his strict rules and detached demeanor. Having won the American Association title in 1925, he was hired by Phil Wrigley to lead the Cubs in '26, despite never having played in the majors, and was immediately regarded by Grover Alexander and other veterans as a "bush leaguer."

Joe McCarthy is greeted by his wife at an airport in his hometown of Buffalo shortly after announcing his resignation as Red Sox skipper. (AP/Wide World Photos)

Fired by Wrigley in 1930, Mac managed the Yankees the following season, but was forced to coddle an aging and embittered Ruth, whose annoyance with having been overlooked as Ruppert's new choice as skipper made him unmanageable. Even when Ruth left and championships followed, Joe wasn't given his due by reporters who resented his disinclination to deliver profound or prolonged pronouncements. Thus was Jimmy Dyke's playful yet unjust poke at fellow skipper McCarthy for the apparent simplicity of leading an exceptionally talented team, labeling him a "push button manager," widely quoted by the press.

It wasn't Mac's fault that he was continuously blessed with superior ballplayers, and it can be argued that the players overachieved partly as a result of the manager's insistence on professionalism. And if his rules that Yankees be neatly dressed at all times and refrain from clubhouse card playing were disliked at first, gradually they came to be respected. So was the manager. It's not surprising that in choosing the better skipper, Lefty Gomez, Phil Rizzuto and other Yankees who played for both Stengel and McCarthy chose the latter.

In 1945, Larry MacPhail became a part-owner of the Yankees and from then on it was a battle of the Macs. McCarthy lost, his quitting the following year a result of resentment over MacPhail's interference as well as frustration over the attitude of talented but rebellious pitcher Joe Page. In 1947, Red Sox owner Tom Yawkey enticed McCarthy with a two-year deal at a salary of $50,000, which was renewed prior to the '50 season.

The decade began optimistically, with Boston winning 31 of its first 50 games in staying close to first place. A turnabout resulted in McCarthy, who in the past had warned such players as Alexander, Hack Wilson and Page against drinking, soothing shaky nerves during games with periodic walks to the end of the bench for whiskey snorts. When the club lost 11 of 13 games to fall nine games behind, 12 in the loss column, Joe decided enough was enough. On June 23, he announced his retirement, claiming "physical exhaustion" as the reason.

Wrote sportswriter Arthur Daley a few days later, "Don't let anyone tell you that McCarthy never could manage. The fellows who know more about it than anyone else, the impossible-to-fool baseball players, say he was the best. Suppose we let it go at that."

Suppose we do.

CHAPTER 44

SLAUGHTER AT FENWAY

Baseball isn't a science, so that the most ingenious of managers and best ballclubs can be foiled on any given day by a bad hop grounder, a wind-blown fly ball, a missed call by an umpire, or simply an off-day by a player. Still, on most occasions when talented teams face pitiful ones, the results are predictable. Such was the case when the last-place Browns met heavy-hitting Boston on June 7, 1950, as the Sox socked their way to a 20-4 laugher in Beantown. The next day, if Sox manager Joe McCarthy was concerned that the humiliated St. Louis Club would be inspired to victory his fears were quickly abated.

After a scoreless first inning, the sparse crowd of 5,000 at Fenway watched Sox starter Chuck Stobbs blank the Browns in the second (Mickey Mantle fans might recall Stobbs as the hurler who surrendered one of the Oklahoman's longest homers in 1953.) Boston then proceeded to thrash St. Louis in a manner unprecedented in baseball history. Their outscoring the opponent by 25 runs remains the major-league record today.

The Red Sox bombarded Browns hurlers for eight runs in the second, five in the third and seven in the fourth. By the fifth, Boston's 20-3 lead had Joe McCarthy breathing easily, and the Sox eased their attack by scoring a mere two tallies that inning, none the next. The temptation to pour it on returned as Boston

Scored a pair in the seventh, another five in the eighth. As the licked Browns took their last licks, Ted Williams stared in disbelief at the scoreboard which indicated what would be the final score — Boston 29, St. Louis 4.

Not surprisingly, Williams played a role in the massacre with five RBIs coming on two homers. The first was hit well into the stands in right field. He then beat the "Williams Shift" with an opposite-field blow over the left-field wall. His firepower was impressive, but there were more productive batters than Terrible Ted that day.

For instance, Bobby Doerr had three homers and a single, along with four runs scored and eight ribbies in what was probably the greatest game of the Hall-of-Famer's career. Then there was Walt Dropo who was only slightly less noticeable with a couple of homers, seven RBIs and five runs-scored. Unlike Doerr, Dropo never made it to Cooperstown, but he did have more exciting moments. In 1952, Walt strung together a dozen consecutive hits, still a major-league record, while matching two other marks by gathering 13 hits in three straight games, 15 hits in four consecutive games.

Johnny Pesky was never peskier with three singles and two doubles against four Browns' moundsmen, scoring three times while driving in two, while Al Zarilla matched Pesky's five hits, four of them being doubles, and scored four. Incredibly, Zarilla was the only Sox player besides pitcher Stobbs to fail to get an RBI.

Others were more modest contributors. Vern Stephens merely stroked a single, double and triple to drive in three. Matt Batts batted well with a single, double and pair of runs and ribbies. Clyde Vollmer, replacing an undoubtedly disappointed Dom DiMaggio who was nursing a bruised leg, might have hung his head after getting only one of the 28 hits had he not set an American League record for a nine-inning game with eight plate appearances — in only eight innings! Even Stobbs contributed with two singles, but not before walking four times in the first four innings, which the Boston Herald reported was a new major-league record for pitchers.

Many records fell that day. The total of 29 runs was the most by any team in the century, a mark still standing, though matched by the White Sox in 1955. Boston had 60 total bases and 29 RBIs, also current major-league marks. Zarilla's four doubles tied the record for most in a game, and he nearly had another his last time up when his drive was caught by Roy Sievers with his back to the center-field wall.

Joe McCarthy had been on the enviable side of many massacres while piloting the Bronx Bombers, but few could have been as impressive as Boston's bashing of the Browns, especially coming on the heels of the rout the day before. Ironically, it was only two weeks later that McCarthy's 24-year career as manager came to an end.

THE DUKE ROCKS
FLATBUSH — TWICE!

F or the 19,000 fans at Ebbetts Field, it had been a memorable Memorial-Day morning of 1950. Philly shortstop
Granny Hamner's weak 10th-inning toss bounced past first
baseman Eddie Waitkus, allowing Bobby Morgan to score the
winning-run and the Dodgers to tie the Phils for the league-lead.
Victory in the afternoon would give Brooklyn sole possession of
first.

It hadn't been a good morning for Edwin Snider, nicknamed
Duke since boyhood. While teammates Jackie Robinson and Roy
Campanella had connected for homers, Snider was held hitless
in five at bats against the Phils' Robin Roberts. The 23-year-old
center fielder from Compton California opted only for a dough-
nut and glass of milk before taking the field for second-game
warmups.

Whether or not his light lunch had anything to do with it,
Snider's day turned around in the matinee contest. Facing Rowdy
Russ Meyer in the first frame, the natural right-hander who
learned to swing southpaw from his father pulled a fastball over
the 38-foot high, right-field screen and onto Bedford Avenue, then
dented the same street in the third. In the fifth inning, Snider
blitzed a Blix Donnelly delivery, the ball landing in the lower
seats in center for his third-consecutive homer. His chance to

become only the fourth player in history to hit four in a game was lost when reliever Bob Miller "held" Duke to a single in the seventh, the ball crashing four feet from the top of the right-field screen so viciously that Snider could advance no further. The appreciative crowd of 34,000 rewarded their newest hero with a standing ovation.

Nearly a quarter of a century following his retirement in 1964, Snider wrote in his autobiography *The Duke of Flatbush*, "I think that game was a decisive point in my career. The home runs caused a big stir in Brooklyn. Suddenly, the reporters and fans were talking about my power." The stats confirm Snider's recall. He accumulated only five homers as a part-timer in his first seasons of '47 and '48, and his total of 23 in '49 was respectable, not extraordinary. By the end of the 1950 season, Snider had over 30 homers, batted over .300, had over 100 RBIs, and was an All-Star (though he was booed at Wrigley Field while playing in the midseason classic), all for the first time. It was also the first time he led the league in a major category (hits with 199).

His success in 1950 was personally satisfying for Snider. It compensated for an early-season confrontation with skipper Burt Shotten over a failed bunt attempt which resulted in Snider's being fined fifty bucks. The year contained its share of heartbreaks, culminating in a nightmarish defeat at the hands of those same Phillies. Following their Memorial Day sweep, the Dodgers fell dramatically behind the Phils, but narrowed the gap to two games in late September, then to one by defeating Philadelphia before a packed Ebbetts Field in the next-to-last game. In the season-closer, Snider had a chance to force a playoff by knocking in the winning run with two outs in the ninth. He came through with a single, but the runner was thrown out at the plate. Dick Sisler, whose 13 homers that year would be a career-high, then reached the seats in the 10th, and Roberts, Richie Ashburn and the rest of the Whiz Kids had the first Philly pennant in 35 years.

Snider became only the third Dodger in history to have a three-homer game. Before the 1950 season ended, teammates Roy Campanella and Tommy Brown would make the feat slightly less uncommon, but not another Brooklyn batter would again belt three in one until Duke became the last to do it, repeating the act almost precisely five years later.

Snider crosses plate after belting one of two homers in Game Six of 1952 World Series. Yogi Berra is the disgruntled backstop. Yanks went on to take the Series in seven over Brooklyn. (National Baseball Library, Cooperstown, NY)

To use Snider's words, "If there was a year that had everything for the Brooklyn Dodgers, it was 1955." They exploded from the starting gate, winning 22 of their first 24. They never trailed in the standings, clinching the flag earlier than any other National League winner. They led the league in 11 categories, including batting average, homers and runs, as well as strikeouts by pitchers and lowest ERA. Last but by no means least, the team was finally able to stifle the fans annual lamentations of "Wait til next year" and "Dem Bums" by beating their perennial rivals, the Yankees, in October, thus earning Brooklyn's sole victory in Series history.

It was also a year that had everything for Snider. His 42 homers was the third of four-straight seasons of 40+ four baggers, while his 136 RBIs easily led the league. He socked two of his longest-ever homers, one traveling 470 feet, the other hit to center at Ebbetts Field, a drive which "was still going up when it landed in the upper deck." Duke even chased the Babe that year, gathering 38 homers by early August when a Johnny Klippstein fastball caught him on the left knee, causing a nagging injury which limited him to only four more by year's end. His hot bat earned him numerous opportunities to appear in commercials, endorsing such products as cigarettes, razor blades and hot cocoa. He put the finishing touch to his monster season by smashing four homers in the Series, earning him an honorary-mayor title in his hometown a few weeks later.

Appropriately, Snider had the most productive game of his career in 1955, coming on the first of June against the Braves at Ebbetts Field. In the first inning, he laced into righty Gene Conley's first pitch, the center-field clout delighting the 18,000 spectators. After being retired in the third, Snider reached for a slant thrown by rookie southpaw Roberto Vargas in the fourth and pulled it over the screen in right, then duplicated the drive with another off Ernie Johnson in the sixth. Two innings later, Snider strode to the plate to the accompaniment of the organists' "California Here I Come" and a thunderous ovation from the hopeful crowd. But his chance to hit four in one game was again thwarted by the high screen in right, with Duke's drive off Lefty Chet Nichols at least earning him a double this time.

Snider remains the only Dodger in history to hit as many as three homers in a game twice. Unlike his first trio of round trippers which were all solo shots, his three on June 1, 1955 drove in six runs. Duke's homers and double that day gave him 14 total bases, the second-highest amount in Brooklyn history behind Gil Hodges' 17 in a game in 1950.

Even as late as the '60s, ballplayers worried about their finances following retirement. After quitting in 1965, Duke became a coach and earned considerably less than his maximum salary of $40,000, forcing his wife and him to adjust to a more modest lifestyle. Snider became eligible for the Hall of Fame in 1969, but had a surprisingly difficult time making it. He had begun to give up hope when sportswriter Jack Lang finally telephoned the good news in 1980. With Mantle having already been elected in 1974, and Mays in 1979, Cooperstown had in its midst the three greatest center fielders of the '50s — Willie, Mickey, and the Duke.

THE CATCH

I n *Romancing the Horsehide*, poet-author Gene Carney writes, "Say Willie Mays and where does your imagination run? You know where."

For Carney and most others, the skillful slugger who accumulated more than 650 homers, 3,000 hits, 2000 runs and nearly 2,000 RBIs is best remembered for one moment of September 29, 1954. It was then that Mays, whose quick reflexes, gifted hands and cunning maneuvers made him equally adept as a fielding larcenist, performed his greatest theft.

The victims — the presumably unbeatable Cleveland Indians, winners of more regular-season games than any other franchise save the 1906 Cubs. The setting — Game One of the World Series at the Polo Grounds. With the score tied at two in the eighth, Giant right-hander Sal Maglie surrendered a walk and hit, leaving southpaw Don Riddle with the difficult duty of retiring the Tribe's next batter, fearsome Vic Wertz, already with a triple and two singles on his line of the box score.

Manager Leo Durocher's desire for a lefty-vs-lefty confrontation had occasioned Riddle's appearance, but on his first pitch, Don's slant was "practically a crime against nature, as pitching laws go," wrote one Mays biographer. Rather than breaking down and away, it hung invitingly, and Wertz took advantage. He blasted the ball to where, as George Will described in *Men At Work*, "Only Superman could catch it. Superman did."

But it was the manner in which this man-of-steal saved the day that left spectators spellbound afterwards. Eyeing the ball at the crack of the bat, Mays turned and ran towards the center-field bleachers. Only once did he take another glance at the horsehide. Pounding his glove, he made an over-the-shoulder catch approximately 10 feet from the wall. Not finished displaying his superpowers, Willie made a 180-degree spin on the run, losing his hat in the act and used the momentum of the turn to launch a 300-foot strike to second baseman Davey Williams. The throw prevented runner Larry Doby, who had tagged and went to third, from continuing on home. Had Mays taken the time to stop running, then thrown to the infield, the orthodox procedure after catching a fly on the retreat, Doby probably would have had time to score.

Having thrown one pitch, Riddle was through. While replacement Marv Grissom walked to the mound, Don proudly strode to the bench, triumphantly declaring, "I got my man." As did Grissom (after yielding a walk), and the Giants wiggled out of the inning unscathed. In the 10th, pinch-hitter Dusty Rhodes became a hero when he dumped a shallow fly ball into the even shallower right-field stands to win it. Rhodes could have thanked Mays in the clubhouse for, as Oscar-winners are inclined to say, making the moment possible.

Hank Greenberg once recalled a catch made by Joe DiMaggio in 1939 at Yankee Stadium that was similar to Willie's snare, only better. DiMaggio never looked at Hank's drive while racing back, and used "sheer instinct" in sticking his glove up to where he thought the ball would drop just prior to corralling it. Sportswriter Arthur Hano remembered a catch by the Giants' Freddy Lindstrom, who ran at full speed, then leaped at the last second before crashing into the fence. He arose from the ground with his head in a spin, the ball in his glove. The Indians' Tris Speaker was the best defensive outfielder of the pre-'20s, renowned for the shallowness in which he positioned himself in center, daring batters to hit one over his head, winning the dare 99 percent of the time. Mays claims his circus catch against Wertz wasn't his best ("I had it all the way," he told teammate Monte Irvin in the dugout), insisting that a barehanded grab at Forbes Field in his rookie season in 1951 and a soaring capture of an apparent Ted Williams home run ball in an All-Star game were better.

To recount all the resplendent robberies by outfielders may be too protracted a project for one book, certainly for one chapter of a book. Suffice to say there have been many. Yet, any discussion of the best inevitably begins with Willie's now four-decade-old catch of Wertz's fly ball. Why? Was that "optical illusion," as broadcaster Jack Brickhouse then described, far greater than any before or since? Aren't equally athletic catches made by modern ballplayers almost on a daily basis? Moreover, the manner in which Mays made the catch — basket style, was actually easier for Mays than for other outfielders, since Willie caught most balls in a similar fashion.

There are even some who believe Mays didn't have to make an over-the-shoulder grab. Cleveland's Al Smith told editor Daniel Peary for the book *We Played the Game*, "Personally, I thought Mays had time to run the ball down and turn around to catch it, but Willie liked making dramatic catches like that and caught it while running the other way." Another, noting Willie's love for the spotlight, quipped, "Mays made the hard ones look hard."

It should be pointed out that the latter two opinions are in a distinct minority, and anyone who has seen the footage of the catch and throw can judge for themselves the splendor and skill in making them. Still, it doesn't explain the inordinate reverence given a play which, grand as it was, wouldn't be a shoe-in for a video featuring the most spectacular in baseball history.

There are several reasons which help explain the fame attached to a defensive play which has become as large a part of baseball lore as Babe's called shot, Gabby's dark shot, Thomson's loud shot, and Maz's Series-ending shot. Some are more obvious than others, the most apparent being the fact that The Catch occurred during the drama of a World Series game. Was the athletic skill of Mays' miracle superior to Kenny Lofton's or Ken Griffey Jr.'s, when they sprinted, leaped and stretched over walls to take homers away from distraught hitters in regular-season games of the '90s? Though the plays received some publicity at the time, little is mentioned of them today. Willie probably made better catches than the one off Wertz, but the settings were different. Magicians need a large audience for their acts to be fully appreciated. No better showcase for gifted glovemen exists than the Fall Classic.

There have, however, been similar stunning Series snatches. In 1969, Tommy Agee made two clutch, running, diving grabs of long fly balls, and Ron Swoboda another. All three were arguably as wonderful as Willie's but, though still talked about, aren't regarded with as high esteem. The reason, of course, is that the plays were made by Agee and Swoboda, not Willie Mays. Both were skilled major leaguers who had moments of greatness, but their overall careers can be described as average. When mediocre players perform the impossible, their acts are revered by some years later, but regarded as flukes by most. When superstars perform the impossible, everyone appreciates, even exaggerates their efforts for decades to come.

Television made Willie's catch more memorable. With Speaker and DiMaggio, you had to be there to have appreciated their moments of defensive brilliance. Though telecasts of other great fielding plays followed, like Sandy Amoros's running stab of Yogi Berra's opposite field blooper in Game Seven of the 1955 Series, Mays' was the first to be seen live by millions of people. (It can be argued that Al Gionfriddo's grab of DiMaggio's drive in the '47 Series, and Billy Martin's desperate lunge of a Jackie Robinson infield pop-up which preserved a Yankee victory in Game Seven of the '52 Series, both came first. The plays were exceptional and timely, but not great. Besides, the '47 Series wasn't seen by a national audience, and though television sets were more numerous in '52, there weren't nearly as many as the 29 million in American homes by '54.)

Conditions in which Mays and others of his era played made it more difficult to field their positions. Outfields were generally more spacious, fences unpadded. Uniforms were far more bulky. And how many running, leaping or one-handed catches (not to mention the "snatch" catches) would be seen today were outfielders forced to use the petite-sized mitts of the past? Those who are quick to praise present players for being speedier and more agile should admit that their baseball instincts are probably inferior to former stars. Is there anyone today who gets as good a jump on a fly ball than did Mays?

Finally, there was the throw that followed the catch. The putout was admirable, but to have both the presence of mind and the agility to instantaneously spin and fire an accurate throw to the infield made the play unprecedented, you might call it a breathtaking two-mints-in-one.

It's not surprising that, with all his accomplishments, the multi-talented Mays is best remembered for "The Catch of 1954." Willie wasn't the only beneficiary of that magnificent moment. Vic Wertz's career would have been better had a bout with polio not interrupted it, but considering he hit over .300 twice, socked 20 or more homers six times, and drove in more than 100 runs five times, it was impressive enough. Yet, few would remember him today had Mays not robbed him in '54. As Wertz acknowledged after retirement, "Willie made me famous."

WAS AARON
UNDERRATED?

I
f asked to pick the top three ballplayers of the '50s and early '60s, many would select Mantle, Mays and Aaron. Yet, Aaron supporters often complain that Hammerin' Hank wasn't recognized as the equal of Mick and Willie until the late '60s. By then, Mantle was close to retirement and Mays in the twilight of his career, while Aaron continued to produce as he edged closer to Ruth's legendary career homer total. Wrote sports columnist Arthur Daley in 1969, "Aaron has long been one of the most overlooked superstars."

Several reasons for Aaron's being ignored can be given. Henry began his career in 1954. Mays was the showcase of the National League by then and detracted from Hank's debut that year by muscling 41 homers and winning his first batting crown, finishing the year with a circus catch in the World Series. And the muscular Mantle was already wowing fans with lengthy launches, like the one in 1953 off pitcher Chuck Stubbs that carried over 560 feet.

Some say Aaron's being black was the reason Mantle received more attention, though it's a weak argument considering Mays' racial makeup didn't hurt his popularity. Others point to the fact that Willie and Mickey played in New York which received more press coverage than Milwaukee, Aaron's club, but Mays lost that advantage when the Giants went to Frisco in 1958. Mantle benefited from being showcased in the World Series every year save two from 1951-1964, whereas Aaron appeared twice. Still, Mays became nationally recognized despite making it to the Fall Classic only three times.

If Aaron was a third choice behind Mantle and Mays prior to the late '60s, could the reason be that he simply wasn't as good during that time? Listed on the following page are their overall totals for the three batting categories generally regarded as most important, covering the periods from 1954-1960, 1961-1965, and 1954-1965.

Hammerin' Hank socks number 715. (National Baseball Library, Cooperstown, NY)

OVERALL STATS FROM 1954-1960

	Batting Titles	RBI Titles	Homer Titles	Average	RBIs	Homers	Homer Rate
Aaron	2	2	1	.318	743	219	1/18.8 ab
Mantle	1	1	4	.312	691	263	1/13.9 ab
Mays	1	0	1	.325	721	255	1/16.0 ab

OVERALL STATS FROM 1961-1965

	Batting Titles	RBI Titles	Homer Titles	Average	RBIs	Homers	Homer Rate
Aaron	0	1	1	.323	562	179	1/16.6 ab
Mantle	0	0	0	.302	409	153	1/12.3 ab
Mays	0	0	3	.308	590	226	1/12.9 ab

OVERALL STATS FROM 1954-1965

	Batting Titles	RBI Titles	Homer Titles	Average	RBIs	Homers	Homer Rate
Aaron	2	3	2	.312	1305	398	1/17.8 ab
Mantle	1	1	4	.308	1100	416	1/13.3 ab
Mays	1	0	4	.318	1311	481	1/14.6 ab

Looking at the stats, Aaron compares equally with Mantle and Mays during the early stages of their career. Mays and Mantle were better homer-hitters, but Aaron's batting average exceeded Mickey's and his RBI total was higher than both. Aaron won five offensive titles, only one fewer than Mantle, and Mays only took two. However, four of Mick's titles were in the more glamorous, but not necessarily more important homer category, helping to boost his popularity.

From 1961-1965, Aaron out-hit Mantle and at least batted on a par with Mays. Willie had more RBIs and homers, but Aaron's average was significantly higher. Henry bettered the Mick in every major category, though it must be pointed out that the Yankee slugger missed many games with injuries, and that his homer rate was superior to Aaron's and Mays' throughout their careers.

The overall stats from 1954-1965 shows conclusively that Aaron deserved equal recognition during that period. He won more titles, accumulated more homers, obtained a higher average than both, and was a mere six under Mays' RBI total.

If Hank wasn't as recognized as Mantle and Mays, perhaps it's because he was consistently great, but never as spectacular. The best seasons of Mantle and Mays were better than Aaron's. Hank never reached the 50-homer plateau. Mickey and Willie did it twice. Mantle captured the fans' imagination by winning the Triple Crown, by hitting tape-measure homers, by chasing the Babe, by limping with pain throughout his career. Mays made basket catches in the outfield, stole more bases, out homered his rival most of the time. All Aaron did was hit between 35 to 45 homers, drive in over 100 runs, and bat over .300 in a nonchalant manner every year. {Insert Photo 29}

If the press and public ignored Aaron, pitchers weren't showing much respect either. Though he was a notorious bad-ball hitter, it's nevertheless astonishing that Aaron drew as many as 70 walks in only one season from 1954-1965. Furthermore, Aaron never led the league in base-on-balls nor ever reached the 100 mark during his career. Mantle drew over 100 walks 10 times, led the league five times.

Still, Aaron was productive for a longer period of time. Mantle had 10 years which can be considered outstanding, Mays 13. Aaron had 18 great seasons. If he was underrated during most of his career, by the time of his retirement in 1976, when he had collected more homers and RBIs than anyone else, Aaron was regarded by baseball historians and fans as, not only the equal of Mantle and Mays, but the equal of any of the game's great hitters.

CHAPTER 48

GRAND GUY IN A PINCH

D**espite his sensational four-hit debut of '59 and a season-ending average of .354, Willie McCovey was still a platoon player by 1960, competing for first-base duty with the Giants' righty-swinging Baby Bull, Orlando Cepeda. With lefty George Brunet on the mound for Milwaukee on June 12, it was southpaw McCovey's turn to ride the bench that day in San Francisco. His absence from the lineup would afford him the opportunity to make history.

One run separated the two teams by the seventh inning. When the Giants loaded the bases in the home half off righty Carl Willey, manager Bill Rigney called for McCovey to pinch-hit for Frisco reliever Johnny Antonelli. Stretch lifted a sky-high fly that, as Brave skipper Chuck Dressen moaned afterwards, his right fielder "would have had to run in to get in Milwaukee." Fortunately for McCovey the notorious winds of Candlestick, either a blessing or curse to batters depending on which direction they happen to be blowing, were favorable on this day. The ball landed 10 feet beyond the right-field fence. The grand slam gave the Giants a five run lead as they coasted to 16-7 triumph.

The victory put the Giants a half-game behind the front-running Pirates but despite being only two games out a week later, Rigney was fired by owner Horace Stoneham. According to Rig, who recalls the canning in *Baseball Chronicles*, the press had overestimated the club's potential, predicting in the spring they'd "win the league by twenty games." Stoneham believed what he read. Bill went on to manage in California, Minnesota and another season in San Francisco, but won a flag only once in his 18-year career, a division title with the Twins in 1970.

For McCovey, the grand slam was not only his first, but the first by any Giant at the three-month-old Candlestick Park. Before his 22-year career ended, Willie would knock a National League record 18 slams out of the park. His hitting a pinch-slam wasn't an unprecedented feat, with 84 other major-leaguers having done it previously in the century, but McCovey would do it two more times. Hitting three pinch slams is an achievement matched by only two others in big-league history (Round Ron Northey and Rich Reese).

Mac had hit only one more slam by September 10, 1965, when in a game against the Cubs in Frisco he again found himself on the bench, though not for the same reason. By then, McCovey had clearly won the battle for first with Cepeda (who'd be traded to the Cardinals after the '65 season), and was merely being given a day's rest. That rest was interrupted in the sixth inning. Willie was sent to bat with the score tied at one and the bags jammed against the submarine-throwing righty Ted Abernathy. Strategy normally dictated Abernathy's removal, setting up a southpaw-versus-southpaw confrontation, but Abernathy was the league's best reliever that year (he'd go on to lead the senior circuit in game appearances and saves) and had previously been tough on Giant batters, McCovey in particular. Cub skipper Lou Klein would rue his decision to keep him in the game.

McCovey was looking for a fastball, and Abernathy delivered one that dipped below the knees at the last second. Mac missed it. Ted let loose with another but this time the ball crossed the plate belt-high. Willie turned on it and rifled a shot that brought the crowd of 20,000 to their feet. The ball easily cleared the right-field fence.

One of the three who scored ahead of McCovey was Willie Mays, who had been intentionally walked to set up the bases-loaded drama. When Mays touched the plate it marked his 12th consecutive season of scoring 100 or more runs, breaking Stan

Musial's National League record. Mays' mark was in turn broken by Aaron's 13th-straight in 1967.

By 1975, McCovey's age had again relegated him to a platoon player, but for a different team. The Giants had traded him the year before, despite the superstar having led the league in homers and slugging percentage three times and in RBIs twice in his 15 years with the ballclub. After socking a respectable total of 22 four-baggers in his first year under Padre and McDonald's owner Ray Kroc, Big Mac was a part-timer on the trading block and on the bench in '75 when the Padres played the Mets at Shea Stadium on May 30.

Willie watched from the dugout as a pair of gifted southpaws — San Diego's Randy Jones, who'd win 20 that year, and Jerry Koosman, who'd win 20 the next year, battled into the eighth. By then, the score was deadlocked at two, but the Padres were threatening with the bases-loaded and only one out. Met manager Yogi Berra brought in his ace righty-reliever Bob Apodaca, prompting John McNamara to counter with McCovey.

The odds seemed to favor Apodaca. The 25-year old hadn't allowed a run in his previous seven outings and had an ERA below 1.00. In contrast, the 37-year-old McCovey was off to a slow start, his average a pathetic .224. Apodaca was quite capable of getting a strikeout when needed, while Willie fanned frequently. Knowing this, McCovey approached the batter's box with the idea of "just trying to meet the ball."

Apodaca began cautiously with two balls, then challenged Mac with a fastball. Willie fouled it off. The next pitch jammed him, breaking his bat, but the powerful Padre got enough good wood on the ball to send it sailing over the right-field fence, 370 feet away. McCovey's poke was the game-winner in a 6-2 San Diego victory.

McCovey's record third-career pinch-hit slam squashed plans to trade him that season and earned him more playing time. He finished the year with 23 homers, his 11th season with 20 or more. Mac was traded in 1976, first to Oakland, then back to San Francisco, where he belted a club-high 28 dingers in 1977 — at the age of 39! In his final season in 1980 he belted one homer, boosting his career total to 521.

Rare have been the instances in which players have come off

the bench to hit bases-loaded homers. McCovey's career accomplishments were numerous, including being one of only 15 players in history to win both Rookie-of-the-Year and MVP awards, but few could have been more satisfying for the Hall-of-Famer than his record three pinch-slams.

MICK'S MISSED MVPS

I n the spring of 1961, Billy Martin predicted that Babe Ruth's 60-homer mark would be broken that year by Mickey Mantle. He was more than half right. Roger Maris surpassed Babe with 61 homers, but not without a huge assist from Mantle.

Throughout the '61 season Maris had the advantage of having Mantle hit behind him. Hurlers preferred challenging Rajah to walking him and facing Mickey with a man on. Had their positions in the batting order been reversed, would Maris have caught Ruth? In all likelihood, he wouldn't even have been in the chase.

Nineteen hundred sixty-one was Maris' big year, but Mantle had the better season. Only a few homers separated the M & M boys going into September, but an injury hindered Mickey's chances and he missed nearly two weeks of the final month. Yet, despite finishing seven homers behind Roger, Mick's homer rate of one every 9.5 at bats was better than Maris', was the best of his career and was the best in major-league history except for three of Ruth's seasons and Mark McGwire's incredible year of 1996. Mickey's RBI total was only 14 fewer than Roger's coming in 76 fewer at bats. He led the league in runs-scored, walks and even slugging percentage. Most significantly, Mantle's batting average was nearly 50 points higher than Roger's.

So why did Maris win MVP honors that year? Sixty-one homers

was a feat too significant to allow anyone else to take the award. Ruth had been the most renowned and idolized sports figure in history. His 60-homer season of 1927 was his ultimate achievement. Such formidable challengers to his mark as Jimmie Foxx and Hank Greenberg had fallen short. How could Maris be bypassed after taking on and defeating a legend?

Mantle may have been robbed of MVP honors in other years as well. In 1955, he led the league in homers, slugging percentage and walks, yet the popular Yogi Berra was chosen despite Mantle's outhitting him by over 30 points. Mantle's 42 homers, 127 runs, and 129 walks were league highs in 1958, but Jackie Jensen took the MVP that year. Since Mantle had won the award in '56 and '57, his being snubbed in '58 prevented his winning an unprecedented three-straight MVPs.

Mantle won his third and final MVP in 1962. He had a chance to become the first player to notch four when in 1964 he compiled a .303 average with 35 homers and 111 RBIs while leading the league in slugging. Much of Mantle's hot hitting came in the final month-and-a-half, helping the Yanks to a come-from-behind pennant. The MVP went to Brooks Robinson.

Since ballplayers of pennant-winners are usually given greater consideration in MVP voting, the Jensen and Robinson selections are particularly puzzling. In 1958, Jensen's Red Sox finished a distant third behind the Bronx Bombers. Robinson's Orioles also finished in the show position behind the Yankees and White Sox in 1964. Though Jensen and Robinson had impressive seasons, their overall stats weren't better than Mantle's. Jensen led the league in one category (RBIs) to Mantle's three. Robinson's RBI total and batting average weren't much better than Mick's, while Mantle hit more homers, scored more runs, and had a better slugging percentage.

Conservatism on the part of voters may have been the reason Mantle was twice denied. By winning a third-consecutive MVP in '58 or a fourth award in '64, Mick would have achieved what such superstars as Ruth, Lou Gehrig, Ted Williams or Joe DiMaggio could never do. Many baseball writers felt uncomfortable with that realization. Present-day scribes are less concerned with precedence. Should Barry Bonds, already a three-time MVP winner, put together another spectacular season, his chances of grabbing a fourth will be better than were Mantle's.

After Maris connected for his record-breaking 61st, Mickey could have complained about his lost opportunity to do the same. He didn't. Nor did he ever whine about the chronic bone disease and frequent injuries which prevented an outstanding career from being more incredible. And certainly Mickey never cried over additional MVPs denied him by sportswriters.

Mantle's admirable character superseded even his remarkable athletic skills.

ROGER'S 62ND HOMER

J uly 17, 1961. The Dodgers' Duke Snider bats eighth for the first time in his career and drives in the winning run late in the game. Warren Spahn and Early Wynn both win, edging closer to the 300-victory milestone. And the Maris-Mantle race is in full gear as the Yankees prepare to play the second of a twinbill in Baltimore, having shot down the Orioles in the opener.

With their club already 10 games out, many in the crowd of 44,000 were focused more on the M & M duel than the Yank-Bird battle. By the fifth inning, their enthusiasm had been fueled by Maris' 36th and Mantle's 34th homers. But as the powerful pair prepared to bat again, a thunderstorm vent its fury on the Memorial Stadium greenery. Sixty-five minutes later, umpire Charlie Berry indicated with a wave of his arms that the Yankee 4-1 lead, and M & M's dingers, were washed away.

As the Yanks and Maris headed into September, they may have reflected on the lost opportunity of midseason. The Bombers were a formidable team that year, considered by some the greatest in history, but in that final month they retained a single-game advantage over the powerhouse Tigers led by Rocky Colavito, Norm Cash and Al Kaline. And though Mantle, who was playing hurt, had fallen behind in the Ruth pursuit, Maris' chances remained good. If he failed by one to catch the Babe, the homer-that-wasn't would return to haunt him.

For the Yanks, their negated efforts of July 17, which came within an inning of being realized, were of little importance when the team won the pennant. But for Maris, his lost homer would have significance.

On the same day he was cheated by the rainman, Maris was informed by Commissioner Ford Frick that he'd have to match the Babe's record 60 in 154 games, not in the 162 scheduled for that first season of expansion. Consequently, by September 20, when Maris and the Yanks returned to Baltimore to play their 154th, with heavy clouds again threatening to spoil the fun, Roger realized he'd need to add two to his total of 58 homers before the night's work was complete.

After being retired on a short fly ball in the first inning, Maris golfed a Milt Papas 2-1 fastball over the 380-foot sign in right-center in the third. Knowing the Yank had at least two more at bats, the crowd of 21,000 must have had mixed feelings — wanting to witness history being made, yet uneasy about the game's greatest player, and Baltimore's greatest celebrity, losing his most cherished record. (Babe was born and raised in Baltimore and, you'll recall, played his first year of pro ball there.)

Wherever the fans' sympathies lay, Maris failed to catch Ruth that night. In the fourth, the slugger was whiffed by reliever Dick Hall. Hall again retired Maris in the seventh, but Rog had another chance in the ninth. Facing knuckleballer Hoyt Wilhelm, he hit a check-swing roller which was grabbed by Wilhelm, who personally applied the coup de grace to Roger's quest. "Why did you swing at that one?" a disconsolate Patricia Maris exclaimed after watching her hubby on the tube from their home in Kansas City. No doubt Hoyt's floater was mesmerizing, but pressure felt from Frick's edict probably contributed to Maris' tentative swing as well.

The Yanks beat the Birds that night, clinching the pennant for rookie skipper Ralph Houk. None of the players, including Maris, cared about the aborted game of July 17 as they guzzled and sprayed champagne in the clubhouse. But that rainout looms large in regards to Maris' record. Had his July home run counted, the four bagger in game number 154 would have been his 60th, not

59th. After matching Ruth's total in the specified number of games, would classifying 62 in 162 as an unequivocal record be disputed? At the least, it would have made the commissioner's insistence that the record be shared more difficult to justify. Even protests that the Yanks had played an extra game, with one in April ending in a tie, and that the contest in Baltimore was actually the team's 155th, could have been refuted easily enough, since the Bombers of '27 played 155 also.

Yogi Berra congratulates Maris after homer number 59. The umpire is Ed Runge. (AP/Wide World Photos)

Announced a relieved Maris in Baltimore after the issues of the pennant and Ruth-chase had been decided, "Now that it's all over, I'm happy with what I got." But it wasn't over. Tracy Stallard served up gopher ball number 61 in the 162nd game, renewing debate over legitimacy of a record established during an extended season. Five years after Roger's death from cancer in 1985, Commissioner Fay Vincent declared Maris to be sole holder of the mark, but some record books continue to equally honor both sluggers.

Longfellow taught us that some rain must fall in every life. On July 17, 1961 in Baltimore, it should have waited another 20 minutes.

ROGER'S
RECORD

T he question as to whose feat was more difficult — Ruth's 60 homers in 1927 or Maris' 61 in '61 is an intriguing one. Looking at the stats, the Ruth argument is strong. Not only did he appear in 10 fewer games, but Babe also had 50 fewer at bats. He walked 138 times compared to Roger's 94, despite having the same advantage as Maris of having a fearsome slugger (Gehrig) waiting to hit next against wary pitchers. Ruth's homer percentage was better, socking one every 9.0 official at bats compared to Roger's 9.7.

What cannot be overlooked as well are the years in which both performed. Nineteen hundred twenty-seven wasn't a time when homers were leaving the ballpark with unusual frequency. Gehrig chased the Babe for the homer crown (until Ruth blew him away with 17 in the final month) and finished with 47, a significant sum in any era. But no one else hit more than 18. Compare that with the production of sluggers in 1961. Besides M & M , four other ballplayers hit over 40 in the A.L., and the league smashed its single-season homer record before the final month began. If hurlers hollered about a livelier ball during the '20s, many made the same complaint in 1961. Whined righty Jim Brosnan, "Don't tell me it isn't a rabbit ball. I can hear it squealing every time it goes over the fence." Cracked future Hall-of-Famer Early Wynn,

"Cut the ball open, and you'll find a carburetor."

Yet, the intangible factor of pressure must be considered. In 1927, Ruth was trying to surpass his 59 round trippers of 1921. Had he failed, Babe could still boast of holding the homer mark. In addition, Ruth had the advantage of having everyone pulling for him, with the possible exception of owner Jake Ruppert, who was nervous about his star's contract demands in 1928. In contrast, Maris was disliked by the fans and press for having the audacity to challenge a legend's most venerable record. Though Mantle's presence in the lineup was helpful to Maris, the popular long-time Yankee also unintentionally increased pressure on Roger by staying in the homer chase, giving fans another reason to root against the sophomore pinstriper.

No argument can counter the fact that Maris broke the record. It wasn't his fault that the circumstances for his accomplishment were different. Frick's insistence on an asterisk was nonsensical. New records are often set in every sport, with conditions having changed. Must they all be qualified by identifying the various factors which allowed former feats to fall? Frick's proclamation was inspired more by personal feelings for his old crony Ruth than fairness. Had Babe's total in '27 been 61 in 162 games and Maris' 60 in 154 in 1961, would the commissioner have insisted that Ruth's old mark be distinguished with an asterisk?

Roger Maris

As prestigious as they may be, records eventually fall after numerous attempts by athletes hungry to take their place in sports history. Many thought Walter Johnson's career strikeout total could never be reached, but Nolan Ryan proved them wrong. Dale Long's streak of hitting a homer in eight-straight games was equaled by Don Mattingly, and again by Ken Griffey, Jr. Ty Cobb's lifetime stolen base record was erased by Lou Brock (and Brock's by Rickey Henderson), as was his lifetime hit total by Pete Rose. And Ruth's World Series home run record was smashed by Mantle in 1964.

Other records remain in tact, but barely. In 1941, Ted Williams batted .400. While some experts believe that mark will never again be reached, Rod Carew, Wade Boggs and Tony Gwynn came close. Rudy York still holds the mark for homers in a month with 18 in August 1937, but Mays fell one shy in August 1965. Even Joe DiMaggio's consecutive-game hitting streak, which many say is an unbreakable record, was approached by Rose in 1978.

Maris' 61 in '61 has gone unchallenged. Indeed, the main pressure came from his teammate that year. Mays (1965), George Foster (1977), Cecil Fielder (1990), Albert Belle (1995), and Mark McGwire and Brady Anderson (1996) all hit in the low 50s, but none were considered serious challengers during those seasons. Roger's feat truly has stood the test of time.

Most record-breakers gain fame when they accomplish the unbelievable. Roger Maris gained notoriety. He was the one

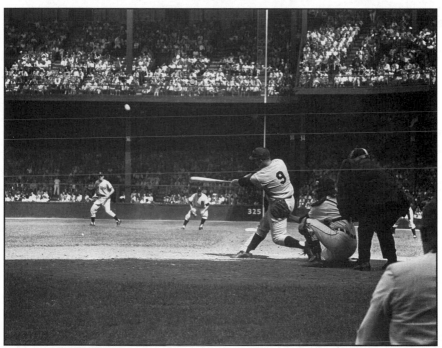

Yankee baserunner Tony Kubek has a perfect view of Roger Maris' swing which resulted in his 57th homer at Tiger Stadium on September 16, 1961. (UPI/Bettmann)

responsible for the undeification of Babe Ruth. Later, when Aaron's assault on Ruth's lifetime mark ended with his conquering it, most of the fans and media applauded his accomplishment. Hank could thank Roger for that. With Ruth thought of as only mortal then, people could accept his other records being challenged, even surpassed.

Roger's will never be fully accepted because he was the first to break Babe. Although baseball's official attitude may be changing, as exemplified by the asterisk removal, Maris remains the villain. Why else would the holder of the most renowned achievement in the game still not be an acceptable inductee for Cooperstown?

The most popular feat in the grandest of games, for fans of all ages, will always be the home run. The older generation will talk about the true superstars of the past and swear that none of the modern sluggers can compare. Younger fans will idolize their heroes, rooting and cheering for them to hit one out in every at bat.

Retired players will continue to rave about their home run accomplishments more than any others. In describing the thrill of connecting on a round tripper, Frank "Home Run" Baker once said, "Thousands of fans on their feet, hands waving, hats in the air and shouting as you round second base is something a man never forgets."

With all the pressure Roger had to endure — the badgering from the press who mistook his straightforwardness for arrogance; the hostility from the fans who thought Mantle a more worthy challenger to a god; the anxiety that built to the point where his hair began falling out — the record was worth setting, though Maris felt otherwise. For when a youngster goes to the ballpark for the first time and sees the ball knocked over the fence, it will remain one of the most memorable thrills of his or her lifetime. And one question likely to come to mind is, "Who hit the most homers in one year?"

That's Roger's record. Perhaps it always will be.

STEALING A
RECORD

With one prestigious and long-standing record having been
erased in 1961, an assault on another began the following season. By 1962, Ty Cobb's mark of 96 stolen bases,
set in 1915, stood for a dozen years longer than had Ruth's homer
record and seemed unsurpassable. Pittsburgh's Max Carey and
Washington's Sam Rice had come the closest when they stole 63
in 1916. But a year after Cobb's death, his cherished record was
stolen by a scrappy switch-hitter from Los Angeles.

Maury Wills was not an unknown when he began the '62 season. He had swiped 50 and 35 bases the previous two years, the
first Dodger ever to win in consecutive seasons (No, Brooklyn
fans, Jackie Robinson and Pee Wee Reese never did it). As a rookie,
Maury bagged three steals to help the Dodgers win the Series in
'59 and, two years later, won the Gold Glove Award for shortstops.

Wills may have been entertaining while strumming on the banjo
at a banquet given by the Baseball Writers Association prior to
Opening Day of '62, but not nearly as much as when running the
bases that year. After a slow start due partly to a pulled ham-
string, the diminutive dynamite added to his eight April steals
with another 19 in May and 15 in June. He slowed down with
nine in July, but sprinted to 32 thefts in August, giving him 83

245

heading into the final month. On September 23, Wills broke for second off Cardinal southpaw Larry Jackson and slid in with stolen base number 96. Three innings later, on a delayed steal off the same hurler, Wills had the record. Three days later, the Dodger became the first larcenist to reach the century mark with a steal of third. Wills ended the season with 104 thefts.

Although Maury's record was surpassed by three others (Rickey Henderson, Lou Brock and Vince Coleman), as Ralph Kiner explained in a baseball telecast in 1992, "Wills really started the stolen-base trend with his 1962 season." His total seems more amazing when compared with former stolen-base specialists. For instance, Cobb was thrown out 38 times in stealing 96, whereas Maury was caught only 13 times. In addition, Cobb stole bases in an era when it was more common to do so. Here are the major league's stolen-base leaders from 1910-1915:

Maury Wills

Year	Player	Team	Stolen Bases
1910	Eddie Collins	PHI	81
1911	Bob Bescher	CIN	83
1912	Clyde Milan	WAS	88
1913	Clyde Milan	WAS	75
1914	Fritz Maisel	NY(A)	74
1915	Ty Cobb	DET	96

Though Ty's record of 1915 was exemplary, others were able to accumulate high season totals during his playing days. Ben Chapman swiped 61 bases in 1931, the only player to gather more than 60 after 1920 until Wills' 104. The closest competitor to Maury in 1962 was teammate Willie Davis who had 32.

Some would say that Wills actually had 105 steals in 1962, the last coming when he won the MVP. Like Mantle the year before, Willie Mays had more impressive overall stats than the record-

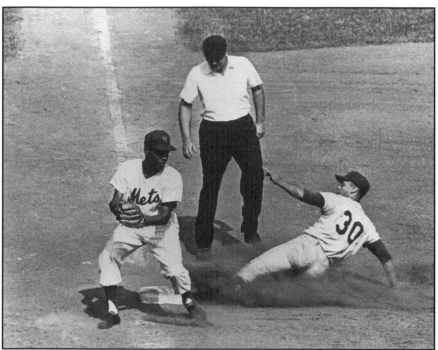

Mets third baseman Felix Mantilla doesn't even attempt a tag as Wills slides into third for steal number 72 on August 29, 1962. (National Baseball Library, Cooperstown, NY)

setter. His major-league leading 49 homers combined with career-high totals of 141 RBIs and 130 runs scored make 1962 perhaps Mays' greatest season. In addition, his team, not Maury's, won the pennant.

But they gave it to Wills, who thus became the first player in history to win an MVP by stealing. The Brocks, Lopes, Hendersons and Colemans that followed could thank Maury for changing the game from the free-swinging, go-for the-big-inning strategy that began with Ruth in the '20s, to the running style that has become so much a part of it during the past three decades.

Sportswriter Jim Murray once illustrated the impact Wills had on the game by offering advice to opposing managers: "The way to play Maury is to mine the approaches to second base. If he lays a bunt, the shrewd thing is to throw instantly to second."

It might have worked.

THE GIANTS ROB
THE DODGERS —
AGAIN!

"**T**he Giants win the pennant! The Giants win the pennant!" You don't have to be a Giant or Dodger fan to be familiar with Russ Hodges' celebrated call of Bobby Thomson's 1951 pennant-clinching poke at the Polo Grounds off Ralph Branca. It was the coup-de-grace to a Dodger dive which enabled the Giants to eradicate a 13-game deficit in less than two months, then erase a three-run disadvantage in the final inning of the final game of a best-of-three post-season playoff. For Giant fans, the sight of the exultant Eddie Stanky leaping on skipper Leo Durocher's back while a triumphant throng awaited their hero at home plate is the supreme moment in their club's history. For Dodger rooters, it remains their worst nightmare.

Eleven years later, the Giants would steal another one from their perennial rivals in near-identical fashion. The Dodgers began the season as the choice of most sportswriters to win, despite the Reds prevailing the year before. By September, their selection appeared justified with a four-game lead over the Giants. It narrowed to two by the final week, but one of the remaining four home games was against the expansion Houston Colt .45s, already losers of 94 games, and the other three were with the mediocre Cardinals, mired in sixth place, 21 games behind. Few

Giant followers could have held much optimism.

On the 27th, the Colts overcame a 4-2 Sandy Koufax lead by erupting for six runs in the final three frames to defeat the Dodgers, but the Giants lost as well. Maury Wills' game-tying single against the Cards the next day went for naught when reliever Ron Perranoski surrendered a two-out RBI single in the 10th. On the 29th, the Dodgers committed three errors behind Don Drysdale in losing 2-0. Yet, with the Giants splitting a double-header, the Dodger's destiny was still in their hands. All they needed was a win.

Like Dandy Don the day before, Johnny Podres pitched his heart out, but the gopher ball he served to Gene Oliver was as crushing a blow as Willie Mays' blast at approximately the same time in San Francisco. Both were eighth-inning game-winners and forced a post-season playoff. When a reporter asked Duke Snider "What happened?," referring to the Dodgers hitting slump which caused them to drop 10 of their last 13 games, Duke answered, "It's right on the scoreboard, no runs and five hits." Replied Giant skipper Alvin Dark when reminded that two of the three playoff games would be in Los Angeles, "I'm just tickled to death to play 'em anywhere. Chavez Ravine or Bayou, Louisiana."

The Dodgers' chance at redemption seemed bleak after being shut out in Game One, then trailing 5-0 in Frisco in Game Two. But they overcame their sluggish slugging with seven runs in the sixth, and despite giving up two runs in the eighth, they won it with a tally in the ninth. In returning home, they still had a chance to close out the Giants. All they needed was a win.

When they overcame a two-run deficit to take a 4-2 lead, it seemed the Dodgers would avoid hot-stove talk of their choking the pennant away. But the apple implanted in their throats the previous month reappeared in the ninth when the Giants fought back with two runs to knot the score. Then with the bags jammed, reliever Stan Williams walked Jim Davenport, giving Frisco the lead. Three quick Dodger outs, and the Giants had the pennant. Former vice president and future president Richard Nixon helped them celebrate in the clubhouse.

Considering their similarities, it's interesting that the Giant pennant comeback (or Dodger drop) of '62 carries far less importance in baseball books than does the one in '51. There are several reasons. The '51 season ended dramatically — with a home run. "The shot heard 'round the world" is a far more fitting finish to an exciting race than "the walk that won it." Furthermore, the miracle of '51 had the chronological advantage of happening first. That the Giants and Dodgers already set a precedent for doing the impossible made its repetition in '62 less climactic. The most important reason is that the battlegrounds took place on the western front, not the eastern, with both teams having taken Horace Greeley's advice in the late '50s. What baseball rivalry could match the Brooklyn Dodgers and New York Giants? Los Angeles versus San Francisco couldn't, and still doesn't, compare.

When the Dodgers lost their final regular-season game of 1962, forcing a playoff, it was Russ Hodges who first brought word to a tense Giant clubhouse in Frisco. Perhaps he put it this way: "The Giants can win the pennant! The Giants can win the pennant!"

FOUR-SEASON
HALL-OF-FAMER

S andy Koufax is regarded as one of the greatest hurlers in history. He won the ERA title five times consecutively. He led the league in strikeouts in four seasons. He threw four no-hitters, one of which was a perfect game. His 27 wins in 1966, his final year, remains the highest one-year total for any left-hander in the 20th century. Sandy's 382 strikeouts in 1965 was a major-league record until Nolan Ryan bettered it by one in 1973. He led the league for six straight seasons in allowing the fewest hits per game. The league's on-base percentage was lower against Koufax than against any other N.L. pitcher for seven years. He led the league in complete games and innings pitched twice and in shutouts three times. He won an unprecedented three Cy Young Awards and is one of only a handful of hurlers to win the MVP.

As great as Koufax was, he wasn't outstanding for the first half of his dozen years in the majors. Control problems stayed with him like an unwanted guest. Once urged by reporters to evaluate his young hurler, Dodger manager Walter Alston responded dryly, "He has one pitch ... high and outside."

Koufax was a losing pitcher from 1955-1960, accumulating a 36-40 record. During those six years Koufax had a winning record in 1959 alone, and only in 1958 did he manage double figures in victories. Although his season-strikeout totals were high, he failed to break the 200 barrier until his seventh season in 1961 when he led the league for the first time. Though he accumulated 18 wins that year and won his first ERA title in an injury-plagued season in '62, Sandy's first year of superstardom was 1963, when he showed the baseball world a sample of the dominating force he would be in the years to come.

Even 1963 began with some worrisome moments. After winning 2-1 on a five-hitter, Koufax yielded five runs in losing his next start to the expansion Colts. He shut them out four days later, but was forced to leave the mound in his fourth outing when he hurt his shoulder throwing a curve ball. Reporters asked afterwards how he felt about the early injury. Sandy joked, "I'm pretty sore about it."

Sandy missed two starts. He returned with a five-hit victory, then pitched the second no-hitter of his career against the defending champion Giants at Chavez Ravine. Harvey Kuenn made the final out, bouncing a comebacker to Koufax who trotted three-quarters of the way to first before flipping to Ron Fairly, precipitating a shower of seat cushions thrown from the stands. In the clubhouse, the perfectionist found fault with his performance, saying, "To pitch a perfect game would have been a better thrill." The lefty would experience that thrill two years later after perfecting the Cubs in Los Angeles.

Sandy Koufax

Koufax went on to win a league high 25 in 1963, while breaking the 300 K barrier for the first time. His ERA of 1.88 was also the league's best, as were his 11 shutouts. His performance in the Series that year is legendary. He defeated New York in Game One, fanning a record 15 Yankees (broken by Bob Gibson's 17 in 1968.) In Game Four, the K man swept the Yankees to defeat with a 2-1 decision, despite Mantle's record-tying 15th Series homer (Mick shattered the mark shared with Ruth the following year with three more).

Koufax, following completion of a perfect game against the Cubs, the fourth no-hitter of a career cut short by tendonitis of the elbow. (National Baseball Library, Cooperstown, NY)

In 1963, Koufax remarked prophetically, "Who knows when it's going to end. I feel that if I could play till I'm 40 and be successful till then, I'd have everything I want. But the thought is always there that it might end quickly."

255

After three more equally incredible years, it was over for Sandy. Following the '66 season, tendonitis in his left arm forced him to leave the game he loved "while I can still comb my hair." But his early retirement didn't prevent his accomplishing what most pitchers have been unable to match, including becoming the youngest player to be inducted into the Hall of Fame at the age of 36. That Koufax was elected largely on the basis of four seasons' work is an indication of how overpowering he was during that relatively brief amount of time.

THE CHANCE OF A LIFETIME

S till suffering from the after effects of the appalling killing of President Kennedy in November of 1963, and the horrifying live broadcast of the alleged assassin's murder, a shaken nation sought distractions by spring of '64. The April opening of the World's Fair couldn't have come at a better time, or a more appropriate place for baseball — Flushing, New York, adjacent to the Mets' spanking-new Shea Stadium. Cassius Clay, who would become Muhammed Ali before the year ended, was showing expertise in throwing jabs with his left in the ring and with his mouth outside of it. Arnold Palmer strengthened his claim to king of golf with his fourth Masters title.

And the baseball season was never more welcomed, especially by American League fans who were brimming with confidence after seeing the mighty Yanks humbled by Koufax and company in the '63 Series. Managers, too, were optimistic. White Sox skipper Al Lopez boasted the "best pitching in the league," while the Tigers' Charlie Dressen stressed that the "Yankees aren't invincible."

Notwithstanding opponents' high hopes, the Bombers would win their final flag of the pre-Steinbrenner era.

One team perhaps lacking confidence in '64 were the expansion Los Angeles Angels. Owner Gene Autry may have wished he was back in the saddle again after his team lost over 90 games in two of its first three seasons. Adding to club miseries was questionable behavior on the part of two of its star performers. Jimmy Piersall, traded to the Halomen in mid-season of 1963, didn't waste time in displaying a well-known temper by knocking down an umpire in his second game. Pitcher Bo Belinsky was a talent, but playboy activities between starts often aggravated front office executives who believed his night life was a distraction, not only to him, but to a fellow fireballer and close crony.

Dean Chance

Righty Dean Chance was a strong, 6-foot, 3-inch, 200 pounder who won 14 games in his first full season in '62. He lost 18 in his sophomore year and was forced to accept the same salary of $20,000 in '64. Though Chance predicted he'd win 20, he had problems early on. After Pat Boone took time between glasses of milk to croon the National Anthem in the home opener, Chance was removed in the first inning due to an index-finger blister. He was sidelined for a couple of weeks.

But unlike roomie Belinsky, who self-destructed by punching a reporter in midseason, leading to his suspension and eventual trade, Chance had a banner year. He became one of two 20-game winners in the league, and his ERA of 1.65 was the lowest in over 20 years. (Some would argue that Spud Chandler's 1.64 of '43 is deceiving, since many of baseball's stars were in the service then.) Dean won the Cy Young Award in '64, the last American Leaguer to do so before the tradition of giving one per league began in 1967.

Most impressive of all was Chance's accumulating 11 shutouts. At a time when American Leaguers were crushing the horsehide, the Dean shut them down more often than any hurler since Walter Johnson's 11 of 1913 and was only a pair shy of Jack Coomb's

A.L. mark of 1910.

With some luck he would have shattered it. His blistered finger forced him to miss four starts. He fired 14 goose eggs against the Yanks in May before leaving the game with a no-decision. Dean was removed in a game against the Orioles in August after pitching six scoreless frames. The most convincing stat is that in eight of his starts he allowed only one run, and some could have been prevented with better defensive efforts.

Sportswriter Ira Berkow, in introducing Michael Fedo's book *One Shining Season*, wrote that there "comes a time in every man's life when he does something right, and not just right, but absolutely, indisputably, gloriously right."

In 1964, L.A. fans witnessed the Chance of a lifetime. Unlike Koufax, who had several brilliant seasons, Dean never delivered for the Angels again. In '65, his record dropped to 15-10, then to 12-17 in '66 before being traded to the Twins the following year. He won 20 in '67, including a no-hitter against the Indians, but also lost 14 and failed to finish more than half his starts. In his remaining five seasons, Chance accumulated a 34-35 record.

Chance's career cannot be characterized as exceptional, but supporters can point to his stupendous season of 1964 as being one of the greatest in hurler history. Opposing managers knew that when the flamethrower from Wayne, Ohio took the mound that year, their team didn't have a chance.

YOGI

Upon hearing of Yogi Berra's recent marriage, Tiger hurler Dizzy Trout shouted to the Yank catcher from the Detroit dugout, "Hey, Yogi. How does your wife like living in a tree?" The joke was reminiscent of another instance when a Bengal yelled to the home plate umpire who had inched closer to backstop Berra in order to get a better view, "Look out! Don't step on his tail!"

If frequent remarks eluding to a simian ancestry (of which even the press was guilty) hurt the squat 5-foot, 8-inch, 200 pounder with a dark complexion, thick eyebrows and prominent ears, Lawrence Peter Berra never let on. Perhaps hearing an inordinate number of insults throughout his life had rendered him immune. As a youth struggling to finish grammar school in St. Louis, Berra had often been the butt of teasing and taunting. His lunches of banana sandwiches served only to foster further comparisons with primates, and his easy-going personality and infectious smile also made him an easy target for good-natured kidding. As an example, his lovable nickname was acquired after watching a flick about India with some friends, who found one of the Hindu characters so humorously appealing that they promptly proclaimed their buddy as a "Yogi" as well.

Having dropped out of high school as a freshman in order to concentrate on ballplaying and earn income for his mom at such jobs as coal yard and shoe-factory worker, soda vendor and newsboy, Berra's limited command of grammar usage later made him easy prey for gags regarding his intelligence. Like the time he kidded Bill Summers about wanting to become an umpire. "The union wouldn't let you in," the veteran ump laughed. "You aren't smart enough to pass the tests."

In fact, "stupid Berra" proved to be an oxymoron, as Yogi was smarter than your average jock, to paraphrase the trademark line of Yogi Bear, a cartoon character purposely patterned after the popular player. Berra's shrewdness led to such financially beneficial endeavors as spokesman for a leading soft-drink company ("Say me-he for Yoo-Hoo," Yogi would advise in commercials), and a bowling-alley partnership with teammate Phil Rizzuto. (In a slump one year, Berra lamented, "I'm bowling 300, but batting .221"). His appeal helped land television appearances on *The Milton Berle Show*, *Sergeant Bilko* and *General Hospital*, where he was typecast as a brain surgeon. (Who says producers have no sense of humor?) If it was fun to laugh at him, Yogi probably found each trip to the bank equally humorous.

Berra's one-liners, known today as "Berrarisms," were as confusing and hilarious as Casey Stengel's more verbose double talk, or "Stengelese," though a few of Yogi's peculiar utterances have merely been attributed to him. As fictional as some may be, Berrarisms have become as cherished a part of baseball lore as Babe's appetite for hot dogs and Satchel's rocking chair.

Berrarisms took many forms. They were often redundant or contradictory. In explaining why he'd make a good Yankee manager when the team hired him in 1964, Berra stated, "I have observed from watching Houk and other managers." As leader of the Mets, he chastised a slumping Ron Swoboda who had been aping Frank Robinson's batting style, "If you can't imitate him, don't copy him." Offering his friend a reason for not wanting to eat at a restaurant, Yogi said, "Nobody goes there anymore; it's too crowded." Asked if he had enjoyed a recently-attended party, Yogi complained, "It was hard to have a conversation with anyone, there were so many people talking." While illustrating the difficulty in playing left field due to the low afternoon sun at

Yankee Stadium, he remarked, "It gets late early out there." Expounding on the attributes of his ballclub, the skipper bragged, "We have deep depth." Economist Berra once described 20th-century inflation by noting that "a nickel ain't worth a dime anymore." After being badgered by reporters in '85, the frustrated manager replied to an oft-repeated question, "I wish I had an answer to that because I'm tired of answering it." Explaining the significance of Opening Day, Berra once philosophized, "A home opener is always exciting, no matter if it's home or on the road."

Berrarisms at times exposed weak arithmetic skills. "I usually take a two-hour nap, from one o' clock to four," said Yogi in describing his activities prior to night games. Approaching a trio of players once, he greeted them with, "You guys make a fine pair." According to teammate Mantle, manager Berra once asked his pitchers to pair off in threes.

Soft-hearted Yogi might be unintentionally insulting. During an outdoor luncheon on a blistering hot day, the host mentioned to her not-so-eloquent guest how nice and cool he looked. Berra's reply, "Thanks lady, you don't look so hot yourself," was meant as a compliment.

Yogi would frequently give odd answers to questions. Asked once "What time is it?" he replied, "You mean now?" To the hypothetical query of what he'd do if he found a million dollars, Berra responded, "If the guy was poor, I'd give it back." A friend once wondered if he'd like to see a triple X-rated movie. Yogi wanted to know, "Who's in it?" At an Italian restaurant, Berra was asked how he'd like his pizza divided. He told the waitress to cut the pie into four slices because, "I don't think I can eat six." After returning from an opera, Yogi was asked for a review. "It was pretty good," he answered. "Even the music was nice." While Berra was reflecting on boyhood days, someone asked what he had liked most about school. His response: "When it was closed." When someone asked if he just had an audience with the pope, Yogi said, "No, but I saw him." A reporter criticizing Berra's production at the plate received the Berra rejoinder, "I ain't in no slump. I just ain't hitting." Asked how he liked his new house, the Jersey resident replied, "It's nothing but rooms."

Of course, Yogi's questions could be as ridiculous as his answers. On the road, he liked nothing better than to spend a quiet evening in bed with a good comic book. Fatigued from reading one night, Berra turned to roommate, teammate and doctor Bobby Brown, and asked, "How did yours come out?" Brown had just put down his medical book. While being introduced to Ernest Hemingway, Yogi was asked whether he was familiar with the writer's work. He shook his head, then politely inquired, "What paper are you with?" Appearing on a radio show, Berra was asked by the host to participate in a game of free-association. "I'll say a word and you respond with the first thing that comes to your mind." When his guest agreed, the host began by saying, "Mickey Mantle." "What about him?" Yog wanted to know. Advised by a teammate to use his brains at the plate, Berra wondered, "How can a guy hit and think at the same time?"

Berra might misconstrue the meaning of what he read. Given a check with "Payable to Bearer" written on it, Yogi requested a new one, explaining, "That's not the way to spell my name." Reading a newspaper feature about himself, Yogi was confused by the word naive. Turning to a nearby reporter for assistance, he became furious in learning that he had been labeled the lowest of scoundrels. The perplexed reporter asked to see the article, then appeased the yelling Yank by explaining that the word in question was naive, not knave as Yogi had pronounced it.

Berra couldn't help being funny. Angry that the water cooler in the Sportman's Park dugout wasn't working, Yogi cried out, "Why don't the owners break down and buy some new water?" Grateful for former Yank catcher Bill Dickey's coaching him on defense, Berra publicly thanked him for "learning me all his experiences." Commenting on a foreign dignitary's first visit to the U.S., the national pastime's ablest ambassador commented, "It could only happen in America."

Fortunately, like Ruth and Dean before him, Berra's conspicuous but delightful off-the-field remarks did little to cloak his reputation as one of the best of all time at his position, rated by analyst A. W. Laird in *Ranking Baseball's Elite* as the third-greatest catcher in history, behind Mickey Cochrane and Dickey, and ahead of such notable backstops as Johnny Bench, Carlton Fisk and Gary Carter. A case could even be made that Berra was the best. He holds regular-season major-league records for most years leading the league in games caught (8) and for most consecutive chances without an error (950), as well as World Series marks for most games played (75), most at bats (259), most hits (71), and most doubles (10). Neither Cochrane nor Dickey accumulated as many as Berra's three MVPs, and didn't duplicate Berra's five seasons of 100+ RBIs and 11 seasons of 20+ homers, missing another by one in 1959 when, as boyhood friend Joe Garagiola explained, "He couldn't keep his dear mom off his mind." (She died in early May.)

Berra was the antithesis of Ted Williams, refusing to let a pitch sail by without hacking at it. Yet, his lifetime average was a solid .285. He walked an average of only once every three games, and his strikeout rate was an admirable one every five games and only one every 18 at bats, compared with Williams' K rate of one every three games, one every 11 at bats.

Many scoffed at skipper Berra but he had a fine managerial career, if his 484-444 record and two pennants in six years is an indication. Actually, Yogi managed part of another season, but was fired by Steinbrenner after 16 games in 1985, in spite of the Boss's preseason promise that the job would be Berra's throughout the year. Justifiably bitter over George's reneging, Berra hasn't returned to Yankee Stadium since.

Yogi should reconsider his self-enforced exile. Though he might say otherwise, Steinbrenner isn't bothered by it, only Yankee fans are. Revenge would be sweeter for the Hall-of-Famer if he chose to appear at the next Old Timer's Day, then saluted the Yank owner with a gesture Reggie Jackson once used to greet Charlie Finley following a tape-measure homer — thumbing his nose.

MICK'S 500
FOOTER

E very baseball fan has a favorite memory. Mine came on a midsummer's day in 1964.

The Yanks were battling the White Sox at Yankee Stadium that afternoon, but it wasn't the closeness of the pennant race that mattered. Yankee games weren't about rooting for the home team. They were about following Mickey Mantle. I made myself comfortable on the living room couch, a bowl of pretzels and bottle of soda within arm's reach.

You could still watch ballgames on free TV, and WPIX had the best broadcasting trio in the business with Mel Allen, Red Barber and Phil Rizzuto. The Old Redhead was at the mike as Mickey stepped to the plate for his second try. The switch-hitting superstar hoisted a high one from the left side, prompting Barber to announce casually, "There's a hiiiiigh fly ball to deep-center." A relaxed tone was common for the laid back Southerner, but even with Barber a degree of excitement could frequently be detected at the prospect of a home run. There was none in his voice this time. Mantle flipped his bat in disgust in reaction to the can-of-corn as his drive soared to the cavernous area of the stadium. I decided to spare myself the pain of watching the putout. Time to get another Coke.

But I stopped heading towards the refrigerator as the Sox center fielder headed closer and closer towards the bleacher wall.

Barber hadn't said another word, not uncommon for broadcasters then wise enough to allow viewers to enjoy the action without obtrusive chatter. (Modern broadcasters may be more sophisticated and knowledgeable, but they're not as enjoyable as their predecessors.) As the ball disappeared above the black backdrop, a surprised Barber shouted (shouting for him, anyway), "That ball is out of here!" Red's home run call wasn't as dramatic as Allen's "Going ... Going ... Gone!" or as emotional as Scooter Rizzuto's "Holy Cow!" but it was wonderful nonetheless.

Memories are magnificent. Research can at times rekindle lost ones. Library microfilms reveal that the Chicago center fielder that day was Gene Stephens, playing in the final season of his 12-year career as a part-timer. At least two New York newspapers carried a photo of Stephens with his back to the wall, looking up at the unreachable sphere. The victim of Mick's monster drive was pitcher Ray Herbert. Herbert was a .500 career pitcher who peaked in 1962 with a 20-9 record, but won only six in '64 while dropping seven, including a 7-3 defeat that day.

The homer was measured at over 500 feet (I remember P.A. announcer Bob Sheppard's precise "501 feet"). *The New York Times* reported that the ball "cleared the bleacher screen 22 feet, 5 inches tall, and landed in the 15th row behind the 461-foot sign." It also correctly pointed out that the tape-measure blast wasn't Mick's longest, reminding readers of his 565-foot blow in Washington's Griffith Stadium in '53, the famed facade homer off Pedro Ramos in '56 which hit two feet from the top of the stadium roof in right (Said Mick later, "Even when I saw it, I couldn't believe it"), and a blast off the A's Bill Fischer off the same facade in '63 which Mantle claimed "was the hardest ball I ever hit."

Said Mickey in the clubhouse after the rocket off Herbert, "I never expected it to travel that far. I saw Stephens running as hard as he could. I still didn't believe it would clear the wall." Though reminding reporters that a strong wind helped the drive, Stephens was nevertheless impressed with Mantle's power, acknowledging that only the mightiest of sluggers could lift a ball that high.

Mantle had a single and another homer that day, slicing a more modest drive into the right-field seats in the eighth. He hit the second batting right-handed off southpaw Frank "The Beau"

Baumann, the 10th and final time in his career he'd connect from both sides of the plate, a major-league record until broken by the Indians' Eddie Murray in 1994.

The beneficiary of Mickey's power that day was a young Missouri righty named Mel Stottlemyre. With the Yank pitching staff struggling, general manager Ralph Houk had made the call the previous day for the promising sinkerballer with a 13-3 record at Richmond and sharp enough control to have allowed only 32 walks in 151 innings. It was a dazzling debut for Stottlemyre. He went the distance, scattering seven hits while allowing only one earned run, "pitching with a poise beyond his years," as sportswriter Arthur Daley observed. Stot would have a fabulous career which included three 20-win seasons, a 2.97 ERA and 40 shutouts, but his most significant season was in '64 when the rookie won nine in the final two months. His arrival that August was one of two turning points in the Yankees' pennant quest.

The game featuring Mickey's mammoth homer was played on August 12. A look at the standings after the win showed the Yanks 3 1/2 games behind Baltimore, 1 1/2 games in back of Chicago. Rookie skipper Yogi Berra was beginning to feel the heat from critics concerned about the Yanks' chances of grabbing a fifth-consecutive flag. A week after Mantle's explosion, Berra exploded at shortstop Phil Linz on a team bus for playfully exhaling into a mouth organ after a doubledip defeat in Chicago. Linz was fined $200. Whether or not some choose to believe today, the incident did "light a fire under us and shake us up," as Yank catcher Ellie Howard predicted it would the next day. They won 30 of their last 42, and finished a game ahead of the White Sox.

The homers gave Mantle a season's total of 25. Roger Maris also connected, his 18th of 26 in 1964, 35 fewer than his record amount three years before. Another homer-hitter that day was Harmon Killebrew, whose fortieth at Minnesota put him on a pace to match Maris' mark. The Killer faltered and finished with "only" 49 to lead the majors. Mantle hit a respectable 35 in 1964, his last outstanding season.

For nostalgia buffs, weekly Yankee afternoon telecasts began at 1:55 and generally lasted between two and two-and-half hours, while competing with such game show gems as *Password*, *To Tell The Truth*, *You Don't Say* and *Queen for a Day*, such enduring soaps as *Another World*, *General Hospital* and *As the World Turns* and repeats of such classics as *Bat Masterson*, *Trailmaster* and *Dobie Gillis*.

Aren't memories marvelous? Or as Yogi might say, it's fun reminiscing about things that already happened.

CHAPTER 58

EXTRA-INNING
UMPIRE

J ust as batters seem to prefer facing particular teams, umpires probably have favorites as well. For Ed Sudol, the Mets
couldn't have been one of them.

Sudol was behind the plate in the second game of a 1964 Memorial Day doubleheader at Shea Stadium, after umpiring at first
base in the opener which the Giants won in two-and-a-half hours.
Frisco built a 6-1 lead in the nightcap, but the Mets delighted the
57,000 spectators with a pair in the sixth, then tied it on a Joe
Christopher three-run blast which barely escaped the reach of a
leaping Willie Mays in center. The inches which separated glove
from ball would make possible the longest game ever played, and
umpired, in National League history.

The game remained deadlocked in the 14th inning when the
first two Giant batters reached base. Orlando Cepeda, whose steal
of home had helped win the opener, lined an apparent tie-break-
ing hit up the middle. Shortstop Roy McMillan stretched and
caught it, then caught the two baserunners by stepping on second and throwing to first. Thanks to the triple play, only the second
in the three-year-old-club's history, Sudol's work behind the plate
was prolonged.

Met manager Casey Stengel sent in Galen Cisco, normally a
starter, to relieve in the 15th. Cisco retired the side easily, but

the Giants' Gaylord Perry struggled in his second inning of work. New York had two runners on and might have ended it but for shortstop Jim Davenport's nifty glovework which helped turn two. When the Mets again threatened in the 17th with a pair on the basepaths, Davenport again saved the day by starting another dazzling twin-killing.

By about 11 p.m. and the 23rd inning, Giant manager Alvin Dark had been ejected by Sudol, Mays had played shortstop, and nearly 40 players had seen action in a game that was seven hours long. Cisco retired Frisco's first two batters, but Davenport drilled an opposite-field triple to right. Stengel ordered an intentional pass to the next batter, knowing Perry would be either forced to hit or forced from the game for a pinch-hitter. The Giants gambled on benchwarmer Del Crandall. Crandall responded with what may have been the highlight of an otherwise mediocre 16-year career — a ground-rule double to right which broke the deadlock. The Mets were set down by another usual starter, Bob Hendley, in the home half, disappointing the 9,000 loyal Met fans who had remained.

The marathon lasted 7 hours, 23 minutes. Including the first game, Sudol's work that day was eight minutes shy of being 10 hours long, still the longest doubleheader in history, with the 32 innings played, also a big-league mark. If it was a day to remember for Sudol, the Mets would oblige him with a few more.

The next one came on April 15, 1968. New York was in Houston's Astrodome in what promised to be a pitcher's duel between hard-throwing righties Tom Seaver and Don Wilson. Sudol had an easy time of it at first, as the game proceeded speedily. After nine innings, however, neither team had scored. Six hours, 14 innings and 10 relief pitchers later, the game remained scoreless. The Mets were retired in the 24th and finally lost in the bottom half when their shortstop Al Weis, who'd be a World Series hero one year later, let a double-play ball scoot between his legs with the bases loaded, allowing a grateful and relieved Sudol to walk off the Astroturf at about 1:30 in the morning.

The Mets hosted the Cardinals on September 12, 1974, and after the game ended, at 3:12 a.m. Sudol was saying, "Why does it always happen to me?" What happened was a seven-hour contest which lasted 25 innings, one short of the Boston-Brooklyn battle of 1920, with 13 pitchers and a total 50 players being used, a record 202 hitters going to bat, 15 dozen balls put in play, and five infield drags taking place (normally, the grounds crew sweeps the dirt surface once — in the fifth inning).

Things had appeared normal to Sudol in the ninth. Met starter Jerry Koosman held a 3-1 lead and had limited Cardinal hitters to four singles. With one out, Larry Herndon walked, and Ken Reitz suddenly tied it with a homer to left. As Commissioner Bowie Kuhn watched from his box, both teams repeatedly failed to score as innings and time passed. By 1:30 a.m. Sudol was in no mood for a dispute with Met manager Yogi Berra over his decision to allow St. Louis slugger Joe Torre first base on catcher's interference and booted Berra from the game.

Sudol's salvation again came in the form of a Met mistake. The speedy Bake McBride opened the Cardinal half of the 25th with an infield single. Righty-reliever Hank Webb, in an attempt to pick off McBride, threw wildly to John Milner. As the first sacker raced to retrieve the ball in right, McBride raced around the bases and headed home. Milner's throw to the plate arrived ahead of McBride, but catcher Ron Hodges dropped the ball. The Mets were retired in the bottom half, despite Brock Pemberton's first of what would become a total four career hits. As brief as was his two-year stint in the majors, at least Pemberton could boast of having participated in a record-setting marathon.

It was an honor Sudol would have preferred avoiding. His 7 hours, 4 minutes of work behind the dish included being hit with foul tips no fewer than five times. Groaned Sudol in the clubhouse, "This neck of mine feels like it's been in a collision with a brick wall."

The Mets were not yet through with their favorite arbiter. Sudol called another Met-Cardinal game on April 19, 1976, played this time at Busch Stadium. Although only 5,000 fans attended, millions watched the nationally televised game which might have ended in regulation had it not again been for Bake McBride's speed and a Met mistake. After fanning the first two hitters in the opening frame, Tom Seaver gave up an infield hit to McBride, who then stole second. A careful Seaver then walked Ted Simmons, but appeared out of the inning when Reggie Smith hit a drive directly at center fielder Del Unser. Unser misjudged the ball, allowing two runs to score.

The misplay cost Seaver the win and Sudol a good night's sleep. Seaver left the game with the score tied at three apiece in the eighth, and neither team came close to scoring again for the next eight innings. With two outs in the top of the 17th, Del Unser made up for his dismal personal performance (besides the boo-boo, Unser had gone zero-for-seven to that point) by driving one of reliever Mike Wallace's fastballs into the seats in right. Mets fireman Bob Apodaca ended it by easily disposing of the Cards in the home half, to the relief of Sudol and television broadcaster Howard Cosell.

Sudol umpired for another season, then retired in 1978 following 21 years of service. Ed's having worked in many lengthy games, mostly involving the Mets, earned him no bonuses, only a nickname — the "Extra-Inning Umpire."

We often marvel at the superb conditioning of our ballplayers, how they're able to take the field day after day for six months. Yet, umpires are equally durable and, unlike the players, work a full nine innings or more. The next time we're at a game which has dragged past midnight, let's show our appreciation for the men-in-blue by rising and giving a hearty shout:

"Long live the umpire!"

Unless, of course, they've been calling 'em against us, in which case the more traditional "Kill the umpire!" will suffice.

CHAPTER 59

THE SPOILSPORT

What do Barry Moore, Dave McNally, Mike Cuellar, Dick Bosman and Catfish Hunter have in common? Besides being former American League pitchers, all have reason to hold grudges against Cesar Tovar.

Tovar was the Minnesota Twins' answer to the A's Bert Campaneris. He batted in the leadoff spot, was an accomplished base stealer, and was comfortable playing anywhere on the field. In a late-season game in 1968, Tovar played all nine positions, matching his counterpart's accomplishment of three years earlier. Though Harmon Killebrew, Rod Carew and Tony Oliva were the major run producers for the Twins, Tovar's 45 steals and 99 runs-scored were instrumental in capturing the division title in 1969. His league-leading 36 doubles and 13 triples, along with 195 hits and 129 runs-scored were the key to the club's repeating in 1970. Tovar led the league with 204 hits in '71, helping him attain a career-high .311 batting mark.

Despite Tovar's obvious talents, a less palpable one led to his only major-league mark. The vexatious Venezuelan had a knack for hitting in the clutch and reaching base in games in which teammates were unsuccessful, as indicated by his having prevented no-hitters on five different occasions. The Reds' Eddie Milner is the only other ballplayer to have ruined as many masterpieces.

Tovar first played the spoilsport on April 30, 1967, in his second year as a full-timer. Southpaw Barry Moore had the better of Twin batters at the nation's capital until Cesar conquered the Senator in the sixth with a two-out single. Moore finished with a one-hit whitewash, the only shutout in an otherwise undistinguished career. If the near-miss was at first disappointing, Moore might have been consoled in hearing how the Orioles' Steve Barber and Stu Miller combined for a no-hitter that same day — and lost!

Baltimore appeared to have another no-hitter on May 15, 1969. Dave McNally had been the hottest pitcher on the Bird staff for the past year-and-a-half, having won 20 of 22 decisions, and was equally formidable that day in surrendering but two walks to the Twins entering the ninth. The Oriole lefty, who'd win 20 for the second of three-consecutive years in '69 and who attributed his success to pregame meals of filet mignon, had the support of the 11,000 fans at Metropolitan Stadium, who responded with an enthusiastic cheer after McNally inched closer to immortality by striking out leadoff batter George Mitterwald. Alas, the no-hit dream ended on a clean single to center by Tovar on the next pitch.

Tovar made another Oriole southpaw suffer three months later. On August 10, after Twins' manager Billy Martin had explained to reporters his reasons for mauling starter Dave Boswell outside a restaurant a few days earlier (boasted the feisty skipper, "He was out before he hit the ground,") his team was manhandled by Bird starter Mike Cuellar. The Cuban screwballer, victorious in four previous decisions and winner of 23 before season's end, breezed through eight hitless frames, helped in part by spectacular catches by outfielders Paul Blair and Don Buford. Their acrobatic saves went for naught as Tovar turned Cuellar's no-hit attempt into just another close call by singling to left-center on an 0-1 pitch to open the ninth.

One year later, Tovar spoiled Senator right-hander Dick Bosman's chance at making the record books, albeit in a far less painful manner than that experienced by McNally and Cuellar. Had Bosman known that Cesar's bunt single to open the August 11 game in Washington would be the only hit he'd yield, he might have reacted more quickly in trying to field it. Bosman faced the minimum number of batters thereafter and attained some measure of revenge by disposing of Tovar to end the game.

Jim "Catfish" Hunter fired a perfect game for the A's in 1968, and nearly had another as a Yank hurler on May 31, 1975. Throwing in front of a capacity crowd of 38,000 at Arlington Stadium, Catfish retired the first nine men he faced, preserved the no-hitter with a sparkling unassisted putout on a bunt attempt in the fourth, and was rescued that same inning by Graig Nettles, who gave a preview of future World Series heroics by diving and snaring a hot grounder, then throwing out the swift Willie Davis.

With two outs in the sixth, Hunter faced Tovar, who had been traded to Texas the year before. Catfish fell behind on the count, then saw his next delivery stroked to the outfield for the Ranger's first hit. Tovar's single and Toby Harrah's reaching base on an error, prevented Hunter from pitching an unprecedented second perfecto.

William Shakespeare philosophized that the world is a stage for each to play many parts. In the world of baseball, Cesar Tovar's greatest role was that of spoiler.

THE LAST
TRIPLE CROWN

Perhaps no player was more anxious to begin the 1967 season than Frank Robinson. The Oriole slugger was coming off his greatest year, having led the league in homers, RBIs, and batting average. No player in history had ever won back-to-back Triple Crowns. Robby felt he had a great chance.

On June 27, Frank slid hard into second baseman Al Weis trying to break up a double play. He arose with double vision. It disappeared a month later, but by then Robinson had missed 28 games. He ended the season with enviable stats of 30 homers, 94 ribbies, and a .311 average, but none were good enough to lead the league.

Yet, the A.L. would boast another Triple-Crowner in 1967 when Carl Yastrzemski batted .326 with 44 homers and 121 RBIs. Consecutive Triple Crowns had been seen only once before, when Lou Gehrig duplicated Jimmie Foxx's effort of 1933. (In '33, the National League's Chuck Klein also took a Triple, marking the only year in which players from both leagues won the Crown.)

As the '67 season headed into the final month, Yaz's dazzling fielding plays, like his ninth-inning robbery of Yank Tom Tresh to preserve a Bill Rohr no-hit attempt in April (which was foiled on an Ellie Howard single with one out remaining), and spectacular hitting, like his two-homer game in May highlighting a slugfest

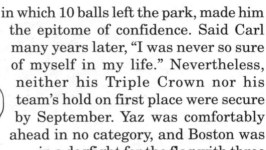

Carl Yastrzemski

in which 10 balls left the park, made him the epitome of confidence. Said Carl many years later, "I was never so sure of myself in my life." Nevertheless, neither his Triple Crown nor his team's hold on first place were secure by September. Yaz was comfortably ahead in no category, and Boston was in a dogfight for the flag with three other clubs. For the benefit of himself and the Sox, Carl would need a strong finish.

Considering the closeness of the race that year, it's not an exaggeration to state that Yastrzemski almost single-handedly won the pennant for Boston in September. When he smashed his 40th circuit off a Fred Lasher fastball a ninth-inning, game-knotter enabling Boston to win in overtime, he became only the fourth Red Sox to reach that plateau. He hit his 41st two days later off fireballer Sudden Sam McDowell, spoiling a shutout, then singled and scored the winning run in the ninth. After promising to hit number 44 for Sox hurler Jose Santiago in the next-to-last game, he connected off southpaw Jim Merritt, sealing the victory for Santiago, then had a double and clutch, game-tying single off hard-throwing righty Dean Chance in the pennant-clinching season finale.

Though he was an outstanding clutch performer throughout his career, it's doubtful he was ever better than in September of '67. Yaz batted .444 that month, .523 the last two weeks. He drove in 26 runs in the last 19 games, 20 in the last 15. He had 10 hits in his last 13 at bats, seven in his last eight. If owner Tom Yawkey had groaned while relinquishing over $100,000 in signing the son of a Long Island potato farmer in 1959, he wasn't griping in 1967 after Carl's super season led to Boston's first flag in over 20 years.

In terms of the 13 Triple-Crown seasons in history, Yaz's wasn't the most dominant. His .326 and 121 RBIs are below the average for Triple-Crowners of .362 and 133 RBIs, though his 44 homers

Carl Yastrzemski, shown hitting in 1967, had his first great season that year. It would be the greatest of his career. (National Baseball Library, Cooperstown, NY)

bests the norm of 36. Carl also falls short in comparison with other winners in outdistancing nearest challengers. His batting average was 15 points higher than runner-up Robinson, compared with the average 20-point margin; his RBI difference over Harmon Killebrew was eight compared with an average margin of 16; and he actually tied for the home run title with Killebrew, only the second instance in which a Crown winner shared one of the titles (Ducky Medwick took the Triple despite Mel Ott matching his 31 homers in 1937), whereas the norm is a seven-homer advantage.

Honors for highs in each particular category go to three different Crowners. Mickey Mantle's 52 homers in his Triple Crown season of 1956 is three better than Gehrig's in '34 and Robinson's in '66, four better than Foxx's in '33. Gehrig's 165 RBIs in '34 exceeded Foxx's league-leading total of the previous year by two, with no other Crowner coming close. Hornsby, who along with Ted Williams are the only players to win the Triple twice, batted

.403 in 1925, beating his own .401 in '22. Rogers' 1922 season is probably the most dominant in baseball history, as he comfortably outdistanced his nearest opponent in batting (by 47 points), homers (by 16), and RBIs (by 20).

If Yaz's Triple Crown wasn't the best, it holds the distinction of being the last. Not since 1909, when Ty Cobb first accomplished the most difficult of batting feats, has baseball gone as long without a Crown winner. In 1997, it's been 30 years since Yastrzemski's majestic season. If we never see another Triple Crown, perhaps it's fitting that the last one was so crucial to the outcome of the pennant race. As Yaz once admitted, "If I had my choice of a pennant or a Triple Crown, I'd take the pennant every time."

MILESTONE FOR
MAYS

G iants manager Clyde King was concerned. Having just
swept the Dodgers three straight in Frisco, his team held
the top spot in the newly formed National League West by
the barest of margins — half-a-game over the Braves, with only
a week remaining in the '69 season. Wanting to begin the vital
road trip with a win, King also realized the importance of doing
so against the Padres who, playing in their inaugural season,
were the worst club in baseball. A defeat against them would be
as bad as losing to the Mets! (In fact, being humbled by the Mets
would be a surprisingly common occurrence in 1969, with the
previously pathetic club winning their first division, pennant, and
Series flag that year.)

Yet, despite playing in a town where they were still undefeated,
in front of a hardly intimidating crowd numbering 4,000, Frisco
was locked in a 2-2 tie heading to the seventh. With the go-ahead
run on base and pitcher Mike McCormack due up, who could
blame King for looking to his bench, especially when one of the
prospective pinch-hitters was one Willie Howard Mays?

Mays hadn't started due to leg damage, a result of hustling to
third on a Stretch McCovey single which led to a tally in the one-
run victory over the Dodgers in the home finale. Prior to the
injury, Willie had been struggling. The pressure of reaching the

600-homer milestone after socking number 599 off Pat Jarvis nine days earlier was affecting the 19-year veteran, much as it had rival superstar Mantle when, after attempting for two weeks to belt number 500, he finally succeeded in May of 1966. For Willie, perhaps it was best he rest completely for one game.

Not best for King, who was feeling a different kind of pressure. With first place in the balance, the temptation to use his sore, slumping slugger was too overpowering to resist. If Mays couldn't run the bases, trotting would suffice if he could connect solidly. Certainly no better clutch homer-hitter ever existed than the man with the most career extra-inning blasts.

To those not familiar with Willie's batting style, he may have appeared nervous after straddling the dish and assuming his stance, repeatedly rocking the bat to and fro before finally cocking it, continuing to fidget with it while awaiting the pitch. Merely his method of timing the delivery. More likely it was rookie right-hander Mike Corkins who was edgy, faced with the most significant out of his career, though unaware of being moments away from securing his place in hardball history.

The ball carried 391 feet, easily long enough to clear the left-field wall at Jack Murphy Stadium, but its distance held further significance for Willie. The Adirondack Bat Company had promised their most famous endorser one share of stock for every foot number 600 traveled. The poke was worth $3,519.

Much more than that if you asked King, the blow being the decider in a 4-2 Giant victory. But San Diego finally beat Frisco the next day which, coupled with an Atlanta win, knocked the Giants into second place, where they remained until the season ended four days later. For the rookie manager, it wasn't a bad finish for a team that hadn't taken a flag in seven years. Nevertheless, King was canned two months into the 1970 season.

Naturally, the homer was worth more than a few grand to Mays as well, even if the sports car he also received is discounted. He became only the second batter in history to reach the 600-homer mark, the first right-hander. Aaron later matched him (and went on to reach a higher plateau), but Willie could boast of socking 600 first. True, he had a three-year head start over his contemporary, but Mays actually needed fewer games and at bats to make it.

Mays is congratulated by teammates after belting number 600 in September of '69. That's Stretch McCovey in the rear. (National Baseball Library, Cooperstown, NY)

"I knew I'd hit 600, but I was beginning to wonder when," a relieved Mays said in the clubhouse after the game. "The pressure was building up. I had been trying too hard to hit home runs." The future Hall-of-Famer, considered by many today to be the greatest all-around ballplayer in history, added a comment which disclosed a team-conscious mentality not unusual for ballplayers of his era and before. Said the Say-Hey Kid, "The big thing is that the homer won the ballgame." If that unselfish attitude remained with ballplayers in the decades that followed, it became increasingly less apparent to the baseball observer.

BALL FOUR
WAS FOUL

I n only his second season in the majors, Yank hurler Jim Bouton won 21 games with an ERA of 2.53, fourth-best in the league. In Game Three of the '63 Series that year, he pitched gallantly in losing 1-0 to the Dodgers' Don Drysdale. The following season, Bouton won 18 with an ERA of slightly over 3.00. He again started Game Three against the Dodgers, this time winning 2-1 on a ninth-inning upper-deck blast by Mickey Mantle and had another complete game victory four days later, forcing the Series to a decisive seventh game.

What better beginning to a career could any athlete expect? Unfortunately, the handsome Newark native with the hard overhand fastball would never again win more than four in one year. His competitiveness and determination, made apparent by the frequency in which his cap flew off on follow-throughs and the nickname "Bulldog" given him by teammates, weren't enough to compensate for lost mileage on his heater, overuse of a "palm ball" leading to an abundance of long balls, and inconsistency with a newly developed knuckleball. By 1969, the righty's 9-24 record and 4.00 ERA, accumulated during the previous four seasons, may have made him sleepless in Seattle following his trade that year, wondering whether the game would ever be as wonderful as the '63 Series when he felt "lucky to be out there, alive on a sunny day, laughing and having a good time."

No longer a success in his profession, Bouton decided to write about his experiences in baseball, exposing off-the-field details of the antics of past and present teammates. *Ball Four* not only became a best-seller, it "sold more hardcover copies than any sports book in the recorded history of the English-speaking language," to use Bouton's own words.

If his book was a financial success, it wasn't a hit with ballplayers. Most objected to Bouton's disclosing information regarding players' private lives, including acts of drunkenness and infidelity. Many criticized Bouton for making some players, coaches and managers appear intellectually inferior, as well as making inferences about their character. Even Bouton admitted as much when he wrote in the sequel *I'm Glad You Didn't Take It Personally*, "I don't blame Elston Howard for not liking *Ball Four*. I was tough on him." The black backstop had been portrayed as a hypocrite and Uncle Tom.

As Bouton continued with his baseball career, he encountered angry reactions. Players turned their backs as he approached, others openly cursed and threatened him. Managers insulted him, and teams banned the reading of his book. Commissioner Bowie Kuhn attempted to extract a public apology from Bouton, claiming the book was a "disservice to baseball."

Bouton's response was to laugh, while wondering what all the excitement was about. He shrugged off the traditional clubhouse motto of "What is said here, stays here," believing instead that "the clubhouse is not a CIA office. If what happens there gets out, no one will die."

If Bouton was truly surprised by the players' reaction, his naiveness exceeded the most outrageous childlike behavior he attributed to them. As one of Bouton's targets, Mickey Mantle, wrote in *All My Octobers* a quarter of a century later, "If the players resented the press for digging into our private lives, how were we supposed to feel when a teammate did it?" Bouton must have understood the ire his book would arouse. Aware that his playing career was near an end he wrote it anyway, but perhaps not only for the money.

According to some ballplayers, like Mantle, Bouton was never popular with teammates, even before he wrote his best-selling book. Former Yankee Stan Williams recalls in *We Played the Game* that the Bulldog "got too big for his breeches" with the Bombers. Another former teammate, Pedro Ramos, states in the same book that "Jim had a big mouth." Though Bouton denied "any sense of retribution," had he felt more comfortable around clubhouses, he might have felt more uncomfortable about writing *Ball Four*.

Bouton welcomed criticism of the book, thanking opponents such as sportswriter Dick Young for generating publicity, thus increasing sales. He defiantly refused Kuhn's apology request, while labeling him "the best commissioner in baseball today."

He was sarcastic in assessing Bowie, but the cynical scribe would have done fans (though not his wallet) a service by listening to "probably the most capable commissioner the owners ever had," as one historian rates Kuhn. Players began to be looked upon not as heroes but as sex maniacs, despite most being "straight arrows," as former pitcher Jim Brosnan maintained. And to be a ballplayer naturally meant you had a drinking problem and were stupid.

Suddenly, the games on the field became less interesting than the ones off the field. Readers were intrigued by autobiographies of players now willing to tell all for the chance of making big bucks. They were equally interested in books focusing on the personalities and lifestyles of past superstars. The media began to pay more attention to the clubhouse, less on the ballgame, eager to report any controversial occurrence.

Bouton's *Ball Four* benefited from the decade which preceded its publication in 1970, a period in American history known for its increasing lack of respect for authority and tradition, the reaction to an unpopular war and civil rights unrest. But if it was a time for change, need it have affected our national pastime? Was it so important that we learn about the transgressions and weaknesses of ballplayers? Would we have been harmed by continued belief in the absolute virtues of our heroes? If our childhood idols weren't perfect, did we have to be told about it? After all, this wasn't about Kent State or Watergate. It was about baseball, our way of escaping from the world's harsh realities.

America lost its innocence during the sixties. With the publishing of *Ball Four*, baseball lost its innocence as well, for which we have Jim Bouton to thank.

FIFTH OF JULY
FIRWORKS

T he Mets didn't need Ed Sudol as an excuse to play into the morning hours, as they showed on an Independence Day game in Atlanta in 1985. Only a year away from a world championship, New York was only slightly less impressive in '85 with a starting staff that included an at-his-peak Doc Gooden, whose 24 wins, 1.53 ERA and 268 strikeouts would lead the majors, and Ron Darling, whose 16-6 mark and 2.90 ERA that year would have made him the ace on most other staffs. In contrast, the Braves were a half dozen years from their first of many successful seasons in the nineties and would finish 30 games below .500 in '85, so that the nearly 45,000 who attended the Fourth of July night game were there as much to watch starter Gooden and owner Ted Turner's post-game fireworks as to root for slugger Dale Murphy and company.

Additional seats might have been occupied had the weatherman cooperated, as rain delayed the starting time for 1 hour, 24 minutes. Rick Mahler, who after the game would profess to have forgotten he had started for Atlanta, retired the first two Met batters, but Keith Hernandez doubled and was brought home on a Gary Carter single. The Braves tied it quickly in the bottom of the first, thus setting the tone for the hard-fought see-saw battle.

The Braves reached Gooden for a one-out single in the third.

Before Doc could deal another pitch the rains returned. Gooden didn't when the showers ended 41 minutes later. Roger McDowell relieved and surrendered a single and double leading to a pair of runs before retiring the side.

The Mets ambushed the Braves with four in the fourth, highlighted by a catchable drive off the bat of Hernandez which became a triple when Claudell Washington slipped on the wet outfield grass. Both teams exchanged single runs in the fifth and sixth, and Hernandez gave his club a 7-3 lead with a homer in the eighth. Fans began thinking about the fireworks.

The Braves showed them some firepower instead. In the bottom of the eighth, they reached reliever Jesse Orosco for two runs, then loaded the bases, leaving the chance to clear them for cleanup hitter Murphy. Atlanta's all-time doubles leader drove a two-bagger between the outfielders, driving in three and giving his club an 8-7 edge. But a one-run lead in the potential final inning wouldn't be enough on this night (as we'll see, two-runs wouldn't suffice either), as New York knotted it in the ninth on little Lenny Dykstra's big infield hit with a runner on third.

Both clubs were held scoreless in the next three frames, but the Mets snapped the tie in the 13th when Ray Knight, who in contrast to Murphy had failed with the bases loaded three times, stroked a two-out single off southpaw Terry Foster, then scored ahead of switch-hitter Howard Johnson's righty homer to left. It was late, but stadium personnel prepared the fireworks nonetheless.

Turner's team wouldn't cooperate. Rafael Ramirez opened the home half with a single and, two outs later, stared intently along with Met reliever Tom Gorman at Terry Harper's drive off a two-strike fastball which sailed down the left-field line. The ball hit the foul screen, and the game played on.

By the 17th inning, Hernandez, who'd hit for the cycle for the first and only time of his career that night, couldn't believe they were still playing ball past 3 a.m. As the Mets took their swings, he phoned his brother Gary from the clubhouse, feeling he "just had to call someone." Had Hernandez waited another hour, he'd have had much more to say.

New York was retired in the 17th, and so were manager Davey Johnson and slugger Darryl Strawberry after arguing a called strike with plate umpire Terry Tata. The Mets regained the lead the next inning, thanks in part to an error by reliever Rick Camp. Given a chance at redemption, Gorman quickly retired the first two Braves and needed only to dispose of Camp who, with no pinch-hitters remaining, was forced to hit for himself. Gorman threw two by the .074 lifetime batter, then fired another. Everyone watching expected the obvious, but what they witnessed instead was Camp's first career homer. For New York, the wrong pitcher had redeemed himself. For Atlanta, and the 10,000 loyal if not sane spectators still remaining, a fatal blow had again been narrowly avoided. It was on to the 19th.

Undaunted, the Met batters struck again. Gary Carter began the inning by drilling his fourth hit. A sacrifice and intentional walk gave Knight another chance to be hero, and the 10-year veteran took advantage with an opposite-field single to right. No longer content with a one-run lead, the Mets put four more on the board against Camp, who afterwards remarked that he "could care less" about his 18th-inning homer which had tied it.

Gorman undeservedly stood to be the winning pitcher if the five-run lead could be held in the bottom of the 19th. Met manager Davey Johnson, no longer in the dugout but still calling the shots, decided Gorman wasn't the man to try. Ron Darling was brought in to save the game, and save the few hours night's sleep remaining. The talented Met right-hander proceeded to load the bases with Braves and then yielded a two-run single to Harper. With two outs, Darling faced the potential tying run at the plate — Rick Camp. At 3:55, exactly 8 hours and 15 minutes past the scheduled starting time, Darling unleashed a two-strike pitch. Camp struck out. Turner then decided that the show must go on and the Fifth-of-July fireworks were ignited, a decision not entirely appreciated by Fulton County residents whose sleep had been interrupted.

What must the retired Ed Sudol have thought of his having missed umpiring yet another Met marathon?

CHAPTER 64

A ROSE BY ANY OTHER NAME

I n the spring of 1990, the baseball world was shocked by news that Cincinnati manager and longtime batting great Pete Rose was under investigation for gambling on ballgames. After subsequent months of sparring, highlighted by commissioner Bart Giammatti's accusations that Rose was in debt for a half a million dollars and had associated with various shady individuals, and Rose's lawsuit which challenged the commissioner's authority, a deal was struck on August 24 in which Pete agreed to drop the suit, Giammatti to drop the investigation.

Though a relieved Rose knew the settlement made forthcoming criminal charges for illegal gambling unlikely (but didn't know he'd be charged, convicted, and sent to prison for tax evasion), peace did not come without a price. The superstar who had appeared in more games (3,562), accumulated more at bats (14,053) and hits (4,256) than any other big leaguer, and who played with an enthusiasm that earned him the nickname Charlie Hustle, was banned forever from the game he so dearly loved. More bad news followed a year later when the Cooperstown election committee decided that this shoe-in for the Hall of Fame was no longer eligible due to questionable moral character.

One source hints at the committee's double standards in electing to the Hall "racists like Cap Anson, assailants like Ty Cobb, drunkards like Rabbit Maranville and Grover Cleveland Alexander, and numerous others who should have come up short of this criterion (moral character)," while banning Pete. A plausible defense of Rose is possible without having to attack past greats. Such seemingly repugnant individuals were far from being isolated cases during their playing days. Anson wasn't the only southern racist, nor Cobb the only violent athlete, nor Maranville and Alexander the only alcoholics. In the first few decades of the century, ballplayers were in fact notorious for bad behavior, which included betting on ballgames. Since then, baseball and American society have evolved to where racism, alcoholism and brawling are condemned often enough. Past players can't be blamed for actions which largely reflected the times. Modern ones should know better.

Pete Rose

But if there's one problem in which society remains lax in combating, it's gambling. If Rose wagered illegally, he too was far from an isolated case. Across the country, thousands of Americans hand over parts of their paychecks to bookies in bars every week. Newspapers do little to discourage, with daily lines on baseball, basketball, football or hockey games. One wonders whether the large majority of modern ballgames are played during prime time for the convenience of baseball fans or gambling enthusiasts.

And where is the justice when one of the game's greatest is banned for life for alleged criminal activity when today's players are repeatedly forgiven for proven criminal behavior? Is it because those in the upper echelons of the baseball hierarchy consider drug use to be less serious a crime than illegal gambling? Perhaps it's a reflection of today's society that drug offenders like Steve Howe and Doc Gooden are treated as victims, not criminals, and sympathetically permitted to continue their profession. Presidents talk tough about solving the drug problem in America, but results might improve if buyers become as equal a target as sellers.

Some point to the Black Sox scandal of 1919 as being a precedent for dealing tough with gambling offenders. Joe Jackson and company were permanently banned from the game for their part in fixing the Series of 1919, and the action was devastating to their economic futures. For sure, none could rely on making much by signing autographs or selling memorabilia, as Rose could. Since then, baseball officials have been outspoken about maintaining the "integrity of the game," careful to prevent any interference with clean competition (though their leniency towards drug offenders would appear to be a contradiction to that principle, since a player's using drugs inadvertently hurts his team's chances of winning.)

The Black Soxers' infraction was quite different from Pete's. They accepted a deal which guaranteed money from gamblers in return for deliberately playing poorly. If Rose gambled on Reds games while their manager, again something never proven, it's unlikely he bet against them or did anything shady to influence the outcome. This doesn't excuse breaking the law but, from a baseball perspective, made his action less threatening to the game's integrity. Certainly it provides a better reason for reinstating Rose than have proponents of Joe Jackson in demanding his Hall induction.

For one of baseball's most prolific, durable and fierce competitors to be forever barred from any association with the game is a harsh sentence for an unproven crime. For purposes of fairness, baseball officials have two choices — lighten up on Rose or toughen up on drug offenders. Common sense dictates doing both.

FROM LAST TO
FIRST

I n July of 1993, I appeared on a syndicated sports-talk show
publicizing the recently published *They Kept Me Loyal to the
Yankees*. As the hour interview came to a close, the radio host
declared, "Let's hope the Yankees finally win one this year," a
reasonable desire considering New York was occupying first place
at the time. Imagine his amazement when I came back with, "It
would be something if the Red Sox won it."

Neither the Yanks nor Sox would take the flag in '93, the Blue
Jays comfortably in first by season's end, but at the time Boston
was the hottest club and appeared to be the chief competition for
the Bombers. That fact, combined with the antagonism Yankee
fans feel for their traditional rival, made the animated host's irate
retort of "You're a Yankee fan?" quite appropriate.

On the surface, it would appear my statement belongs among
baseball's biggest bloopers. Yet, a logical explanation was offered,
either unheard or ignored by the animated interviewer. The Sox
had finished last in the standings the year before, and it seemed
historically significant that after going nine decades without a
club climbing from last to first in consecutive seasons, there existed the possibility that a third team in three years would turn
the trick. I hadn't said I wanted Boston to win, only that it would
be something if they did. Even the most ardent Yankee fan would

have admitted as much.

The Minnesota Twins were the first American League team to make the long, rapid climb. In 1990, mild-mannered manager Tom Kelly, a hero three years earlier when the Twins won it all, may have appeared too complacent for some after his team hit bottom for the first time in eight years. Not so in 1991, when the reborn savior led his team to the top for a second time.

Amazingly, the Atlanta Braves became the first National League bottom-to-top club that same year. Their pennant winning season of 1991 was more dramatic, however, since it followed not one, but three-straight basement finishes. The Battle of the Cinderellas in the Series couldn't have been more exciting. The trailing Twins prevailed by winning the sixth and seventh games, each going extra-innings.

Divisional play had begun in 1969. With fewer teams competing for first place, it was easier for the Twins and Braves to make the jump. That there have been other clubs which came close since '69 is not surprising. In the first season under the new format, the Mets took advantage by capturing the flag, thus detracting from a notoriety for ineptness previously earned with seven-of-nine last-place finishes. Their "improvement" to ninth in 1968, escaping the cellar by one game, prevented baseball's premiere worst-to-best franchise.

In 1990, the National League's oldest team had, not a revived manager, but a new one. Cincinnati's Lou Piniella replaced the banished Pete Rose, and his club responded by winning its first nine games in cruising to division, pennant, and Series victories. It was a terrific turnabout from the tumultuous '89 season, which saw the Reds finish fifth after a multitude of injuries to key players and the distraction of an ongoing gambling investigation had effectively disrupted team efficiency.

The Reds defeated the Eastern Division Pirates in the Championship Series of 1990. The Bucs' road to the top had been identical, winning their division after injuries led to a next-to-last position in 1989. They saved their best for last in '90, reeling off eight-straight wins to pull away from the Mets in September.

Though giant leaps to the top in two seasons have been nonexistent prior to divisional play, there have been a couple of near-misses. The Red Sox would have been the first to pull it off in 1967 had they been a wee bit more pathetic the year before. They escaped the bottom berth by being a half-game better than the Yanks. New York's first cellar finish in over half a century must have been a pleasant consolation for Sox fans.

Ironically, the Yankees were the first to nearly pull off the rags-to-riches miracle. In 1925, Babe Ruth's bellyache contributed to his worst season of the decade and, not surprisingly, his club did better than only one other (you guessed it, the Red Sox). Ruth had a more typical year in 1926, and the Yanks captured the flag. When Babe had a monster season in 1927, they easily won again. Despite the Ruth factor, it's hard to believe that a team, which most experts rate the greatest ever, came so near to finishing in the basement two years before.

I still maintain it would have been something had the Red Sox won in '93. I'm still glad they didn't.

CHAPTER 66

MR. OCTOBER'S SEPTEMBERS

A ccording to Reggie Jackson, some irony is connected with the origin of his celebrated nickname "Mr. October." Rival teammate Thurman Munson, still angry over insulting comments made by Jackson months earlier in a preseason 1977 magazine interview, first used it as a sarcastic stab following Reggie's two-for-sixteen performance in the championship series with the Royals, won by the Bombers in five games. When Jackson then exploded with five homers in the Fall Classic, three in the Series-ending sixth game, a far-different meaning to the nickname took root.

Unquestionably, the lefty-swinging Pennsylvanian with an ego as large as the muscles on his 6-foot, 200-pound frame was a preeminent post-season performer. In 27 World Series games, Jackson batted .357, nearly 100 points better than his career average and ninth on the all-time list of Series players, and he attained a record slugging percentage of .755. Reggie's 10 homers, 24 RBIs and 21 runs-scored are all among the top 10 as well. Not as successful during championship series competition, Jackson's six homers in 45 games nevertheless boosts his post-season total to 16. Mantle, with 18 Series homers, is the only player to have amassed more.

Mr. October thrived on hitting in the limelight, but the cameras would have focused elsewhere had his team failed to take the division during the regular season. Consequently, the question begs being asked: How big a factor was Reggie in September during the club's final drive for the flag? Was he a clutch performer in the month arguably even more significant, since participation in the league championships and World Series necessitates first winning the division? Does Reginald Martinez Jackson deserve the additional sobriquet "Señor September?"

Jackson's career September averages for four offensive categories appear below, along with his pre-September and career output. (Note: A few regular-season October games were played in most seasons and are therefore included among the "Post-August" averages.)

	HR rate	RBI rate	B.A.	S.A.
Pre-September	1/17.1 ab	1/5.8 ab	.264	.492
Post-August	1/16.7 ab	1/5.7 ab	.255	.479
Career	1/17.5 ab	1/5.8 ab	.262	.490

It would appear that Jackson's play in September wasn't particularly outstanding when compared with that of other months and his entire career. Though his homer rate was noticeably better than both, his RBI rate was about the same, while his batting and slugging averages were considerably lower. (To compute slugging percentage, divide the number of total bases on hits by the number of at bats.) Shall we conclude that Jackson didn't raise his level when it counted?

Not just yet. During his career, which began in 1967, Jackson at times played for non-contending ballclubs. He appeared in only nine September games in '67 when Kansas City finished the season in 10th place, and though he played the entire final month the following year, the relocated A's were again out of the running, though improving to sixth place. Oakland took second place in '69 and '70, but badly trailed the formidable Twins throughout September making the final month meaningless in both years. Following five division titles, Jackson said sayonara to antagonist Finley and played for a Baltimore club in '76 which finished 10 1/2 games behind the Yankees.

Helping those same Yankees to pennants in '77 and '78, Jackson had a solid September in '79, made meaningless by New York having already dropped out of the race by then. The Yanks rebounded to take the flag in '80, and though repeating in '81, it was the year of the strike-shortened split-season. Having already taken the first half, the Yanks finished below .500 in the latter half, holding sixth place by the end of September. In 1982, Reggie was an Angel when the franchise took the division flag, but the team was a distant fifth in '83. Following three-consecutive contending years, Jackson ended his career with the last-place Angels in '87.

A more accurate method of judging Jackson as a late-season clutch performer would be to review his September contributions playing for pennant-contenders. Listed in the following table are Reggie's pre-September and post-August stats for the dozen seasons playing for a contender. His career stats are again included as a basis for comparison.

	HR rate	RBI rate	B.A.	S.A.
Pre-September	1/17.4 ab	1/5.6 ab	.273	.504
Post-August	1/15.7 ab	1/5.3 ab	.251	.496
Career	1/17.5 ab	1/5.8 ab	.262	.490

Again, the stats are inconclusive. Jackson's homer rate was far better during the final month, and his RBI rate slightly superior. Yet, his post-August batting average was dramatically worse, while his slugging percentage, though higher than his career mark, was lower than his pre-September average.

A look at post-August stats from each contending season may be helpful, and are listed on the opposite page. You'll note that Jackson socked six or more homers and had 16 or more RBIs in nine of the dozen seasons, attaining a slugging percentage over .500 in six of those nine years. Still, his batting average was below his career mark in six of the nine seasons, under .220 in three of them. Reggie's September performance in the other three seasons, from 1972-1974, can be described as poor, and though the A's were impressive during that span, capturing three World Series flags, they clinched the division late each year, so that it cannot be suggested the final month was merely a formality.

Judging from the chart, we can confidently conclude that Jackson was a superb September contributor in 1971, 1977 and 1980,

Jackson's Post-August Stats From Pennant-Contending Years

Year	Games	At Bats	Homers	RBIs	Batting Average	Slugging Average	Team Position
1971	26	101	7	19	.307	.554	First
1972	30	110	3	11	.282	.427	First
1973	18	53	1	12	.245	.377	First
1974	25	86	2	10	.209	.314	First
1975	25	94	7	16	.191	.457	First
1977	28	100	10	29	.310	.660	First
1978	29	108	8	25	.241	.481	First
1980	29	101	7	18	.307	.604	First
1982	31	104	7	17	.260	.548	First
1984	28	105	6	18	.190	.371	Second
1985	28	89	7	18	.236	.528	Second
1986	24	77	7	18	.219	.521	First

and was very helpful in 1978, 1982, and 1985. Reggie produced the late-season long ball in 1975, 1984 and 1986, but also hurt the Angels with a pitifully low batting average. As mentioned in the previous paragraph, Jackson wasn't a factor in the other three seasons, perhaps a detriment.

Jackson's September homer totals were impressive, averaging five a month in 21 seasons, six a month while playing for contenders. Yet, stats can be deceiving. Six of his 72 homers during contending years came after his team had already clinched or been eliminated from the division race, and at least a dozen others came with his club leading or trailing badly, hardly clutch clouts. Jackson's blasts usually came early in the game when the pressure was off, his pre-fifth inning homers outnumbering his post-fourth frame wallops by nearly a two-to-one margin.

That's not to imply that Jackson didn't have his share of clutch September round trippers. In 1971, his 10th-inning homer off the Twins' Pete Hamm on the 11th won the game for the A's. Reggie's two-run, ninth-inning belt on a full count pitch won it for the Yanks on September 14, 1977. With the Angels trailing by one in the eighth in a 1986 game, Jackson hit a two-run homer, the game-winner clinching a tie for the division.

Jackson had other late clutch hits for contenders. His eighth-inning two-run double in mid-September of '71 scored the only Oakland runs in a 2-1 squeaker. In 1978, Jackson stroked an RBI single in the eighth to break a 1-1 tie, giving the Yanks a much-needed win on the 29th, enabling Bucky Dent to play hero in a one-game showdown with the Red Sox three days later. On September 18, 1982, Jackson singled and scored the winning run in the ninth for the Angels, and his eighth-inning sacrifice led to Brian Downing's scoring the winning run one year later.

Jackson often provided his club with early leads. Fifteen of his September homers for contenders were the first runs of the ballgame. At times, he would break open games single-handedly. In 1975, his two homers were the spark in a 13-2 division-clinching rout on the 24th. Jackson's first-inning grand slam on September 29, 1977 helped the Bombers coast to victory and clinch a tie for the flag. In 1986, one season before retiring, Reggie became only the third 40-year-old player in history to have a three-homer game (Ruth and Musial being the others) when he blasted a trio on the 18th, with the Angels reaping the benefits of Jackson's power surge in an 18-3 laugher.

But what Jackson gave, he often took away with sloppy fielding, foolish baserunning, and a proficiency for fanning. (When asked in 1986 how he felt about Reggie's surpassing his career total of 536 homers, Mantle retorted, "He passed me on the all-time strikeout list a couple of years ago and nobody asked me about that.") Jackson fanned three times in a meaningful September game on seven occasions, and in three instances whiffed four times. In a 1980 contest, he struck out three times, stranding six runners, fanned four times the following day leaving a total of seven men on base, and two weeks later whiffed with the bases loaded in the eighth in a 4-1 Yankee loss. On September 9, 1985, Jackson was called out on strikes in the ninth with the go-ahead run on third and one out, as the Angels lost to the Orioles in the bottom of the inning. A year later, California lost in extra-innings after Reggie had failed to make contact with runners on second and third in the seventh frame.

Jackson frequently showed peculiar judgment in baserunning. In a 1977 game, he was nailed trying to go from second to third on a grounder to short, was again thrown out at third two innings later while attempting to advance two bases on a single, and was picked off first base the next day. He was equally untrustworthy on the field. On September 21, 1977, Jackson's outfield error allowed a run to score in a 4-3 Yankee defeat. In 1980, Jackson's 10th-inning boo-boo resulted in two go-ahead runs for Toronto, and he was equally charitable to the Canadian ballclub two years later when his 12th-inning dropped ball cost the Angels a game in the standings.

Researcher Walt Wilson, in providing many of the stats for this chapter, noted that Jackson's eighth-inning solo blast giving the Yanks a 5-2 lead in the 1978 playoff game against the Red Sox and which turned out to be the winning run is a somewhat forgotten blow in comparison with Dent's three-run drive over the Green Monster at Fenway which catapulted the Yanks to the lead an inning earlier. True, but Jackson had previously gone hitless in three at bats while his club was trailing, his late-game homer coming when the pressure was not nearly as intense. His contribution that day typifies his career as a September performer — an important but not necessarily key contributor, and not one which warrants a regal title similar to his deserved Mr. October.

INTERVIEW WITH A RECORD-SHARER

Cincinnati-born Karl "Tuffy" Rhodes played in the minors for seven years. He was brought up to the big leagues in 1990 by Houston. He was traded to the Cubs in 1993.

On April 4, 1994, in a game against the Mets in Chicago, Tuffy became the first National Leaguer in history to hit three opening-Day homers. (George Bell is the only other major-leaguer to do it.) Since he had homered in his final at bat the year before, Rhodes became the 22nd player in major-league history to hit four baggers in four consecutive at bats. (As of this writing, he is also the last player to hit four-straight.) Six weeks later, Tuffy spoke with me on the telephone about his record-matching performance prior to his taking the field under the Wrigley lights:

My first career homer came in my first season in 1990. The funny thing is that I hit it against the team I'm with now, the Cubs, and at Wrigley Field where I had that big day this year.

In the last game of the '93 season, I hit the first of four-straight off Marc Davis in my final at bat. Actually, that wasn't the first time I ended the year with a homer. In Triple A, I homered in my last at bat of the championship series.

When I hit the three homers on Opening Day this year, I wasn't really trying for a homer in any of those at bats. The only time I might have been trying to hit one out was in my final at bat in the ninth. With the fans hollering for me to get the fourth one, I guess I got caught up in the excitement and swung for the seats the first couple of pitches. But then I settled down and just tried to hit a line drive.

I wasn't really aware that I had a chance to set a new record of five-straight homers though. It wasn't until after the game in the clubhouse, when everyone was telling me that I tied the record, that I knew anything about it. All I cared about at the time was helping the team win the game. I took a lot of kidding from my teammates after the game, too. Some of the guys were calling me Babe Ruth or saying things like, "Thanks for showing up the team." But it was all in fun.

The first homer I hit that day was off a curve ball, but the next two came off fastballs. I felt very comfortable at the plate each time up. Again, I wasn't trying for homers just trying to make contact. I'm especially proud that all three homers came off as great a pitcher as Doc Gooden. I have the utmost respect for Doc. He's got such great pitching ability. I was just fortunate to get three pitches I could handle.

After the three homers, I came to bat in the seventh facing Eric Hillman. He tried to get me to nibble at a bad pitch, but I didn't go for any of them. He kept the ball away from me with a couple of sliders and fastballs, and I took them all and took my walk to first.

In the ninth, I got a single off John Franco. I was quite satisfied, even though I lost the chance to hit four in one game. It gave me four hits in four at bats, and more importantly, gave the team a good start to the inning. At the time, we were down by four runs and a homer wouldn't have meant much. We still would have been down by three runs. As I said, I did lose my focus a bit on the first two pitches, but after I swung for the seats, I stepped out, took a deep breath, and told myself to try to just hit the ball back up the middle. Actually, I feel my last two at bats, when I walked and singled, were my best of the game as far as keeping focused on what I wanted to do.

Even though I'm off to a fast start with the long ball this year (Tuffy had seven in the team's first 33 games), my hitting philosophy won't change. I'm just going to try to make good contact

The Cubs' Karl "Tuffy" Rhodes. (National Baseball Library, Cooperstown, NY)

with the ball and not think about hitting home runs. I'm more concerned with the things I can do to help the team win, like maintaining a high batting average and on-base percentage and scoring a lot of runs. If the homers come, that's a plus, but I'm not

311

going to worry if they don't.

I'm proud that I share the record with such great players as Gehrig, Foxx, Williams, Kiner, Mantle and others. Those guys were all great hitters, Hall-of-Famers, but I hope the fans don't overexpect and will understand that the game is tough enough to play without more pressure being put on than is given to you already.

CHAPTER 68

GEHRIG'S CURSED STREAK

O n the evening of September 6, 1995, in Baltimore, a roar
filled Camden Yards for 22 minutes as Number Eight trotted around the ballpark on a victory tour. Not surprisingly,
President Clinton and Vice President Gore were among the cel-
ebrants, perhaps hoping to benefit from Cal Ripkin Jr.'s popularity.
After all, it wasn't every day that a player competed in his 2,131st
consecutive game.

Ripkin's record streak was a remarkable achievement in durability and dedication, made more apparent in an era when
players prefer the bench to the field due to the slightest injury.
Furthermore, this was not simply a case of putting in time.
During the 14-year run, Ripkin won two MVPs and two Gold
Glove Awards. Most noteworthy was that the streak surpassed
a legend's most renowned, though not greatest, accomplishment.

In *The Biographical History of Baseball*, Lou Gehrig is correctly
labeled "the most underrated player in the history of the game,"
suggesting as the reason his having such noticeable teammates
as Ruth and DiMaggio. The authors also hint at a less obvious
cause when stating that "He is almost always thought of as the
Iron Horse whose consecutive game streak was ended by a disease later named after him."

Gehrig played in his first game in 1923, but his streak began two years later when he pinch-hit on the first of June. He remained in the lineup for 15 years before voluntarily removing himself from a game at Detroit on May 2, 1939, realizing it was physically impossible to continue.

That the streak was snapped by a disease which would prove fatal only added to its legendary status. The impossibility of it being surpassed became accepted dogma among baseball experts. His having played in 2,130 consecutive games became more noteworthy than his accomplishments during that span. Lou Gehrig was the Iron Horse, owner of the unbreakable record for endurance.

So when Ripkin surpassed Gehrig, the inevitable comparisons began. If a Hall-of-Famer's greatest achievement was surpassed, doesn't logic dictate the new record-holder deserves equal recognition? Wasn't the streak even more difficult for Ripkin, playing in an era when additional teams and a longer schedule made travel more tedious? Wasn't the shortstop position, often a target of sliding baserunners, more conducive to injuries than the first-base job? True, a healthy Gehrig may have continued playing for several more years, but neither was Cal finished with his streak after breaking the mark.

In regards to their streaks, comparisons between Ripkin and Gehrig are justified. Both did well to take the field on a daily basis for so long a period, often disregarding illness and injury. How ludicrous, however, to suggest that Cal was Gehrig's equal in any other aspect.

As of this writing, Ripkin is approaching the end of what has been an exceptional career. Some regard him as the greatest shortstop in history, a claim not totally outrageous despite such superior batters as Honus Wagner, Arky Vaughn, Joe Sewell, Luke Appling and Joe Cronin. Nevertheless, Ripkin was never a superstar in the class of a Gehrig, a fact easily proven by statistics.

Cal never led the league in homers, RBIs, or batting; Lou led in batting once, in homers three times, in RBIs five times. Cal ripped 30 or more homers once; Lou did it ten times, nine consecutively. Ripkin drove in more than 100 runs three times; Gehrig 13 times, all consecutively. Ripkin hit better than .300 three times; in his 17-year career, Lou missed the .300 mark only three times, twice

Delirious fans celebrate after Cal Ripkin appears in his record-breaking 2,131st consecutive game.

in his final two seasons when the debilitating disease hindered his ability to perform. Ripkin never won a Triple Crown, nor is among a handful of players to hit four homers in one game, nor played in as many as seven World Series. He doesn't hold records for most career grand slams, RBIs in a season, or total bases in one game. Ripkin's career totals won't come remotely close to Gehrig's .340 average (15th on all-time list), .632 slugging percentage (3rd), 1990 RBIs (3rd) or 493 homers (16th). The most telling stats are Ripkin's totals from his greatest season in 1983. His .323, with 34 homers and 114 RBIs would have been an off-year for Gehrig, who in his 14-year career as a full-timer *averaged* .340, with 39 homers and 141 RBIs.

GEHRIG AND RIPKIN AS COMPARED WITH LEAGUE AVERAGES			
	Years	Batting Average	League Batting Average
Gehrig	1925-1938	.340	.282
Ripkin	1982-1993	.277	.262
	Years	Avg. Hrs/ Season	Avg. Hrs/ League Leader
Gehrig	1925-1938	35	49
Ripkin	1982-1993	23	43
	Years	Avg. RBIs/ Season	Avg. RBIs/ League Leaders
Gehrig	1925-1938	141	164
Ripkin	1982-1993	90	129

Ripkin loyalists might maintain that it was easier for Gehrig to accumulate better numbers in an era known for its hitting. Listed above are the career batting averages of both players, along with their season average for homers and RBIs as a regular (in the case of the still active Ripkin, until 1993). They are compared with league batting averages for the corresponding periods, as well as the average homers and RBIs by league-leaders during that span. Gehrig rates the significantly more productive batter, even when both are compared with contemporaries.

When Ripkin retires, his consecutive-game streak will be his greatest achievement. Gehrig's wasn't his greatest achievement, only the most famous. Sadly, he will now be remembered by many as the man whose sublime streak was snapped by Cal Ripkin, Jr.

DON WAS
A DANDY

D ave Winfield was recognized as one of the best hitters in
baseball by 1984, but had never won a batting title in his
dozen years in the majors. Now, with one game remaining
in the season, the 6-foot, 6-inch slugger held a two-point lead
over 23-year-old teammate Don Mattingly.

Mattingly was finishing his first season as a Yankee regular.
The lefty-swinging Indianan, who played Little League in his
youth and was a three-sport high-school star in his home town of
Evansville, was a 19th-round draft selection and played in the
Yankee farm system for five seasons. He was batting .340 in Columbus in 1983 when the big club called him up on June 20, his
roster spot replacing that of longtime Yankee Bobby Murcer. (As
a rookie, Murcer had been heralded as the "next Mickey Mantle,"
but the Oklahoman's career, though impressive, fell considerably
short of his club's optimistic prognostication.)

Don impressed more with the glove than with the bat in his
first year, seemingly incapable of pulling the ball or hitting with
power. He ended the season with only four homers and a .283
average. Secure in the spring that the first-base job was his,
the sophomore blossomed in 1984, leading the league in hits
and doubles going into the final day, as well as gathering 23
homers and over 100 RBIs. To steal the batting crown in the

curtain-closer would be the perfect ending to a grand season.

Winfield was popular during his nine years with New York, but the crowd at Yankee Stadium appeared to be on Donnie's side on September 30, especially after he stroked hits in consecutive plate appearances. Winfield failed in his first two tries, then managed one hit in his final two chances, dropping his average one point to .340. Mattingly finished with a flourish, slicing two more hits to boost his average to .343 in taking the title.

What had appeared to be a dream season was only the beginning. Mattingly was even better in 1985, leading the league with 145 RBIs, the league's highest total since Cleveland's Al Rosen drove in the same number in 1953. He led the league in doubles and total bases, collected over 200 hits, socked 35 homers, batted a healthy .324 and won his first of nine Gold Glove Awards in winning the American League MVP.

The next year, the Hit Man led the league with 238 hits, the A.L.'s eighth-highest total in the century, as were his 53 doubles, his third-straight season leading in that category. Don's slugging percentage and total bases were also a league-best, and his .352 average would have been good enough to take the batting crown in most seasons, but Wade Boggs was five points better in 1986. Mattingly again topped the 30-homer and 100-RBI marks, making him the only player in junior-circuit history to do so while collecting as many as 238 hits.

Donnie Baseball's phenomenal career continued with 30 homers, 115 RBIs, and a .327 average in 1987. Though he failed to lead the league in any category, he matched Dale Long's major-league record of homering in eight-consecutive games during a July power-surge that ended in Texas on an opposite-field double in his last at bat. He tied another mark the next day with 22 putouts at first base, and belted a still-standing record six grand slams by the end of the year.

Mattingly showed signs of fading after the '87 season. His average slipped to .311 in '88, to .303 in '89, his homer totals to 18 and 23. He drove in only 88 runs in '88, though he rebounded with 113 the next year. A combination of back problems and hurlers adjusting their strategy by using more off-speed pitches were the main factors contributing to the decrease in production which continued into the next decade. From 1990-1995, Donnie hit .300

only in the strike-shortened season of 1994. Not once did he manage as many as 20 homers, nor as many as 90 RBIs. He remained the best fielder at his position, but was little better than ordinary with the stick.

Throughout his career, even during the struggling seasons, Mattingly was known for an admirable work ethic and affable attitude towards fans. He'd spend hours daily at the batting cage, working on a variety of stances. Don would spurn card show appearances, freely offering autographs instead. His style of play was characterized by a boyish enthusiasm which seemed an anachronism alongside major-leaguers often displaying little emotion. Once, after a vain attempt to catch a foul fly near the stands, Mattingly reached into a boy's popcorn bag for a midgame treat, leaving the awe-struck youngster with a delightfully unforgettable moment.

The man selected as Yankee captain in 1991 had a flair for the dramatic even during the lean years, often winning games with late-game homers and RBIs. In 1995, his stats of seven homers and 49 ribbies were the lowest of his career as a full-timer, but he rekindled memories of the old Mattingly in his premiere performance in post-season play. His late-game RBI single helped the Yanks defeat Seattle in Game One, and his homer helped them win the next day. After losing the next two in Seattle, the Bombers were deadlocked in the sixth inning when Mattingly rocked a two-run double, which went for naught when a nervous David Cone later walked the lead away, and Edgar Martinez rocked Jack McDowell with a series-ending hit.

Following the '95 playoffs, an impatient George Steinbrenner wanted change. Longtime Yankee general manager Gene Michael was replaced by Bob Watson, and the popular skipper Buck Showalter gave way to Joe Torre. Randy Velarde, with the club for eight seasons, was gone, as was the productive, power-hitting catcher Mike Stanley. Mattingly had hinted at retirement during the season, and by late fall, Steinbrenner hadn't sufficiently convinced him that he was still wanted. With some reluctance, Don announced he wouldn't be returning with the Yankees in 1996.

There will be some debate as to whether his career stats justify Mattingly's induction into the Hall of Fame. Should he remain retired (as of this writing, his return was a possibility), his lifetime stats of .309 average, 222 homers and 1099 RBIs don't warrant his inclusion. Yet, what must be considered is that for four-consecutive seasons, from 1984-1987, Don was the dominant hitter in baseball. (Boggs' average for those seasons was higher, but his power numbers weren't even close.) During those years, he set records, took a batting and RBI crown and won an MVP. For the two seasons that followed, Mattingly continued to pro-

Don Mattingly was a dominant hitter from 1984 to 1989, but his stats fell sharply during the '90s. (National Baseball Library, Cooperstown, NY)

duce, though not as spectacularly, and was runner-up to Ruben Sierra in RBIs in 1989. Those who remember the mediocrity of the second half of Mattingly's career shouldn't ignore the magnificence of the first half.

There was one other incredible Mattingly achievement. His reasons for leaving the Yankees in 1995 were vague, prompting much speculation immediately afterwards. The question, however, shouldn't have been why Mattingly chose to end his employment with Steinbrenner, but instead, what took him so long? There are many enviable records in baseball, but Donnie's playing an unprecedented 14 seasons for the overbearing owner isn't one of them. By itself, that amazing accomplishment rates Number 23 a spot in Cooperstown.

CHAPTER 70

THE TRAGEDY OF
MICKEY MANTLE

Actor Peter Falk is best known for his television role as a quaint police detective, but one of his most memorable performances, for this writer at least, came when he abandoned the drab suit and short cigar of Lieutenant Columbo to play the part of a man stricken with cancer who becomes involved with a lady with the same deadly disease. The tearjerker's climax, which has his friend dying first, is followed by a poignant finish in which a grief-stricken Falk, furious at the injustice of life, trods in a daze along a quiet street wielding a baseball bat, bashing side windows of each of the parked cars along the way.

So it was with Mickey Mantle. Unable to cope with the early deaths of family members, and fearful that cancer would claim him as well, Mantle reacted by bashing through life. He didn't bash car windows. He bashed baseballs, hitting them farther than anyone else. He bashed his own, already vulnerable body on the field with hard slides and hustle on the basepaths, though he had the best excuse for taking it easy. Off the field, he bashed his body as destructively, if not as admirably, by drinking heavily, knowing that cancer would beat a damaged liver in the race for his life, drinking as if there was no tomorrow, or that his last tomorrow would be coming too quickly.

So when he was informed by doctors in the summer of 1995 that he had cancer, the only surprise for Mickey was that the number one killer in the country, outside of heart disease, hadn't struck until he was 63 years old. He had joked that if he knew he'd be living as long as he did, he'd have taken better care of himself. Now, the nightmare had become reality.

A valiant attempt was made to save him. On July 8th, Mick was given a liver transplant. News reports were optimistic, but doctors were aware even before the operation was complete that the cancer had spread throughout his body, and that Mantle had little hope of recovery.

Mickey had always feared death, but he faced it bravely as it creeped closer. His deathbed acceptance of Christ comforted him, and eased the mind of preacher and former teammate Bobby Richardson, who reported that Mickey told him the news "with a smile on his face." He died on August 13, barely two months after the transplant. Said Richardson at the funeral, "Mickey is now in God's Hall of Fame."

Mantle speaks to reporters a month after his liver transplant. Mickey died one month later. (AP/Wide World Photos)

He died even a greater hero than before. His last recorded message to Yankee fans at Old Timers' Day in July had included "Don't be like me," reminding everyone of the dangers of alcohol abuse, and "Be a hero. Be an organ donor," bringing the virtually ignored issue of the need for donations to national attention.

But Mantle's death carried with it a tragedy. It wasn't that his 63 years was a dozen shy of the average life span, for few people who died at an older age accomplished as much. It wasn't that he drank himself to an early death for, as doctors reported afterwards, his drinking wasn't what killed him, though it may have if cancer hadn't interfered. Nor was it the fact that Mantle's gloomy prognostication had been correct after all.

The tragedy of Mickey Mantle is that this greatest of sports heroes, whose death more than a quarter of a century following his last game made the front page of every major newspaper, whose funeral was covered by major television networks, who remained the focus of news and talk shows weeks after his passing, this man who had touched the lives of so many Americans, died thinking himself a failure.

Mantle died with the irrational notion that he hadn't performed well enough in baseball, that if he had taken better care of himself he would have done better. As if 536 home runs, a near-.300 career batting average, four homer titles, a Triple Crown, two 50-homer seasons and more World Series homers than Babe, Reggie, or anyone else who'd claim the title Mr. October, all accomplished with a body so battered with leg injuries that his own team doctor acknowledged it was a miracle he performed as well as he did, wasn't good enough. Mantle died convinced that he failed as a husband and father, forgetting, as teammate Tony Kubek once tried to explain, that travel demands placed on ballplayers make it difficult for them to be there for their families. Mantle died thinking he hadn't been a good role model, unaware of how fans marveled at his courage in limping through 18 painful seasons.

Perhaps it was because Mantle was always hard on himself that in the end he belittled his skills, and ignored the positive influence he may have been for his family, and certainly was for the public. Or was it that Mantle was impressionable, unduly influenced by the criticisms of writers and commentators, who zealously point out players' faults, as if their own lives are beyond reproach?

The truth is that Mantle was nowhere near a failure as a ballplayer. And no one — not friends, writers, not even Mantle, could judge whether he failed as a family man better than his wife and kids. Let them be the ones to decide, in the privacy of their own minds and hearts.

At Mantle's funeral, Roy Clark sang his classic hit of the '70s, "Yesterday When I Was Young," a last request from his dying buddy. The song relates how a man in his late years ruefully reflects on a life filled with wasted opportunities. It concludes with:

"There are so many songs in me that won't be sung.
I feel the bitter taste of tears upon my tongue.
The time has come for me to pay
For yesterday when I was young."

Poor Mickey. He never understood how enormous was the joy his life gave to millions of other lives.

CHAPTER 71

BASEBALL THEN AND NOW

S everal years ago, I sent questionnaires to members of the Society for American Baseball Research asking them to compare modern baseball with that of the past. Here are some of the responses:

Van Nightingale, journalist, Orange California
Players of the first two decades lived and breathed baseball. They knew the game inside and out, and knew the correct play to make in any circumstance.

Bill Whiting, syndicated baseball radio host, Birmingham, Michigan
Early-day players knew the game better, and had a fundamental knowledge of the basics. Who wants to bunt today? Who can, besides Alan Trammel?

Phil Wood, sportscaster, Reisterstown, Maryland
Many players today know little of the rule book, and zero about the game's history. Many wouldn't walk across the street to watch a game.

Anonymous
At a time when artificial turf has made contact with the bat more rewarding, batters handicapped by basically larger parks are swinging too much for the fences. Strikeouts kill rallies, as does lack of team play — trying to hit behind runners or bunt. Lack of bat control is depriving fans of what they want most — runs!

Jerald McCanlies, principal, Burleson, Texas
The talent pool has not increased as fast as team expansion. Simple logic — if baseball expanded to 1,000 teams, I would have a great chance to play major-league baseball, even at the age of 49. And as long as George Steinspender owns the Yankees, I still have a chance to become a big-league manager.

Tom Knight, baseball writer, Brooklyn, New York
Since 1961 (first expansion year), baseball quality has declined each year. It is so bad, I can say honestly we are no longer seeing major-league baseball. I can remember when the poorest clubs had at least a few good major-league hitters or pitchers. It's sad but true — people under the age of 40 never saw good baseball. If I had my way, every record set since 1961 would have an asterisk after it.

Jack Lang, sportswriter, Fort Salonga, New York
Many great athletes now concentrate on other sports, and as a result, baseball loses potential players. The game is going to have to concentrate on better development than the minors now provide. They have to get behind college programs, motivating them to develop players the way football does.

Kenneth Johnson, former minor-leaguer, Schenectady, New York
I coached a Connie Mack (Little League) team from 1974-1991. I saw a change in the kids' willingness to practice. Some would rather make money.

George Stone, sportswriter, Bristol, Tennessee
Is there the quality of play that existed in the '50s and '60s? I think not. Just imagine at one time Mays, Aaron, Banks, Mantle,

Koufax, Clemente, etc., all playing at the same time. I find it hard to come up with five names from today's players who could come close to filling those shoes.

William O'Grady, accountant representative, Cleveland, Ohio
Some players upset me with their greed and lack of respect for such a great game. The next time I pay $5.00 to park, $3.75 for a 'hot dog', and $15.00 for a ticket, Julio Franco, Rickey Henderson and Albert Belle will be too old to dog it around the bases. Good riddance to greed and sloth. Hello water polo.

Tom Ferrick, former major-league pitcher, Upper Darby, Pennsylvania
The umpires have a strong union and get all they want in demands. Underpaid minor-league umpires seldom get promoted. There are some incompetent major-league umps that can never be fired. (Ferrick died in October of 1996.)

Bernie Kennedy, sportswriter, St. Clair Shores, Michigan
Expansion has diluted the talent not only of players, but umpires, too. There are too many umps who simply are not major-league performers.

John Jackanicz, expediter, ballpark vendor, Chicago, Illinois
The most important change has been the incredible shrinking strike zone. It results in the counts being so long and the game so slow.

Doug Palmieri, stockbroker, Princeton, New Jersey
What a paradox it is that a game played without a clock is being so harmed by the length of its contests. In all the reading and research I've done on early baseball, I have never found a complaint from any era that a game suffered by being played too quickly. I feel abused by a four-hour, nine-inning contest filled with endless car and beer ads and ten or twelve pitching changes.

Philip Meneely, biologist, Seattle, Washington
The quality of play and the athleticism of the players are much higher today than 25 years ago (in my memory). Players are bet-

331

ter conditioned, facilities are better (for the players, not the fans), scouting is better, and players are used better for their abilities. People who say the game was better 25 years ago have faulty memories.

Anonymous
I think we tend to like the teams and players of the past — those who made an impression when we were impressionable. Thus, the 1949 Yankees were the greatest to a 15-year-old Bronx kid, and still are.

Ben Rader, history professor, author of *Baseball: A History of America's Game*, Lincoln, Nebraska
Consider that ballplayers are from a much larger population pool than when African-Americans and the Caribbean population were excluded. Consider, too, that in all sports, the quality of play has increased greatly.

Stephen Bray, baseball writer, Olympia, Washington
Economic imbalance, long-term contracts and expansion have hurt the quality of play, along with 'new' pitches and use of weights which result in more injuries.

Jim Leas, business consultant, Dublin, Ohio
Baseball can only be judged in the context of eras. From era to era, the many parts of baseball change for better and worse. General judgments are difficult in most respects.

Bruce Bohner, cable television-access coordinator, Lakewood, Ohio
Dilution of the talent pool has coincided with the larger number of African-Americans and Hispanic players that play now and were not allowed in the 'old days.' And there were egos then as there are now (Cobb, Delahanty, Ruth for example) who were every bit the prima donna as some are today.

Richard Shook, sportswriter, Plymouth, Michigan
Player-pay is tied to statistics which begets stat-oriented players. It would be different if credit were given for advancing runners, sacrifices, hit-and-runs, etc., but maybe fans don't care about

those things anyway. Early baseball is in no manner similar to today's high-tech game.

Jack Charles, retired teacher, Aurora, New York

Baseball past and present is so big a part of my life that I just want to sit back and enjoy it, hoping that it's larger than the sum of its problems, anticipating my yearly visit to Fenway Park, looking forward each day to the box scores, and conversing on the subject with my friends.

Thanks to all SABR members who responded to the survey.

AT THE OLD
BALL GAME

Baseball is a slow-moving game. Batters step out of the box frequently. Pitchers take their time delivering the ball. Managers make numerous trips to the mound. Coaches flash a myriad of signals. The time between innings is lengthy. It's not unusual for a fan to fall asleep on the couch before the four-hour struggle concludes.

Contrast that sport with hockey, where fast-skating forwards, rugged defensemen and lightning-quick goalies keep the game moving quickly and the excitement level high. Or with basketball, always filled with plenty of scoring, and whose athletes may be the most gifted in the world. Or with football, where strategy combines with skill to make it more attractive to spectators than any other American sport.

Television has made all sports more popular. Despite the owners' complaints, baseball has a larger number of followers than ever before. However, the percentage of those who watch it over other sports is smaller. Ask today's fan which he prefers and chances are baseball will be third on the list, and if the trend continues, hockey will soon overtake it as well.

Yet, the factor which makes baseball less appealing to the television observer — its relaxed pace, makes it more attractive for those attending in person. When the action stops at the game, your sight isn't limited to what some producer or editor decides is interesting. While the cameras may be spying on a shortstop opening or closing his mouth as a means of giving a sign to the second baseman, you can view the entire infield, speculating for yourself as to who'll be covering the bag. Rather than watching the ever-popular walk by the catcher to the mound, you can keep track of the competition by checking the scoreboard. A prisoner of the screen may have to watch an outfielder stand motionless while announcers talk endlessly about his superstar status, but an in-person viewer might prefer a scan of all the outfielders' positions. A manager speaking on the telephone might be fascinating to fans at home. Those at the game who feel differently aren't compelled to watch.

Another advantage of attending baseball games is that it's played outdoors, though residents of Houston, Seattle, Minneapolis and, sometimes, Montreal and Toronto (retractable roofs) have been denied that opportunity by short-sighted owners. Fans can enjoy watching a game in the sunshine, munching on hot dogs or peanuts, getting a tan in the bleachers, or just taking in the beauty of a day at the ballpark. At night, a glance at the stars and moon can be a pleasant diversion. No matter how often one attends, there's always a certain thrill that comes from viewing the ballpark after walking through the runway leading to your seating section.

What's there to see at a hockey or basketball game? Playing dimensions are symmetrical (with one or two exceptions in hockey), and the arenas are equally monotonous. When the action stops for a television time-out or during intermission, one is forced to listen to recorded music (it was better when they had organ music), or watch a fan's imbecilic attempt to score a goal at mid-ice or a basket from half-court.

It's true, football is played outdoors, but assuming you're rich or lucky enough to get hold of a ticket, do you really want to be there in 20-degree weather? The game moves along well, but it has its lapses too. And is there anything more boring than those half-time shows? To borrow that infamous Spiro expression, "If you've seen one, you've seen them all." Soccer is the only other team spectator sport played in the sunshine, but that advantage is lost when one falls asleep from boredom.

For in-person entertainment, baseball has them all beat. The action may not proceed as steadily, the players' skills not always be as evident, the results not always as climactic. But what's better than being at the ballpark on a sunny day, arguing with the guy next to you over strategy, yelling at the umpire while knowing he can't hear you, cheering the home team, mocking the opponent, or just settling back and wondering when you'll have a chance to return?

You can still take me out to the ballgame, even if there isn't a crowd.

BIBLIOGRAPHY

Alexander, Charles C. *John McGraw*. NY: Viking, 1988.

——— .*Our Game — An American Baseball History*. NY: Henry Holt and Company, 1991.

———. *Rogers Hornsby —A Biography*. NY: Henry Holt and Company, 1995.

———. *Ty Cobb*. NY: Oxford Universtiy Press, 1984. Anderson, Dave.

———. *Pennant Races — Baseball at Its Best*. NY:Doubleday, 1994.

Anderson, Dave, and others. *The Yankees — The Four Fabulous Eras of Baseball's Most Famous Team*. NY: Random House, 1979.

Anobile, Richard J. *Who's On First?* NY:Avon Books, 1972. Asinof, Eliot.

Asinof, Eliot. *Eight Men Out —The Black Sox and the 1919 World Series*. NY: Henry Holt and Company, 1987.

Bak, Richard. *Cobb Would Have Caught It*. Detroit:Wayne State University Press, 1991.

Blake, Mike. *Baseball Chronicles — An Oral History of Baseball Through the Decades*. Cincinnati: Betterway Books, 1994.

Boston Herald. several articles.

Bouton, Jim, with Shecter, Leonard, Editor. *Ball Four*. Twentieth century edition. NY: Macmillan Publishing Company, 1990.

——. *I'm Glad You Didn't Take It Personally*. NY: William Morrow & Company, Inc., 1971.

Broeg, Bob. *Superstars of Baseball*. South Bend: Diamond Communications, Inc., 1994.

Carney, Gene. *Romancing the Horsehide — Baseball Poems on Players and the Game*. Jefferson: McFarland & Company, 1993.

Carruth, Gorton. *What Happened When — A Chronology of Life and Events in America*. NY: The Penguin Group, 1991.

Cataneo, David. *Peanuts and Crackerjack — A Treasury of Baseball Legends and Lore*. Nashville: Rutledge Hill Press, 1991.

Charlton, Jim. *The Who, What, When, Why, and How of Baseball*. NY: Barnes and Noble, Inc., 1995.

Clark, Dick, and Lester, Larry, Editors. *The Negro Leagues Book*. Cleveland: The Society For American Baseball Research, 1994.

Creamer, Robert W. *Babe — The Legend Comes to Life*. NY: Simon & Schuster, Inc., 1992.

——. *Baseball in '41*. NY: Viking Penguin, 1991.

——. *Stengel — His Life and Times*. NY: Simon & Schuster, 1990.

Curran, William. *Big Sticks — The Batting Revolution of the Twenties*. NY: William Morrow and Company, Inc., 1990.

Debs, Victor Jr. *Still Standing After All These Years*. Jefferson: McFarland & Company, 1997.

——. *They Kept Me Loyal to the Yankees*. Nashville: Rutledge Hill Press, 1993.

Dewey, Donald, and Acocella, Nicholas. *The Biographical History of Baseball*. NY: Carroll & Graf Publishers, Inc., 1995.

Dickson, Paul. *Baseball's Greatest Quotations*. NY: HarperCollins Publishers, 1991.

Edwards, Bob. *Fridays with Red — A Radio Friendship*. NY: Simon & Schuster, 1993.

Girardin, G. Russell, with Helmer, William J. *Dillinger — The Untold Story*. Indianapolis: Indiana University Press, 1994.

Gorman, Bob. *Double X*. NY: Bill Goff, Inc., 1990.

Gregory, Robert. *Diz*. NY: Viking Penguin, 1992.

Halberstam, David. *October of 1964*. NY: Ballantine Books, 1995.

———. *Summer of '49*. NY: Avon Books, 1989.

Hano, Arnold. *Willie Mays*. NY: Grosset & Dunlap Publishers, 1966.

Hart, Captain B. H. Liddell. *The Real War — 1914-1918*. Reprint. Boston: Little, Brown and Company, 1964.

Helyar, John. *Lords of the Realm*. NY: Ballantine Books, 1994.

Henderson, Rickey, with Shea, John. *Off Base — Confessions of a Thief*. NY: HarperCollins Publishers, 1994.

Honig, Donald. *Baseball in the '30s — A Decade of Survival*. NY: Crown Publishers, Inc., 1989.

Isaacs, Neil D. *Innocence & Wonder — Baseball Through the Eyes of Batboys*. Indianapolis: Masters Press, 1994.

Kashatus, William C. *One Armed Wonder — Pete Gray, Wartime Baseball, and the American Dream*. Jefferson: McFarland & Company, 1995.

Katz, Lawrence S. *Baseball in '39 — The Watershed Season of the National Pastime*. Jefferson: McFarland & Company, 1995.

Kavanaugh, Jack. *Walter Johnson — A Life*. South Bend:Diamond Communications, Inc., 1995.

Kelley, Brent. *In the Shadow of the Babe*. Jefferson:McFarland & Company, Inc., 1995.

Knight, Tom. "Diamond Reflections." *Staten Island Register*. August 15, 1995.

———. "Diamond Reflections." *Staten Island Register*. November 21, 1995.

Laird, A. W. *Ranking Baseball's Elite*. Jefferson: McFarland & Company, 1990.

Liebman, Glenn. *Baseball Shorts*. Chicago: Contemporary Books, 1994.

Los Angeles Times. several articles.

Lowry, Philip J. *Green Cathedrals*. Reading: Addison-Wesley Publishing Co., Inc., 1992.

Mantle, Mickey, with Herskowitz, Mickey. *All My Octobers*. NY: HarperCollins Publishers, 1994.

Maranville, Walter. *Run, Rabbit, Run — The Hilarious and Mostly True Tales of Rabbit Maranville*. Reproduction. Cleveland: The Society For American Baseball Research, 1991.

Mead, William B. *Two Spectacular Seasons*. NY: Macmillan Publishing Company, 1990.

Mead, William B., and Dickson, Paul. *Baseball — The Presidents' Game*. Washington, D.C.: Farragut Publishing Company, 1993.

Meany, Tom. *Baseball's Greatest Players*. NY: Grossett & Dunlap Publishers, 1953.

Minor League Baseball Stars. Volume III. Cleveland: The Society For American Baseball Research, 1992.

Murdock, Eugene. *Baseball Players and Their Times: Oral Histories of the Game, 1920-1940*. Westport: Meckler Publishing, 1991.

Nash, Jay Robert. *World Encyclopedia of Organized Crime*. NY: DaCapo Press, 1993.

New York Times. several articles.

Oakley, J. Ronald. *Baseball's Last Golden Age, 1946-1960*. Jefferson: McFarland & Company, 1994.

Okkonen, Marc. *Baseball Uniforms of the 20th Century*. NY: Sterling Publishing Co., Inc., 1991.

Okrent, Daniel, and Lewine, Harris, Editors. *The Ultimate Baseball Book*. Boston: Houghton Mifflin Company, 1991.

Okrent, Daniel, and Wulf, Steve. *Baseball Anecdotes*. NY: Harper & Row Publishers, Inc., 1990.

Peary, Danny, Editor. *We Played the Game*. NY: Hyperion, 1994.

Philadelphia Inquirer. several articles.

Rader, Benjamin G. *Baseball — A History of America's Game*. Chicago: University of Illinois Press, 1992.

Reichler, Joseph. *Baseball's Great Moments*. Updated edition. NY:Bonanza Books, 1982.

——. *The Great All-Time Baseball Record Book*. Revised by Ken Samelson. NY: Macmillan Publishing Company, 1993.

Robinson, Ray. *Matty — An American Hero*. NY: Oxford University Press, 1993.

San Francisco Chronicle. several articles.

Seaver, Tom, with Appel, Marty. *Great Moments in Baseball*. NY: Birch Lane Press, 1992.

Seymour, Harold. *Baseball — The Early Years*. NY: Oxford University Press, 1960.

——. *Baseball—The Golden Age*. NY: Oxford University Press, 1971.

Snider, Duke, with Gilbert, Bill. *The Duke of Flatbush*. NY: Zebra Books, 1988.

Sowell, Mike. *The Pitch That Killed — Carl Mays, Ray Chapman and the Pennant Race of 1920*. NY: Macmillan Publishing Company, 1989.

Sporting News. several articles.

Staten Island Advance. several articles.

The Baseball Encyclopedia. Ninth edition. NY: Macmillan Publishing Company, 1993.

The Sporting News Complete Baseball Record Book. 1995 edition. St. Louis: The Sporting News Publishing Company, 1994.

Thorn, John, and Palmer, Pete, Editors. *Total Baseball*. Third edition. NY: HarperCollins Publishers, 1993.

Trimble, Joe. *Yogi Berra*. NY: Grosset & Dunlap, 1965.

Vescey, George. *Baseball's Most Valuable Players*. NY: Random House, 1966.

Ward, Geoffrey C., and Burns, Ken. *Baseball — An Illustrated History*. NY: Alfred A. Knopf, 1994.

Ward, John Montgomery. *Base-Ball — How to Become a Player*. Unabridged republication. Cleveland: The Society For American Baseball Research, 1993.

Will, George. *Men At Work*. NY: Macmillan Publishing Company, 1990.

Williams, Ted, and Prime, Jim. *Ted Williams' Hit List*. Indianapolis: Masters Press, 1996.

Williams, Ted with Underwood, John. *My Turn At Bat*. NY: Simon & Schuster, Inc., 1988.